ANDY BOUNDS, *FIN*

"*Outcast* takes you inside one of t
in the merger boom of the late 1⁹
leaks and tears as Andrew Cook, one of the last industrial titans of northern England, fights for the independence of his family firm.

"It is populated by a fascinating cast of characters from the City and the media. But at the centre is Sheffield steel man Cook, who once slept on a camp bed in the foundry as he saved the firm from bankruptcy. The self-confessed autocrat ran the listed company as if it were his own, breaching the corporate codes of the day and exposing it to takeover. Ginns does not spare the physical and emotional trauma inflicted on him and his young family. The story based on Cook's diaries and interviews is inevitably partial.

"Ginns make us ask whether manufacturers and their defence critical technology are safest in the hands of industrial engineers or financial ones – a relevant question today. Cook's pay is targeted for criticism by shareholders and analysts earning far more for doing less. As he noted wryly when Cook settles his bills with his advisers: 'The bank always wins'."

MARTIN VANDER WEYER, BUSINESS EDITOR, *THE SPECTATOR*

"Bernard Ginns has written a gripping true-life takeover drama with a complex protagonist, Andrew Cook, at its centre: this is the cut and thrust of business, in and out of the City of London, as it really happens."

MARK CASCI, BUSINESS EDITOR, *THE YORKSHIRE POST*

"This is a hugely enjoyable book. It brings to life one of the standout business battles of recent times and transports the reader back to Britain of 1996-97, a time of great social, economic and political change and the dawn of a new era.

"A quarter of a century has passed since these dramatic events took place but the underlying themes of destiny, family, greed and truth are eternal. I thoroughly recommend this book to anyone with an interest in business, modern history and underdog stories."

GARRY WILSON, MANAGING PARTNER, ENDLESS LLP

"Andrew Cook has a unique approach and is one of the most interesting people in British business. He doesn't play by other peoples' rules because he knows business can be done better than that. He's a battler and an innovator and I've had one hell of an experience dealing with him on several occasions in my career. His guiding principle that nothing can take the place of persistence has stuck with me ever since I first met him. A fascinating story well told by Bernard Ginns. Read and learn."

CELIA WALDEN, *DAILY TELEGRAPH* & RICHARD & JUDY BOOK CLUB AUTHOR

"A great new voice in narrative nonfiction. Tense, taut and beautifully paced. I read it in one sitting."

OUTCAST

COOK VERSUS THE CITY

BERNARD GINNS

For L, R and C

CHAPTER 1

Beware hostile bid imminent

It was November 12, 1996, a dark day at the fag end of the Major government. Bill Clinton was interned as President of the United States of America and the Spice Girls were riding high in the UK charts with 'Say You'll Be There'. Andrew Cook, meanwhile, was heading south, down the A1 to be precise.

The chairman of William Cook plc, an engineering group quoted on the London Stock Exchange, relaxed in the cream leather interior of the company car, a Bentley Turbo R – licence plate AC-3. He had recently employed a driver to take on the endless journeying around the company's seven foundries across Yorkshire and the North East and was using the extra time to catch up on paperwork.

Martin Connolly was pleased with his new berth. He had previously been retained by another Sheffield industrialist but Cook offered much better wages. Forty per cent better in fact, much to the delight of his wife (initially at least, until she became annoyed with the early starts and late finishes that came with her husband's new role). There was little small talk but from time to time Cook would break the silence with a humorous remark. He could be an amusing man. He preferred to sit in the front passenger seat, finding it more comfortable during the long journeys and easier to give navigational instructions, which he did repeatedly.

Cook was in good shape for his 47 years, the legacy of an extreme fitness regime and abstemious lifestyle during his twenties and thirties. It gave him plenty of stamina, which helped with the itinerant lifestyle and relentless demands of the role.

The daylight was fading as the dark blue Bentley joined a traffic jam. Cook was leafing through the files, his plume of silver hair hanging down as he glanced through various reports. In profile, his face was dominated by a large aquiline nose. His blue eyes scanned the lines, assessing and absorbing information, while he jotted down notes and instructions in black ink.

These were the days before email. The Bentley's cavernous 550-litre boot doubled as a filing cabinet with a big box of files containing company paperwork, plus the chairman's two or three briefcases. In addition, Martin would often arrive with the latest post and it was to this that Cook turned his attention, leafing through the usual correspondence when something extraordinary caught his eye. A piece of paper on which words, cut out of what appeared to be a dictionary, had been arranged to make a sentence. "Andrew Cook", read the anonymous letter, "beware hostile bid imminent".

It looked like something from a TV thriller and aroused a sense of puzzlement rather than anxiety. A hostile bid? He was the undisputed king of the castings industry. He had saved the family firm in the early Eighties and then over the course of that decade set out to save Britain's steel castings sector, largely succeeding. True, the early Nineties hadn't entirely run to plan, with all that bother in the United States and a near-fatal car accident. But the company was on an even keel and while the share price was a little on the low side, the earnings were good and shareholders seemed happy enough, didn't they?

The question hung in the air as Cook picked up the car phone from its plastic cradle and called loyal secretary Jane to request the number of an old friend who worked in the City. Simon Metcalf was an investment banker, formerly of County Bank and now a director at NatWest Markets. He had acted for Cook previously and while the outcomes weren't as desired – we won't mention Metcalf's enormous fees – they had become friends and Cook trusted his judgment. He also liked the man.

"Simon, it's Andrew. We should meet up soon. It's not particularly urgent. End of next week the earliest? That's fine. I will see you at your office at 10am on November 22. We should have lunch. Very good. Until then."

Cook marked the date in his pocket diary and returned the anonymous letter to the post folder and gazed out of the window into the darkness. A hostile bid imminent. Possible, but unlikely. With that, he consigned the thought to the back of his mind and closed his eyes as Martin drove the chairman home to Froggatt, a village in rural Derbyshire. The traffic had eased and Cook would be back before the children went to bed.

CHAPTER 2

Virtually his flesh and blood

The intensity of the Cook morning routine had eased somewhat. Back in the early years of his chairmanship when he was fighting to save the company, he would sleep on a camp bed in the office for up to six nights a week, devoting all waking hours to the task at hand. The old regimen was equal parts militaristic and monastic. The alarm would ring at 5.40am, triggering a learned response in the semi-conscious Cook who would roll off the bed and land on the floor with a thump, rendering him awake. After ablutions, he would be prowling the shop floor by 6am, orchestrating the show with his iron fist and eagle eye.

Now a made man after many years of toil and sacrifice, the daily start was a little more civilised. Cook would arise at 7am, don one of his Dege & Skinner suits, skip breakfast and be out of the house by 7.30am for a working day involving a series of site visits, customer and management meetings and lots of miles in between.

Today was Friday, November 15, and it started no differently. Cook was due to finalise some financial business at the head office in Sheffield and was midway through his morning routine. Alison, his wife, was making breakfast. The weekend was William's eighth birthday and last-minute preparations were needed for the fancy dress party. Cook had promised to take William to Toys R Us to choose a present and both father and son were looking forward to it.

Cook had emerged from the shower when Alison called his name. "Andrew, it's for you. It's Colin Cooke," she said, handing him the receiver. The name was familiar but strange at the same time. Not Colin Clark, the new chief executive at customer Vickers Defence Systems? No, Colin Cooke, the chairman of Triplex Lloyd, a rival and adversary. In an instant, Cook understood the reason for the call – and the anonymous letter three days earlier.

"I am calling you as a courtesy," began Cooke, in his Welsh accent. "To let you know that we are launching a takeover bid for your company."

The words had barely landed when Cook, never one to falter in confrontation, issued his response. "This is absolutely reprehensible behaviour," he said. "To do this without any prior contact or discussion is quite outrageous."

Taken aback at the instant hostility, Cooke said: "Well, we didn't think you would listen."

"I promise you a fight to the finish," said Cook, taking the upper hand. "And what's more, at the end there will be a pile of smoking ash and it won't be me."

Cooke hung up, leaving Cook in a state of anger and outrage, heart pounding as the ramifications swirled through his mind. "Hostile bid," he gasped, looking at Alison. To phone him at home was more than an insult. It was an assault on him personally, or so it felt. The firm was his life; his great-great grandfather had founded it more than 150 years earlier. Cook had rescued the company from near death and transformed it into the biggest manufacturer of its kind in Europe. William Cook was his life's work. It was virtually his flesh and blood. And now the battle had begun to try to take it from him.

Cook finished dressing, said a hurried goodbye to Alison, got into the Bentley alongside Martin, who was waiting outside, and off they sped to Sheffield and the Parkway offices of William Cook plc.

Shortly after 7.30am, the regulatory news service of the London Stock Exchange included the following update, which lit up on screens across the City of London and Fleet Street: "Triplex Lloyd announces the terms of an offer to be made by Schroders on behalf of Triplex Lloyd for the whole of the ordinary share capital of William Cook. The offer values each William Cook share at 309p and William Cook's issued ordinary share capital at approximately £57.7m."

In the release, Graham Lockyer, chief executive, said: "William Cook shareholders are suffering from their management's loss of ambition and its failure to pursue new growth opportunities successfully. Our offer fully values William Cook and gives its shareholders the opportunity to participate in the future success of the enlarged Triplex Lloyd group."

As soon as the Bentley reached the top road over the moor, the Motorola car phone picked up a signal from a nearby mast and trilled electronically. It was Simon Metcalf, offering his help. "Thank you Simon," said Cook, instinctively in need of a friend he could trust. "I want you to lead the defence."

"The cavalry is coming," reassured Metcalf as confidently as he could muster, "we'll be up as quick as we can."

Cook replied with his thanks, replaced the handset and,

perhaps unusually for a captain of industry astride a multi-million pound enterprise, burst into tears. Martin shifted uncomfortably in his seat. "My god," sobbed Cook, the feeling of an icy hand gripping his vital organs. "This is going to run and run and it will be a fight to the finish."

CHAPTER 3

What misfortune to have been a widower

Looking like a metal coffin on legs, the long iron box dominated the hospital room. At one end was a set of bellows. At the other, the patient's head. In the middle was an airtight chamber, encasing the patient's supine body. The rhythm of the machine forced her chest up and down, filling and emptying her diseased lungs, breathing on her behalf. It was an extremely painful procedure.

Barbara Jean Cook was 24 years old and, in the words of her brother John Gale, "a beautiful girl, who radiated sparkle: she lit up a room!" Her husband, Andrew McTurk Cook, was besotted with her. They had married in 1948 and enjoyed wonderful Swiss holidays together aboard the Engadine express. She gave him two beautiful children, Andrew in 1949 and Angela in 1950.

Polio was sweeping across Europe after the ravages of the Second World War, killing half a million people worldwide each year. Some sufferers were lucky: they escaped with weakened limbs. Others less so. Polio reached Barbara's lungs in 1951 and despite the best efforts of the doctors and their iron lung, she did not survive.

In the last hours of her life, Cook and his sister were presented

14

to their mother as a final farewell. Due to the advances of the illness and the heaving exertions of the iron lung, Barbara would have been in a state of delirium. Cook was just 20 months old, his sister seven months. He had no memories of his mother and only one of the time when she was still alive, a recollection of him holding the hand of an older child and gazing at a stream at the bottom of the garden in the family home in Fulwood, Sheffield. She died on June 13, 1951, and her death would cast a long shadow.

McTurk, then aged in his early thirties, was sick with grief and never fully recovered. He moved as far south as was possible, settling near Sandbanks between Bournemouth and Poole to be close to his mother-in-law, the kindly and supportive Eve Gale. McTurk looked for a nanny for the children and set about developing a new group of friends in an effort to distract himself from his bereavement.

It was an affluent place to be and there were plenty of distractions to be found. Social life revolved around the sun terraces, bars and lounges of the Royal Motor Yacht Club, the Poole Yacht Club, the West Hants Tennis Club and Parkstone Golf Club. McTurk's new friends contrived to find him a new wife. After all, the young widower was chairman of a sizeable industrial concern and a man of considerable means. Some prospects arose, but McTurk was unable to shake off his feelings of grief and guilt from the death of his wife. He could not rid himself of the sense he was being punished for his success.

Instead of rebuilding his life, McTurk focused only on his bad luck. "I have the misfortune to be a widower," was his sole response to any unfairness that would beset the family. Sometimes, he would wonder aloud whether the Cooks were cursed. His life became a series of disappointments and failed projects. He would rue missed opportunities but was unable to fully apply himself to see anything through to completion. Some men would have turned to drink in his situation. For McTurk, the shock of bereavement simply turned his mind.

Money made no odds. In 1956, McTurk had floated William Cook on the London Stock Exchange, raising the tax-free sum of £250,000 through the sale of a majority shareholding to help pay for professional managers to run the company on his behalf. In today's money, it was the equivalent of more than £5m. He was a wealthy man, but a desolate one. He had little interest in the company and no real liking or understanding of its power and potential.

The nanny, Miss Procter, was a strict governess who applied a firm regime to the children's lives while her employer was out and about lunching and dining with his wealthy leisured friends. She was caring in her way, playing games and taking her young charges on walks and to the beach in the summer. Behind her buttoned-up exterior, she was an extraordinary woman and had served as an airborne nurse during the Second World War, helping evacuate wounded soldiers after the D-Day landings.

The children grew to love Miss Procter as a de facto mother, but McTurk deeply resented having to live with a woman who was not his wife. He reasoned he could not marry again because he felt it would betray her memory. He chose his children's happiness over his own with traumatising consequences. Miss Procter was steadfastly loyal to her employer, taking his side and reinforcing his world view on the children: "If your mother was alive, this would not have happened." She stayed loyal for many years. Perhaps the nanny hoped one day he would marry her.

Cook learned early that one of the few things he could rely on from his father was an unstinting lack of support. More often, McTurk would be critical, demoralising and cross, clearly disappointed his son was not sociable, gregarious or good at games instead of fiddling around with model railway and Meccano sets. His hostility would manifest itself in verbal and sometimes physical outbursts. For his part, Cook was a sickly child, prone to chest infections that caused great anxiety in his father, himself a hypochondriac. In all, it was a desperately unhappy beginning to life – even before the involvement of Britain's 'world-class' public school system.

CHAPTER 4

The school oddball who ran away

The boys sat in rows along tables the length of the dining hall. A portrait of the youthful Queen Elizabeth II hung at the end wall, peering down at her subjects. The daily fare was a grey stew of indeterminate origin, garnished with gristle and fat and served with lumpy mashed swede or boiled cabbage. It was gag inducing. After lunch, the headmaster would rise from his seat at the top table next to the fireplace and announce which boys he wished to see in his study. Malcolm Galloway, known as Gallows, was fond of the cane. He had joined Chafyn Grove School as an assistant master in 1937 and returned after war service to run the school with his wife. He was not the only ex-military man on the staff: the school near Salisbury Plain employed at least three retired Army officers. The general ethos was to shout, scold, threaten, denigrate and, when pupils had committed an apparent infraction, administer a caning.

Not yet nine, Andrew Cook was a sensitive, frightened and sickly child. He found the school terrifying and impossible to comprehend. When his surname was called out by Mr Galloway, he was led shaking to the headmaster's study and then ordered to bend over. The experience was frightening, humiliating and painful. The physical marks faded over a few days, the psychological scars were much longer lasting.

The adults Cook encountered at school were neither pleasant nor kind. At best, they were stern and unsympathetic. At worst, they were sadistic and abusive, even predatory. Perceived transgressions resulted in corporal punishment, acts of violence committed by adults against small children. And despite the institutions charging hefty fees, the standard of teaching was routinely appalling. From the ages of six to 13, Cook's experience of life as a day boy within the private school system seemed akin to Soviet Russia or Communist China. In a regime of ill-defined and arbitrary rules, a boy could end up confessing to non-existent crimes just because a man in a position of authority was questioning him aggressively.

Cook would attend six different schools during these years, each their own house of horrors. His father moved the family frequently, heading slowly back north to the family business he was neglecting. It was an unsettled and unsettling time and Cook was by now suffering from numerous terrors. Despite his unhappiness, he was showing academic potential, winning prizes and developing his love of model-making and trains. He was never a sporty child, dreading the compulsory games sessions and the plunge baths filled with foul-smelling water, where he could recognise the boys who had been caned by the bruises on their buttocks. Cook was selected for the top class on the basis of his unusual intelligence but he didn't understand the subjects, couldn't do the work and was frightened of the teachers. He started to fall behind.

His father McTurk decided that radical action was needed to straighten out his wayward son – he would become a boarder which would prepare him for public school proper. When the dreaded day came, McTurk loaded the family Mercedes with trunk and child and drove off to school. En route, his father suddenly and inexplicably burst into tears and Cook, already scared and now confused to boot, had to comfort him. On arrival, there were no friendly greetings from the other boarders, just surprise that an unpopular low achiever was joining their ranks. The boarders filed into the dining room for their supper. It looked and felt like a prison. Cook sobbed into his cold, brown soup.

He was now an outsider. A former day pupil turned boarder, fitting in with neither group. His hell had extended from nine hours a day to 24. After three days, Cook simply walked out, jogging along the road to the nearest town until a groundsman apprehended the absconder and returned him to school by car. The headmaster called his father and they decided it would be a good idea to end the boarding experiment. Cook was the outsider who had also run away. The school oddball.

To everyone's surprise, Cook passed the common entrance exam and won a place at Oundle, one of England's largest boarding schools. During a tour, he had been impressed with its engineering facilities, which included a pattern shop, foundry and machine shop, features he recognised from the family firm. But as the new term drew nearer, Cook became increasingly anxious, pleading with his father not to send him away again. McTurk refused to listen and Cook resorted to desperate measures, locking himself in the lavatory and refusing to come out. By the time he emerged it was too late to drive to school, so Miss Proctor took Cook to the cinema to calm him down. The choice of film, about someone being repeatedly sent to prison, was not helpful.

In the event, the school was not so bad. The teaching was a big improvement, especially the Latin, and the engineering facilities were indeed very good. The teachers were not frightening and the headteacher was not so fond of caning boys. But by this point, Cook was beyond help. He was consumed with feelings of isolation and loneliness and lived in fear that something dreadful would happen. He just wanted to go home to his father. Halfway through that first term at Oundle, he walked out, caught a bus and then a train home.

Of course, McTurk returned his son immediately but the die was cast. Not long after, Cook ran away again, catching a bus and then hitchhiking north on the A1 in the dark, heading towards Sheffield and the new family home. He phoned his father on arrival in the Steel City. The police were alerted and Cook found himself in total disgrace. His father's shame was so great it caused Miss Procter to have an asthma attack.

Private education is an effective machine for producing the country's elite, the future leaders in politics, business and the City. But it spat out Cook. His final destination was High Storrs in Sheffield, a selective grammar school. Again, he started late – it was January 1964 – and again, he was the outsider. This time, he was the boy who spoke with a posh accent, a source of constant mockery. Bullies picked on him, but he learned to fight back and that the hardest punch wins. On more than one occasion, Cook's would-be assailants were left bruised and battered. The fighter was forming.

The teaching at High Storrs was generally excellent and corporal punishment was rare. Cook steadied himself in this new environment and began to show some promise, achieving 10 good O-levels and four straight A grades at A-level.

McTurk had designs on Oxbridge, but Cook regarded these as extensions of the hated boarding school life. Instead, he chose University College London and law. Although it was clear by now he was a natural-born engineer, the subject would give him another string to add to his bow and he soon showed promise in argument and debate.

Cook had also made another decision. He wanted to join the family business, but his father was against it. McTurk had never encouraged his son's interests. Cook was exceptional with railway modelling, the construction toy Meccano and generally working with his hands but was kept short of money to develop his obvious skills. All his father saw was a let-down, the son who ran away and failed to conform. Oh, what misfortune to have been a widower was the constant, self-pitying refrain.

CHAPTER 5

The more acrimonious, the better

It was a cold, wet Sunday afternoon at the Manor House with rain turning to sleet and Andrew Cook was deep in the woods, laying a trail for William's birthday party and getting soaked in the process. He was dressed as the Wild West lawman Wyatt Earp, hero of the gunfight at OK Corral, and his outfit of blue jeans, waistcoat, checked shirt and cowboy hat offered little protection against the northern elements. Shivering in the conditions, Cook was determined to put on a good show for his son and was setting clues among the trees in the search for the golden tomahawk. He could hear the boys playing nearby, shrieking with excitement as they took turns to ride in William's new electric car, which father and son had chosen on a trip to Toys R Us the day before.

Cook was consumed with thoughts of the hostile takeover bid, the words of the Triplex Lloyd press release and subsequent newspaper coverage repeating in his restless mind: "William Cook appears to have given up… its acquisition in the USA failed… its attempt to diversify failed… its search for opportunities failed… shareholders are suffering from their management's loss of ambition… its failure to pursue new growth opportunities successfully." *The Times*, Britain's paper of record, noted "the predator had delivered what may be a decisive blow" with its move for the company. He hadn't slept properly since the news broke on Friday, his disquiet worsened by the growing concern there was a mole in the camp, leaking damaging information to be used against him. Who could it be?

Upstairs in the Manor House, the ever-loyal secretary Jane was in the study, typing up Cook's handwritten notes for the first draft of the defence document. Nanny Cherry was downstairs in the kitchen, getting the candles ready and watching through the window as Cook, in sodden Stetson, gathered the boys together and led the rowdy bunch around the rain-drenched estate before heading inside for the birthday cake and singalong, leaving a dozen pairs of muddy boots in the hallway. Jane joined the party for the singing and discretely handed Cook the 11-page document. The noise in the house was deafening, but the children were having fun, filling themselves with chocolate cake. William was elated.

Cook leafed through the document and scanned the headings, concerning the strengths of William Cook and its underlying profitability, the weaknesses of Triplex Lloyd and why its outrageous bid undervalued the company he had saved from near extinction in 1982 and grown into a market leader. As ever, Jane had done a decent job deciphering his scrawl and with the addition of the headed paper, Cook felt it resembled the beginnings of a compelling argument but whether the people he would be paying to help defend his company would understand it – or even read it – remained to be seen. It had been a long weekend, but he had not allowed William's birthday to be spoiled. Wyatt Earp had seen off the Clanton cowboy gang, leaving three of their number dead in the dust at Tombstone, and so would he.

Any sense of calm did not last long. Aside from the anger Cook felt, there was the unsettling sense that someone on his side was passing secrets to the enemy and exposing him to danger. These suspicions had arisen on Friday and he thought through the events of a drawn out and difficult day. He had arrived at the head office at 8am to scenes of confusion and dismay with Jane struggling to hold back tears and managers solemn and tight-lipped. There were none of the usual cheery "good morning, Mr Cook" greetings. What would become of their jobs, their incomes and their families?

The phone was ringing constantly with advisors offering their services and journalists requesting comment. The City loved a hostile takeover bid. It would generate enormous fees for the bankers, lawyers and PR advisers. It was game on for them and a troupe had filed north from London to Sheffield, hoping for a piece of the action. At 9.30am, the company was due to stage an extraordinary general meeting for shareholders to approve some financial matters – a long-term incentive plan known as an LTIP for senior employees – and Cook decided to press ahead. The company's ageing non-executive directors, Robert Pickford and Ian Porter, were in attendance for the EGM but out of their depth with the hostile bid. The boardroom filled up as various pin-striped professionals arrived from London. Cook took his seat at the head of the table, cleared his throat and set out the beginnings of his defence: the Triplex offer undervalued William Cook and the company without him as the driving force was no business at all. The response from the floor was muted. Cook tried again, adding the possibility of a monopolies commission ruling preventing the takeover going ahead and some options for a technical defence based on legal and regulatory matters. Again, the response was muted – they were not convinced. Did anyone believe in this company apart from Cook? He scanned the faces in the room. John Caldwell, the newly promoted finance director and a cool-headed individual, seemed to be alone in nodding his support.

"The cavalry has arrived," exclaimed Cook as Simon Metcalf entered the room with his diminutive sidekick, introduced as Margaret Young. Metcalf was the first investment banker Cook had dealt with, back in the Eighties, and while he was undoubtedly hard work at times, Cook respected his judgment and had come to understand the vital role of investment banks in helping companies to raise capital through the underwriting, distribution and brokering of shares. They were powerful institutions. Metcalf was followed shortly afterwards by David Cheyne, an expensive but trustworthy partner at Linklaters, the Magic Circle law firm. Cheyne was rock solid, the son of a professional soldier who had entered the City with no real contacts but established himself as one of London's best mergers and acquisitions lawyers. Cook felt relieved that some people of stature had arrived at last and amused even as Metcalf started arguing almost immediately with the sharp-suited men from UBS about whether or not they would be joint defence advisors. Formerly the Union Bank of Switzerland, UBS was William Cook's broker and responsible for matching buyers and sellers of the company's shares. It was also one of the world's biggest investment banks and a major force in the City of London.

"Let the client decide," said Metcalf as tempers rose, handing Cook the first of many big decisions he would have to make over the coming weeks. Make the wrong call and he could be finished. He asked Cheyne for his learned view. Of all those present, Cook respected his opinion the most. "Let your judgment decide," replied the lawyer. Win or lose, the advisors would get paid regardless, the ultimate racket, but for Cook it was the survival of the company that bore his family name at stake. After weighing the options, he chose Metcalf and NatWest Markets as lead defence advisors, to provide opinion to the company on whether the financial terms of any offer were fair and reasonable, and UBS would continue its role as broker. The men from UBS did not take the news well, losing out on such lucrative fees, and fell into a barely-disguised sulk.

The defence team hashed together a preliminary press release and secured the services of a PR man recommended by Metcalf. Tony Carlisle was the chain-smoking managing director of Dewe Rogerson at London Wall and an accomplished City spinner who made his name during the privatisations of BT, British Gas and BP during the Eighties. "Don't expect any change out of £80,000," he told Cook in response to the question of his fees. In the end, it would be more than three times as much. The agreed release was faxed out to City desks across Fleet Street with Cook's stern rebuff for the Triplex offer as "grossly undervalued" and "extremely unwelcome".

For the City hacks, a hostile takeover bid could generate acres of entertaining coverage and the more acrimonious, the better, with the more experienced hands well versed on the colourful corporate raiders of the previous decade. What's more, they hunted as a pack and could scent blood. The *Evening Standard* was first to the punch with its West End Final edition of 3pm, the page buzzing through the fax machine with its headline

'Triplex fires a £58m broadside at William Cook' accompanied by a picture of the grinning CEO Graham Lockyer saying the target's poor performance was all down to its management. Lockyer warned ominously that Triplex had "done its home-work" with institutional shareholders, including Phillips & Drew Fund Management with its 20 per cent stake. Cook was already uncomfortable about PDFM, the company's largest shareholder and a subsidiary of UBS, and this declaration made matters worse. He found it difficult to read the true feelings of its fund managers and analysts. They did not speak their minds and kept him guessing. He was not sure they could be trusted.

The crowd in the boardroom had thinned out by late afternoon, leaving Cook and finance director Caldwell with anointed advisors Metcalf and Young. The two non-executives Pickford and Porter were still clucking about, not quite know-ing what to do but consuming lots of coffee and biscuits. Young phoned her City broker husband to tell him she would be late home that evening as she had joined the defence team for William Cook plc. His response was typical of the gossip in the Square Mile: "Isn't that the bloke who has been talking down the shares so he can take the company private?" She shared this with Cook. As he wondered what he had got himself into, Metcalf took him to one side and asked, "what's this I hear about you buying a rather expensive aeroplane?" Cook gave an evasive reply – how on earth did Metcalf find out about that? – and agreed to meet him on Monday morning at NatWest's towering offices in the City. Metcalf didn't dwell on the matter and told Cook he was starting to feel quite bullish. Indeed, the company share price had shot up during the day, suggesting Triplex would have to raise its offer to close the deal.

The driver Martin chauffeured a pensive Cook the 15 miles home to Froggatt, fighting through the Friday rush-hour traffic. Cook greeted Alison and his children, forgetting his worries for an hour during the bedtime routine with young William, Hannah, Jenny and Alice. Once they were safely tucked in, Cook retreated to his study with an ice-cold bottle of pink champagne and picked up the phone to his Spanish friend. Enrique 'Henry' Lartundo was a wealthy foundry owner in the Basque Country region of north-west Spain. They had met during Cook's European odyssey, his David and Goliath battle to take on anti-competitive business practices in the Continent's castings industry. Henry had been in tight corners himself and had once been sentenced to death by the armed separatist group ETA for refusing to reinstate sacked workers. He was a tough businessman but a kindly and loyal friend. "Andrew," he said, "tell me what I can do to help." "You can buy some shares Henry," replied Cook, finishing his second glass and pouring a third, still thirsty and in need of solace. Lartundo was a multi-millionaire and could help strengthen the share price further in Cook's favour with a large purchase of shares, but his response suggested it was not something he would be prepared to do. His friends could make sympathetic noises, but in this fight Cook would be on his own.

The champagne helped take the edge off a difficult day. Blurred thoughts swirled around Cook's mind but something was becoming clearer. PDFM, the fund managers, would be key to his future and whoever they backed would win. Cook had found them inscrutable and Janus-like, facing in both directions. Indeed, as well as holding shares in William Cook, PDFM had recently bought into Triplex Lloyd. Was there something taking place silently behind the scenes, an invisible hand manipulating events and moving against him? The phone rang loudly, shaking Cook's train of thought. It was the oily voice of Carlisle, the PR man, still puffing away on a cigarette at 11.15pm. "Andrew, sorry to bother you at this ungodly hour. I have been asked to ask you about flying and the purchase of a company plane. I am told there are troubles with the taxman too. Does this mean anything to you?" My god, thought Cook, how did Carlisle know about the Inland Revenue investigation? Tax inspectors had been probing the company for months and were focusing on the chairman's extensive use of light aircraft and appeared very well informed, leading Cook to suspect someone on the inside, past or present, was feeding information to the taxman. Was the same insider now whispering to journalists? Who could it be? Was there a conspiracy to destroy him?

CHAPTER 6

A strategy of retreat

The thick wedge of newspapers thudded onto the mat and settled with the faint sound of rippling leaves. The morning had not yet broken but Andrew Cook had been awake for hours, unable to calm his racing mind or quell the feelings of outrage and injustice. Fleet Street's finest would do nothing to lift his mood as he sat in the Manor House study in dressing gown and slippers, the latest editions of Her Majesty's Press spread across his Chippendale oak desk, and an umpteenth cup of tea in his hand. The front pages carried reports of the Duchess of York's royal family tell-all interview with US chat show queen Oprah Winfrey – "they tried to behead me" – the latest internecine battles within John Major's Conservative Party and Michael Jackson's secret marriage to a nurse. Cook went in search of the business sections, tucked away between TV and sport. The Triplex bid was all over them.

The Daily Telegraph, edited by Old Etonian Charles Moore, observed how the Triplex bid "shook the quiet world of industrial engineering", carried the personal criticisms of Cook and said analysts had embraced the aggressor's logic for the deal. Correspondent Charis Gresser observed that institutional investors would play a major role in determining the outcome of the bid. *The Guardian*, which usually held its nose while reporting on the cutting edge of capitalism, said Cook was "clearly taken by surprise by the move, taking several hours to dignify it with a response before spitting out its opposition". The paper added that a glance at its accompanying graph should tell its own story – it showed a sharp uptick for William Cook's share price, the biggest riser of the day.

The Independent, under the editorship of Andrew Marr, had the pick of the quotes and had sought the views of Triplex chairman Colin Cooke, although misspelt his surname ("it's Cook with e", his PR advisors would bemoan repeatedly over the coming weeks). Cooke told the paper he was prepared for "a long and acrimonious" battle for the company and, twisting the knife, said "we feel it is a very fair price given Cook's poor rating and recent track record". The one-sided report continued, adding that analysts admired the management trio that had revived Triplex's own fortunes and were less impressed with Cook's management. Analyst John Dean of stockbroker Albert E Sharp said the proposal "offers William Cook shareholders a fairly nice premium, which could go a bit higher. If I was a shareholder I would be delighted". The Triplex chairman had the last word, saying "we would love to be able to agree a recommended deal but I don't think Andrew Cook will listen". Cooke also spoke to *The Herald* of Glasgow, the longest running national newspaper in the world, revealing he had called Cook on the morning of the hostile bid announcement. "He listened politely but seemed a little upset," said Cooke, with some understatement. Reading this particular article, faxed over by his PR agency, Cook nearly spat out his drink and muttered a short expletive.

He tossed these papers to one side and picked up the *Daily Mail*, the voice of Middle England as dictated by its leader Paul Dacre. Never knowingly out-punned, the Mail informed its readers that William Cook had "lost the recipe" for growth and had sought the views of Paul Compton of Merrill Lynch, a once-friendly engineering analyst who had turned against Cook and had been advocating his removal to improve the fortunes of the company in recent research notes, some of which had bordered on the defamatory in Cook's eyes. Compton told the *Mail*: "I do not expect another bidder, or a materially higher offer from Triplex. Cook investors should accept shares in Triplex, an excellent company." In the style of the editor, Cook uttered a double expletive.

There was little respite in the rarified *Financial Times*. In an interview with correspondent Richard Wolffe, Triplex CEO Graham Lockyer damned his target with faint praise: "William Cook did quite a good job in the 1980s in bringing steel casting foundries together. But in the 1990s it is evident that any strategy for growth has disappeared. This offer makes tremendously good sense for us. We believe it has great opportunities for getting growth back into this business, with lots of complementary markets and customers. It is also relatively low risk because it is in our core competency of casting." Wolffe pointed to William Cook's two recent share buybacks totalling 15.5 per cent and the EGM of November 15 in which the company proposed to purchase a further 10 per cent of company shares as part of the long-term incentive plan for senior employees. Companies tended to buy back their shares because management considered them undervalued or had nothing else to do with their money. In a phone interview the previous day,

Wolffe had challenged Cook over his strategy. Cook told him: "Triplex have made no attempt to talk to us, which is frankly silly because it is going to cost them dearly. There is a wholly wrong perception that we are going around rudderless, but my team is in fact totally dedicated to wringing every last penny out of the business. This is a ludicrously cheap price for our shares which were already underrated. That is why we diverted some cash into buying the shares back." It was a fair account of their conversation but Cook felt troubled at the picture that was being painted. However hard he argued, he was on the back foot.

The Yorkshire Post was bottom of the pile but the shrewdest of the lot, characterising the Triplex announcement as "a blistering opening salvo in what looks like developing into a bitter war of words", noting the "aggressive move for Cook came without warning or negotiation and left analysts questioning for how long the company could hold on to its independence". *The YP* had also spoken with Triplex CEO Lockyer, who condemned the share buyback programme as a "strategy of retreat" and promised job losses at William Cook's head office, no doubt starting with Cook himself. It gave the last word to Paul Spencer, an engineering analyst at stockbroker Granville Davies. He said: "I think Andrew Cook is going to find it extremely difficult to defend this bid." Christ, thought Cook, even the YP thinks the game is up.

CHAPTER 7

Forces beyond his control

A weary Andrew Cook took his seat aboard the 7.45am train from Sheffield to London, named the Master Cutler in honour of the head of the Company of Cutlers in Hallamshire, a historic trade guild dating back to 1624. Cook had little time for this particular company but was aware of the long line of famous industrialists who had held its office, names such as Firth, Vickers and Hadfield, men who had forged the city's reputation during the first Industrial Revolution. Cook scanned the faces in the first-class carriage and saw – or imagined – the eyes of his fellow travellers dart back down to their morning newspapers. The quality front pages led with the Shadow Chancellor's promise to hold a referendum on joining the European single currency should Labour win the general election in the spring.

Cook was a recognisable man and not just because of his distinctive features and intense gaze. He had often appeared in the press, locally, regionally and nationally, over the years. Unlike many business leaders, Cook was unafraid to speak his mind and journalists knew he made colourful copy. His recent speech to the Sheffield Chamber at the Cutlers' Hall had the lubricated audience rolling in the aisles with its attack on the uselessness of non-executive directors (*The Star* had covered the story under the headline, "Boss blasts board 'Old Fogeys'"). His acquisition spree of the Eighties had attracted much coverage, culminating in the Confederation of British Industry naming William Cook its company of the year in 1989. Cook's outspoken views on the uneven playing field of Europe had seen him invited onto TV shows like BBC's *Newsnight* with Jeremy Paxman; the trained barrister frequently winning his arguments but failing to prevent Britain's ever closer union with Brussels.

There was no-one he recognised this Monday morning, but it was the first time in years he had caught the Master Cutler service to the capital, preferring to spend his time in his factories and with his customers instead of playing the game in the City. He categorised the first-class clientele as grey men in grey suits, senior employees of the new industry in Sheffield – the civil service. New public sector organisations, offices and agencies were taking root in the city and starting to spend hundreds of millions of pounds in taxpayers' money in the name of regeneration after globalisation had done for the metal bashers and miners of South Yorkshire.

As the tatty Midland Main Line train trundled south from Sheffield station, Cook reflected that some successful entrepreneurs had emerged from this painful period of transformation. The 1.4 million sq ft Meadowhall shopping centre had opened in Sheffield in 1990 and would turn its Hull-born co-founder Eddie Healey into one of Yorkshire's first billionaires. Healey and his business partner Paul Sykes realised their dream of bringing the North American retail experience to the UK, pioneering Sunday trading, late-night Christmas shopping and celebrity openings. Catherine Zeta Jones, the star of ITV's

Darling Buds of May, had cut the ribbon at Warner Cinemas' new 11-screen multiplex, and singer and activist Bob Geldof had opened its HMV record store, now doing a roaring business in high-margin compact discs. Yes, retail was another new industry of sorts and employed lots of people, but it also relied on the purchase of consumer goods, usually on credit, rather than making things and selling them.

Meadowhall's domed Mecca had been built on the site of Osborn Hadfield steel foundry, Sir Robert Hadfield being the inventor of the uniquely tough and impact-resisting manganese steel and the first major manufacturer of general steel castings, essential components for most major engineering achievements from the late 19th century to the present day. Cook had acquired the residue of Osborn Hadfield during his consolidation of the failing UK steel castings industry in the 1980s, merging it into one of his steel foundries, David Brown, another famous name saved from closure, and keeping alive some of the skills and capabilities which otherwise would have been lost forever. A statue by sculptor Robin Bell of foundrymen working a crucible stood in one of the Meadowhall galleries, a nod to the area's illustrious past, but this was later moved outside, presumably to stop it from obstructing shoppers.

Cook succeeded in catching the eye of a train crew member and ordered a full English breakfast, understatedly described as a 'grill' on the menu. The chairman often skipped the first meal of a day, sometimes grabbing a KitKat on the way out of the house or having some fruit later in the office. The meal fortified him for the uncertainty of the day ahead.

NatWest Markets was based at 135 Bishopsgate, a giant of a building designed by the Chicago architects Skidmore, Owings

& Merill and part of Broadgate, the largest office scheme in the Square Mile. Margaret Thatcher had broken ground on the development with a British digger in 1985 and said she hoped the site would become "a monument to the virility and vitality of our times". "We are not only building architecture, we are preparing for the commerce of the future," declared the Iron Lady in her speech. A year later, she would transform the City by tearing up rules and regulations, introducing electronic trading and welcoming foreign banks with their macho deal-making activities into the fold. The Big Bang unleashed a new era of unbridled growth in the power and prevalence of financial services.

Cook clambered out of his black cab near Liverpool Street Station, tipped the driver and walked into the atrium, spotting Simon Metcalf near the lifts. Metcalf had an imposing stature and a pleasant, open face which lit up with a friendly grin on seeing his client. Cook was pleased to see him. Metcalf was part of the City establishment, no doubt, but not so much as to be constrained in thought and deed. He was an insider, sure, but he had sympathy for the outsider and his client in this instance was the rank outsider. With his genial manner, Metcalf had the air of someone who had glided rather effortlessly through life from public school prefect in the Shires to corporate finance director at an investment bank, but he was pragmatic in outlook, aggressive when necessary and gave good counsel on how best to operate within the City, which was still effectively run as an Old Boys' Club.

They greeted each other, caught the mirrored lift to the 11th floor and paced along the gilded corridor to the double doors of the first meeting room. The doors opened and inside was a large throng of suited advisors, actual and putative, physically jostling for chairs around the large boardroom table, pushing each other out of the way in some cases to get a seat and hopefully a slice of the pie. "This is ridiculous," said Cook. "Haven't you got a bigger room Simon?" After a quick call to reception, Metcalf led the group of two dozen men and women out of the meeting room and back along the corridor to another room, twice the size of the first. Everybody found a seat and Metcalf called the meeting to order, swiftly dismissing the hangers-on and no-hopers and whittling down those that had gathered to the core defence.

One of the men from UBS lingered on, still aggrieved that Cook had not chosen the Swiss bank as joint defence advisor after the work UBS had done for William Cook with the recent buying back of shares on behalf of the company. The tall and elegantly dressed young man would not let go and virtually accused his client of disloyalty. Cook felt a flash of anger, but stopped himself exploding at the impudence of the banker. No good purpose would be served by falling out with UBS. But surely it could have foreseen the trouble ahead, especially given that PDFM, Cook's biggest shareholder and a new investor in Triplex Lloyd, was also part of UBS. Don't these people talk to each other? And weren't they supposed to be giving Cook the heads-up on this sort of thing? Or were they in it together?

As the room thinned out, Metcalf tapped Cook on the shoulder and asked for a quiet word in the corridor. Cook knew what was coming – it was time to talk money. After 15 years as chairman, he had paid out a small fortune in fees to various bankers, lawyers and accountants, but he had never been on the receiving end of a hostile bid.

"Our advice and services will cost you just £750,000, plus an additional sum to be agreed if things get, shall we say, complicated." Metcalf was always matter of fact when it came to discussing money.

"I'd prefer to have something contingent on success," replied Cook, his legally trained mind rising to the argument.

"Very sorry Andrew, that's no-can-do from our perspective. These are complicated, demanding matters and we need to be paid fairly. We all hope our reward is great in heaven but I have a divorce to pay for, old chap!"

Cook's will to argue fell away. For all Metcalf's humour, he absolutely did not want his main defence advisor in a state of discontent. "Okay Simon," he sighed. "We can argue about the fees when we have won."

"That's the spirit Andrew!" Metcalf flashed his grin. "Dinner's on me tonight. I've booked us a table at the Savoy Grill."

A couple of hours later, Cook, his finance director John Caldwell and Metcalf were seated in the Art Deco dining room, one of London's most famous restaurants whose past patrons included Sir Winston Churchill, Frank Sinatra and Oscar Wilde. The opulence on this occasion was lost on Cook who felt the familiar gnawing of anxiety in his gut. It was accompanied by a sense of deja vu. It was nearly a decade to the day that he had begun his last major battle with his decision to buy Weir Foundries, a deal he had celebrated rather prematurely with Metcalf in the very same dining room. The acquisition had taken him to the edge of the abyss as he struggled to turn around the troubled company without it taking down William Cook as well. Ultimately, he had prevailed and grown stronger as a result. But on this occasion the stakes were higher and forces beyond his control in the City seemed to be conspiring against him. It was going to be the fight of his life and he knew it. Cook glanced around the elegant dining room – it was busy for a Monday evening – and studied the faces of the other diners. They all looked so happy and untroubled. The feeling of foreboding rose up and he pushed his plate of food to one side, sick at the thought of what lay ahead.

CHAPTER 8

Fight them on the breaches

The sun rose over the City of London, shards of sunlight breaking through the dark steel and glass towers stretching across the skyline, the grey blue of dawn irradiated by orange rays. Despite the early hour, the offices of the Square Mile were hives of activity, the capital markets never sleeping and following the sun around the world. At 26 Finsbury Square, a Fifties building updated with a brash new facade in the Eighties, the trio at the helm of Triplex Lloyd set about their task with the help of strong coffee and an overhead projector. The chairman, chief executive and finance director took it in turns to drive home the arguments for their takeover of William Cook, a move compelled by industrial logic to create a specialist castings group with common technologies and complementary markets that would be a world leader in its field. They were the dynamic predators and their prey a sitting duck, which had been lacking direction, ambition and a strategy for growth for too many years. It was only a matter of time before they got their teeth and claws into it and the day would be theirs.

The case presented met with resounding approval from the audience, a collection of largely male analysts from the stock-broking houses, the City institutions which buy and sell shares on behalf of their clients and on their own account. They were impressed with the slick presentation and said as much in their notes to investors and comments to the press. John Dean, engineering analyst at Albert E Sharp, told the *Financial Times*: "There is consolidation due in the small engineering sector and all businesses are becoming more international. You leave yourself at risk if you do not keep pace with these changes in the market." The share buybacks by William Cook were, he argued, a sure sign the company did not know what to do with its cash and had no intention of developing the business.

Triplex Lloyd, on the other hand, was held up as a shining example of how to run a business in the Nineties, having overhauled its management team and restructured the group with the shedding of loss-making divisions to concentrate on complex castings for the power and automotive markets, sectors with high barriers to entry. The Triplex strategy was working, on paper at least, as pre-tax profits and sales started to soar. Sandy Morris, engineering analyst at historic broker Hoare Govett, told the *FT*: "The interim figures were really good, with profits and cash flow showing that the strategy made sense and the management had credibility. It was time for Triplex Lloyd to get going. The management had knocked out all the old problems and this is a very sensible value-adding bid to make." The analysts were won over. The shares they owned in William Cook had shot up in value, the shares they had recently bought in Triplex were going up as well and it was all set to be a very good year for their bonuses.

Job done, the men from Triplex strolled out of the building and into Finsbury Square with a spring in their steps, the series of dawn briefings with City analysts now complete. They were going to be rich and powerful. The leader of the group, chairman Colin Cooke, paused to rummage in his woollen overcoat, alerted by the bleeping of his clamshell Motorola mobile. "Hello, yes, very well," he answered in his Welsh accent. "All is going according to plan."

The same could not be said for Cook, camped out across the City in an airless room at 135 Bishopsgate. Simon Metcalf, Margaret Young and the rest of the team at NatWest Markets were taking an age to gather the facts and figures for the defence argument. As predicted, they did not seem to have read the 11-page document that Cook had prepared over the weekend and faxed out to his advisors. They kept asking him questions which were answered clearly and concisely in the document. Had they not bothered to read it? Good lord, how much was he paying these people? At least they were starting to understand that William Cook was indeed an undervalued company, its underlying profitability masked by heavy expenditure on the refurbishment of its foundries. The argument that the bid undervalued the company was looking strong, almost to the surprise of the advisors, but the question of corporate governance was proving trickier to answer.

"The problem we have is this, Andrew," said the PR advisor Tony Carlisle, puffing away on his nth cigarette of the day, "you are chairman and chief executive of the company, so nobody really can hold you to account over the decisions you make. Your board of directors, made up of loyal timeservers, certainly doesn't. Pickford, Porter and Pratt are relics and sound like something from a Dickens novel and are nearly as old. They are incapable of offering any independent scrutiny or oversight of your actions. I am hearing that your father and your wife are on the payroll. And your sister was too, until she joined the government as a Treasury minister, no less. You pay yourself well over the odds compared to senior management at other companies in your sector. Anyone could say quite reasonably that you have been running this company like your own private fiefdom. It's not a good look and it will be difficult to counter. You know how seriously the City takes corporate governance."

At this, Cook exploded. "If some little pipsqueak in red braces is going to tell me what I can and cannot earn then I am quitting now," he stormed. Margaret Young looked at the floor, Metcalf out of the window.

Carlisle took a deep drag on his cigarette, exhaled and calmly repeated his points. "Corporate governance counts Andrew. It's not your company, yet you behave like it is. William Cook is around 85 per cent owned by institutional investors in the City of London, but you are chairman and chief executive, your family is on the payroll, you appear to be buying a company plane and, I'm reliably informed, the taxman is looking at your affairs."

Cook shot back through the cloud of smoke. "I think I am worth every penny I earn in view of what I have done, my achievements and what I continue to do. Without William Cook a great slice of British engineering would be in very severe difficulties, quite apart from our strategic importance in the defence world as the only British supplier of tank tracks and the fact that we keep 2,000 good, honest working men and their families in full-time employment, not to mention all our dependent suppliers. I am earning less than a quarter of what some of these City types are earning and if they disappeared down the drain tomorrow, who would miss them?"

"Andrew, it doesn't matter what you think. It's how it looks. Corporate governance is going to be a big issue in this battle, you are on the back foot and we need to get on the front foot. It's not as if you haven't been warned." Carlisle tossed Cook a press cutting across the glass table. It was an article from the *FT* published in the summer and headlined 'Shareholders told to fight on the breaches' which singled out William Cook as an egregious example of the failure of smaller companies to comply with the new City codes of conduct. The codes were named after their authors, the City grandees Sir Adrian Cadbury, former chairman of Cadbury Schweppes, and Sir Richard Greenbury, chairman and chief executive of Marks & Spencer, and had become bywords for what was considered best practice on board leadership and effectiveness, remuneration, accountability and relations with shareholders.

Cook glanced through the article and recalled its critical content and tone. He had dismissed the story at the time, but with hindsight it seemed prescient. "Mr Ronald Pratt joined William Cook, the castings manufacturer in 1949 and became a director in 1953," began the journalist William Lewis, a rising star on Fleet Street. "He now sits as one of two non-executive directors at the publicly quoted Sheffield-based company, the other being Mr Ian Porter. Mr Pratt and Mr Porter, unlike non-executives at most public companies, do not sit on William Cook's audit committee. That is because the company does not have one. Nor does it have a separate remuneration commit-tee to set executive directors' pay." As such, the company was committing serious breaches of the Cadbury and Greenbury codes, claimed the writer.

Cook had responded vigorously at the time, telling Lewis

"there are a large number of smaller companies that do not see it as relevant to their businesses to comply lock, stock and barrel" with the codes. He also wrote a letter to the editor, Richard Lambert, defending his board's actions and criticising the demand for separate remuneration and audit committees as unnecessarily bureaucratic and divisive. Cook laid into the codes as "hasty and ill-considered, being rushed into being as a result in the case of Cadbury of overt boardroom misbehaviour and in the case of Greenbury of public opinion – the good old British envy syndrome again", concluding that "Britain's public company boardrooms are in danger of being coerced into putting code compliance before what their real job is, namely, running their businesses". He was satisfied to see his letter in print and considered the matter closed with more pressing matters at hand.

Looking back that morning in 135 Bishopsgate, surrounded by people who made a handsome living on the back of the various codes, rules and regulations of the City, spoken and unspoken, Cook wondered whether this article had been a warning after all, an early shot fired by the forces that seemed to be massing against him and his family.

CHAPTER 9

Fields giving way to factories

In the early 19th century, life on the land was hard with long hours all year round, come wind, rain and snow. The Cook family lived at Oldcoates, a village near Worksop dominated by a flour mill and surrounded by rolling countryside and ancient woodlands. Born in 1816, William Cook was the third of eight children and destined to follow in the footsteps of his father and grandfather as an agricultural labourer, tending to the fields in the service of local landowners, but by early adulthood he had seen and done enough. He wanted away, to make a new life for himself in a city, a place where great fortunes were being made by ordinary people like him. Family folklore tells of a furious row between father and son over his desire for a brighter future. In a classic act of youthful rebellion, young William left and his decision to travel all the way to Glasgow by foot, a distance of 220 miles, with just a few pennies in his pocket shows a decisive break with his past and determination to succeed.

The fast-growing Scottish city could not have been more different from rural Nottinghamshire. Glasgow was establishing itself as the second city of the empire and home to dynamic new industries producing cotton and textiles, chemicals, glass, paper and soap and the giant shipbuilding yards of the Clyde. It was a place of great opportunity and also extreme poverty and squalor with no guarantee of success and thousands of new incomers arriving every day with the same dream of making it in the city. The pull proved irresistible for William Cook.

His early years labouring in the fields gave him a core of physical strength. He had a commanding presence, characterised by high cheekbones and piercing eyes, distinguishing features that would pass down the family line. He was certainly resourceful and soon found work as a saw-maker. In 1840, he married Helen Cumming, a cotton reeler six years his senior and the daughter of a mercantile clerk who hailed from Blantyre, the birthplace of explorer David Livingstone. They would have five children together. William Cook was good at his work, earning enough to support his family and then take on employees. The first mention of his eponymous company came in 1856 in a listing for the Glasgow Post Office Directory, advertising saws, files, edge tools and cutlery, "all kinds of implements required in saw mills and by mill-wrights, engineers, house and ship carpenters and joiners, cabinetmakers, sawyers, coopers, masons, bricklayers, plasterers kept in stock". It had a logo of sorts, a circular toothed pattern to illustrate its wares.

The flourishing business afforded the family a move to the more affluent western districts of the city close to Kelvingrove Park. The elder sons William and Andrew became saw makers in their teens and joined the family firm. The youngest son Thomas pursued his own passion and joined the whisky trade as an enthusiastic apprentice. William Cook added '& Sons' in 1871, by which time it was employing 30 people and serving the shipbuilding, coal mining and railway industries of Great Britain and her growing empire. "William Cook's success mirrored that of the city of Glasgow and indeed of the Victorian age," noted the historian Philip Hansen. The seeds were sown for a dynastic family company.

Even as his standard of living improved, William Cook was not content to stand still. He commissioned a purpose-built factory in Elliott Street, a sturdy redbrick building with two storeys, tall attic and striking white brick design around its circle-top windows. It is still standing today, the painted sign bearing the legend William Cook & Sons still visible.

The Cook sons and daughters grew up, married and bore children of their own and many would enter the family firm. The founder spread his net further and in 1881 opened a subsidiary in Sheffield, specifically to produce crucible steel castings to complement the output of the Glasgow business, setting up shop in Washford Road in the Attercliffe area of the city, south of the River Don, where fields were giving way to factories, churches and pubs. Like Glasgow, the city was undergoing a huge industrial expansion and rapidly attracting both capital and workers.

The years passed and as his physical health declined, William Cook took steps to get his considerable affairs in order, notably establishing the Glasgow and Sheffield operations as separate entities. His body may have become frail but his strength of character endured and he remained fully *compos mentis* in his latter years, his sage advice always heeded. As the founder of a third generation family firm, he had earned the respect due as the white-bearded patriarch who had left behind a life of rural toil and built up a sizeable industrial concern. In the last months of his life, he moved south to live with his eldest daughter Christina, who had settled with her family in a village near Worksop. William Cook had returned home. He died in 1906 at the ripe old age of 90, a proud and successful man who was loved by his family. He was buried with his wife and two eldest sons at the Southern Necropolis, a cemetery in the Gorbals area of Glasgow, under a monument bearing the inscription 'And Whither I Go Ye Know / And The Way Ye Know'.

CHAPTER 10

All slaves to the shining metal

Pessah Bar-Adon was a grizzled, pipe-smoking writer and adventurer who had devoted his life to the study of Israel and once lived as a shepherd with Bedouin tribes to immerse himself in the land of antiquities. He was a friend and mentor to Vendyl Jones, the Texan scholar who directed archeological quests to find biblical artefacts and reputedly helped inspire the Hollywood film *Raiders of the Lost Ark*.

In 1961, Bar-Adon was leading a team of archeologists and soldiers in a search for Dead Sea scrolls in the Judean desert when he discovered the opening to a cave at Nahal Mishmar. It was perched high above the dry riverbed in one of the desert's deepest canyons and practically inaccessible.

Using ropes and ladders, Bar-Adon and his colleagues carefully descended into the chamber and started digging through debris until they came to a large round boulder blocking their way. With great exertion, they dislodged the rock and sent it tumbling down the canyon side. Where the rock had been, Bar-Adon shone his lantern and saw several metal objects glinting in the light. "Probably archeologically sensational," said the 53-year-old Polish emigre, with some foresight. Wrapped in a straw mat was treasure that would make Bar-Adon's name as

Israel's answer to Indiana Jones.

The collection included more than 400 intricately crafted copper objects, including crowns, sceptres, mace heads, statuettes and orbs, many featuring geometric patterns, herringbone and rope designs. It was dated back to 4,000 BC, the Chalcolithic period. The discovery shed new light on the ancient art of metallurgy and raised many questions over the mysterious practices of the people who made them.

"There are hundreds of metal objects, and though metal seems simple to us, then it was precious," said Osnat Misch-Brandl, a curator at the Israel Museum in Jerusalem. "How did people so long ago make these objects, and why did they make such an effort to take this whole load and bury it in a hole at the end of the world? And why make these beautiful things in the first place? Who were these people? And what did they look like? Looking at these objects, we want to know all of these things — these people were our ancestors, after all," she told *The Times of Israel* in 2012.

The Nahal Mishmar Treasure is the earliest recorded example of a complex casting method known as the lost-wax process, or *cire perdue.* This is a method of casting in which a mould is formed around a wax model that is subsequently melted and drained away. The empty space is then filled with molten metal. Some 6,000 years later, this technique remains one of the most reliable means of producing precise shapes in metal. Casting really is as old as time.

The story of metallurgy is the story of civilisation: gold, found in native form, the easiest for early man to acquire and shape; silver, copper, tin and meteoric iron also found in natural form and conducive to early metalworking; tin, lead and copper extracted from their ores by the smelting of rock and capable of wider applications; the combination of copper and tin to create an alloy called bronze and the beginning of a new epoch.

In the Bronze Age, the Mesopotamians poured molten metal into moulds to create the tools and weapons for their expanding kingdom. The practice developed and spread across the world as humankind emerged from the caves of their primitive societies. It was a time of great advancement with the invention of the wheel, the establishment of early writing systems and new innovations in agriculture, construction, warfare and the law. Powerful empires rose throughout the Near East, rulers immortalised in ancient histories and heroic tales of the search for eternal life recorded for the ages in the earliest surviving examples of literature.

The days of our years are three score and ten, but tried and tested techniques are passed down through the generations, spanning centuries and bridging millennia. Sons followed their fathers, iterating and innovating as they went along to solve the technological problems of their times through the Bronze Age, the Iron Age and the advent of steel and the Industrial Revolution when new companies like William Cook & Sons made fortunes for their founding families through the modern mastery of ancient methods.

The times might have changed but the fundamentals remained the same, the delivery of liquid metal into a mould containing a three-dimensional negative impression, the cooling, the extraction, the fettling and the finishing, an age-old manipulation of the four basic elements of earth, water, air and fire and the addictive power behind the rise of humankind from the caves to the skyscrapers. "We are all slaves to the shining metal," noted the 19th century *Punch* journalist Douglas William Jerrold. It was highly profitable work: the self-made merchant prince of Rudyard Kipling's poem 'Mary Gloster' boasted that his Clyde foundry paid him a margin of 60 per cent.

Following the discovery of the Cave of the Treasure at Nahal Mishmar, scholars have disputed the origin and purpose of the strangely beautiful objects, but one theory has stood out. The writers Gilead and Gosic argued the casting was part of a ritualised process. "The master of the craft created copper artifacts as a master of ritual," they wrote in 2015. "By transforming the stones into metal and by further casting a sacred symbol out of it, he demonstrated his unprecedented control over the material world."

The ability to exercise such control has long stirred the human imagination. In the late 19th century in the city of Glasgow, where William Cook was busy building his manufacturing business, the chemist and bibliographer John 'Soda' Ferguson amassed a substantial collection of books on the subject of alchemy, the forerunner to chemistry, metallurgy and medicine. His extensive library, now the preserve of Glasgow University, includes a 16th century work entitled of *The Mirror of Alchimy, Composed by the Thrice-Famous and Learned Fryer Roger Bachon*. The book describes "a science, teaching how to transforme any kind of mettall into another... by a proper medicine... Alchemy therefore is a science teaching how to make and compound a certain medicine, which is called Elixir, the which when it is cast upon metals or imperfect bodies, doth fully protect them". Thus the field has attracted so many speculators, charlatans and opportunists, spurred on by visions of wealth and power.

Back in the Judean desert, Pessah Bar-Adon and his team of archeologists and soldiers explored the rest of the cave at Nahal Mishmar. They made another discovery – human remains bearing the signs of violent death. Where there is treasure, there will be blood.

CHAPTER 11

Never trust a smiling journalist

Andrew Cook swept into his office, past the old framed notice hanging on the wall. It was the certificate of incorporation for the family's Sheffield works, signed by his great-great grandfather William Cook. He took a seat, a deep swill from his cup of tea and crunched into an apple.

He glanced at the newspapers and saw more tales of woe for Prime Minister John Major battling with his party sceptics over Britain's relationship with the European Union and OJ Simpson due to take the witness stand for the first time, accused in a Los Angeles court of stabbing to death his ex-wife and her male friend. Next to the morning's press was a growing pile of papers relating to company sales, performance and projections.

It was Friday, November 22 and Cook had another busy day ahead after yet another sleepless night, tossing and turning in bed as his over-stimulated mind tried to make sense of what was happening to him and his company. Triplex Lloyd and its co-conspirators were threatening to steal his life's work and seemed to have the support of the City and Fleet Street. How was he, one man, going to prevail?

Earlier in the week, Tony Carlisle, the London PR man, had persuaded Cook to do a couple of confessional-style interviews with select journalists to deal with the corporate governance issue once and for all. "The reason being, Andrew, if the other side are going to play this card, it is better for us to play it first," said Carlisle through clouds of cigarette smoke. "At least we will have some control over what is said and how it is said." Cook had begrudgingly agreed, seeing some wisdom in the argument.

"I have just the journalists and titles in mind," said Carlisle, whose firm Dewe Rogerson represented many quoted companies and dealt with City editors all the time, trading information and favours in the ebb and flow of the financial news industry. The *Evening Standard* had once described him "the dark master". "Of course, there can be no guarantees of favourable coverage in this game Andrew," he added, "and once again never trust a smiling journalist, old boy."

Charis Gresser of *The Daily Telegraph* arrived at William Cook's head office at 10am prompt, was greeted by Jane and shown up to the chairman's office. "Mr Cook, your guest is here," she announced, opening the door. Cook sprang from his seat and walked around the large desk to greet the journalist, a short-haired woman in her twenties. Cook scrutinised her as he smiled. She sounded well-spoken. Oxford, no doubt, he thought, and he was right: a graduate of philosophy, politics and economics, like so many of the rising stars of the new establishment. Gresser took a seat, pulled out her notebook and started the interview, asking Cook about the pictures of trains and boats adorning the office walls to warm him up. He was soon in entertaining mode and a long, colourful conversation ensued, covering his background, management style and views on business and the Triplex takeover bid.

"All my career, I've battled. I've had to battle with customers and suppliers and management," he told her.

"Tell me about what happened with your father when you took over the company in 1980. That sounded like quite a battle," asked Gresser, innocently.

"A difference of views arose," said Cook. "I said the company could be run either by me, or by him, but I couldn't stay there and implement his policy. There was a board meeting and he was persuaded to withdraw. It was acrimonious; actually it was harrowing. But it was put to one side as the sinking ship was being rescued."

He told her the struggle of getting his workforce to accept automation in the early years and the battles he fought as he completed a string of acquisitions of failing foundries throughout the Eighties and transformed William Cook into a catalyst for consolidation in the steel castings industry. Cook was in full flow, distracted from the concerns of the day, fielding questions on anything and everything and making a fair few throwaway remarks to his attentive audience. He dismissed Triplex's commercial logic argument with a flourish: "It's like saying that merging *The Daily Telegraph* and the *Beano* comic makes sense because they are both printed on paper."

An hour or so later, a knock on the door interrupted their talk. "Mr Cook, your next appointment has arrived," said Jane, prompting Cook to draw the interview to a close with Gresser, who he had found quite charming, and seeing her out of his office. He glanced out of the window and saw Gresser getting into a taxi. She looked happy, he thought, without a care in the world.

Next up was Richard Wolffe who had been waiting patiently in reception. He was the bespectacled Midlands correspondent of the *Financial Times* and another Oxford graduate. "Good day Mr Cook," he said. "We have spoken on the phone but it's nice to meet you in person." He was holding a spiral-bound notebook and dressed in a long overcoat.

"Hello!" said Cook, cheered by the interaction with Gresser. "We are going outside to the factory. I am going to show you our operations so you can see for yourself our excellent growth prospects." Wolffe was polite but reserved as Cook led him on a tour of the facilities, including some of the more sophisticated tools for machining steel castings for all kinds of industrial applications, and introducing him to some of the engineers and apprentices, strong and skilled men dressed in dark blue boiler suits embroidered with the company logo. Cook felt good to be doing something to fight his corner and always enjoyed being with the men on the shop floor but Wolffe did not seem particularly impressed with what he was seeing or hearing. Cook moved into confessional mode.

"I have made a mistake, which I regret now, of not keeping the shareholders up to speed on what I was doing," Cook told him. "I have been busy running and shaping the business whilst the shareholders thought it was going nowhere. They thought it was a one-man band, who was lining his pockets and that is why the share price has not moved. But in fact we have spent £17 million improving our operations over the last three years to improve efficiency across the group. We have delivered profits and sales growth over the last four years and I guarantee that will continue in the second half of this year." The journalist nodded as he jotted down the comments, then bid his farewells and followed Gresser back to London with a notebook full of shorthand.

Cook returned to the office. Martin the driver had returned from the cafe with lunch and a plate of fruit and sandwiches was laid out on the desk. Cook sat back down into his seat and exhaled loudly. His leg was aching, a legacy of the car crash which nearly claimed his life in 1990 and a sign of incipient stress. He reached for the plate when his Nokia rang, its ring-tone filling the room. He looked at the number on the screen beginning 0171 and thumbed the top-left button with the picture of the green handset to answer.

"Andrew, it's Tony," said his PR adviser. "I trust the inter-views went well. They should take some sting out of the attack." Before Cook could respond, Carlisle went on. "Triplex Lloyd has published its offer document and we need to get our response together for the press, and sharpish. The phone is ringing off the hook here with requests for comment. It is being faxed over to you now. Speak soon," he said, ringing off.

At that moment, Jane walked into the office and handed a sheaf of paper to Cook. It was warm to the touch and carried the familiar smell of the fax machine. "It's marked 'urgent' for your attention. Hope it's good news," she said. "Chance would be a fine thing," he replied. Top of the pile was a press release issued by Schroders on behalf of Triplex Lloyd announced the posting of the offer document to William Cook's shareholders.

In the release, Graham Lockyer said: "We are delighted at the favourable reception we have received for our Offer as evidenced by the strengthening of Triplex Lloyd's share price. We believe that our offer document clearly shows the benefits of combining Triplex Lloyd and William Cook – a powerful combination founded on industrial logic. I urge all William Cook shareholders to accept the offer."

Cook leafed through the pages, feeling anger rise as he scanned the words. "Triplex Lloyd – a success story," read the title above a list of achievements and tables charting growth in operating profit, sales and the order book, summarised by a splashy pull-quote from ABN AMRO stating the company "has made excellent progress under the new management team and we see no sign that it is about to lose momentum".

William Cook, it claimed, was "a story of disappointment" for its shareholders. £100 invested in January 1994 would be worth just £96 before the offer was announced; the same sum invested in Triplex Lloyd would be worth a handsome £175, claimed the document.

Triplex's PR advisors had done quite a cuttings job, selecting quotes made by Cook since 1990 to decorate a damning timeline of supposed corporate failures of the decade to date, namely the aborted bid to buy struggling locomotive maker Telfos, the doomed project to expand into the United States and a fruitless search for acquisitions in Europe.

"William Cook, under its chairman and chief executive Andrew Cook, has lost the ambition to develop new businesses in overseas markets," the document said. "Instead, it has chosen to invest in getting smaller by offering its shareholders the chance to sell their shares back to the company. William Cook – a strategy of retreat." Acceptances of the offer, valuing the company at £58.4m, should be despatched as soon as possible and received no later than 3pm on December 13, it added. The clock was ticking.

Cook phoned his lead defence advisor Simon Metcalf, who answered on the second ring. "Simon, it's Andrew. Yes, I've just finished reading it. If you can bear to hear the truth that you have spoken twisted by knaves to make a trap for fools…" he said, quoting Kipling, one of his favourite writers. He wondered whether he could watch the things he gave his life to, broken. Should he lose, would he have the strength to build them up with worn-out tools? He was not so sure.

He said: "Simon, they are a gang of knaves who have successfully achieved a good set of figures and assiduously courted the City to gain a fan club of lap-dog analysts. I know them for what they are. You will recall I bought a foundry business called Lloyds Burton from them in 1990. They are skilful at covering their own mistakes and flattering their few good points. Creative accounting is the breath of life to this bunch, but then that's the creed all over the City, as you well know. They follow the ritual of rules and regulations okay, but they know every loophole there is. To the outside world, Triplex Lloyd is the model of a well-run, sanitised plc, in total contrast to William Cook. How far from reality."

Having got it off his chest, Cook finished the call with Metcalf and arranged to see him at NatWest Markets in London on the Monday morning. He wrote out in longhand a statement for PR man Tony Carlisle to share with the journalists, advising shareholders against taking any action on the bid. "It is financial engineering wrapped up in a spurious industrial logic and use of selective statistics," he wrote, his pen pressing hard against the pad. "Our defence document will make plain just how far the Triplex Lloyd offer undervalues William Cook and, indeed, how far they apparently fail to understand our business." Cook faxed it off, had a go at the growing pile of paperwork for a couple of hours and then headed home to the family at Froggatt for the evening in hope of some respite.

It didn't last long. The fax machine in the study started churning out screed at 11pm with the first editions of the following day's papers, the big-selling Saturday editions. Emblazoned across the front of the *Telegraph*'s business section in bold black type screamed the headline, 'Triplex target in breach of City codes', accompanying a report from Charis Gresser informing readers that William Cook was in breach of both the Cadbury and Greenbury codes. Cook's heart quickened as he read on, a litany of alleged misdeeds – a five-year rolling contract for his services, the lack of audit and remuneration committees, the advanced ages of the non-executive directors Pickford and Porter and consultancies for his wife and father. At least the journalist had found someone to stick up for him. The boss of a rival castings company Brian Cooke – no relation to the Triplex chairman – had told the newspaper: "Andrew has made a real success in a very difficult industry. He has rubbed some people up the wrong way, but then you don't become successful by being nicey-nicey to everyone."

The front-page article turned inside to a feature headlined 'Cook faces up to the heat', describing him as "unashamedly autocratic" and "the kind of tough northerner who runs things his way" and playing back the comments he had made to Gresser earlier that day. "I'm not frightened of having to justify this," he said, of the company's paid retainers for family members. His wife Alison, a trademark lawyer and former company secretary in ICI's paints division, was on the payroll for £35,000 a year. Cook claimed he would have had to pay twice as much for the same services on the open market. Alison herself told the journalist: "I feel I jolly well work for it. Obviously, you shouldn't dish out contracts to family like confetti. But I'm actually of some value to the company." Cook had said his father's consultancy was in lieu of a pension, adding in an off-hand way "the poor old sod has been on £15,000 since he retired or kicked out, as he would say". Cook added: "£15,000 is not going to make much difference to our total results. And he's a good icebreaker, you know, on open days with our defence customers. He can field the old buffers." Reading these words in black and white, he instantly regretted them.

The *Telegraph* relayed how Cook trained as a barrister but was an "engineer by instinct" and had a gift from a young age for understanding how things work, making models of cars and planes as a boy with the toys getting bigger as the boy grew up. Charis wrote: "He now holds a pilot's licence, drives a Bentley turbo and flies the company helicopter when the traffic looks bad. None of this is luxury, Cook insists." Fast cars, helicopters, planes and family members on the payroll, Cook saw his life coming across as a Yorkshire version of Dallas, the US soap opera about an oil-rich family in Texas, with a monster like Robert Maxwell, the crooked media tycoon who plundered the pension fund of his workers, as the antagonist. And the company didn't even have a helicopter, only renting one from time to time. "I am autocratic because that's how you win wars and business is a war," he had told Gresser. "You can't have too many committees in a war." It was all very dramatic, thought Cook, as he headed to the bedroom and collapsed into bed.

"Andrew," said Alison, shaking her husband. "Miss Procter is on the phone." Cook opened an eye and saw it was 8am. His thoughts gathered, remembering everything at once. The bid, the battle, that bloody article in the *Telegraph* and now his former nanny, phoning to complain. He sat up in bed and took the handset from his wife.

"What's all this about you referring to your father in a national newspaper as an 'old sod'? After everything he has done for you. This is how you repay him. What would your poor mother think?"

Cook rang off and got up. His whole body ached. Alison asked him if everything was okay. Of course it's not, he thought to himself, not wishing another argument. The world was closing in on him and nobody was there to offer full-blooded support, not even his closest family.

CHAPTER 12

The greatest show on earth

Andrew Cook spent Saturday evening in the company of his eldest daughter, 10 of her little friends and an audience of nearly 14,000 children and their families at the Disney on Ice spectacular at the Sheffield Arena. Hosted by Mickey Mouse and with support from Minnie Mouse, Goofy and Donald Duck, the show promised the very best in entertainment from figure skaters starring as Disney princesses, appearing under licence to the US production company that owned the Ringling Bros and Barnum & Bailey Circus. It was Hannah's fifth birthday party and Cook was determined not to let his growing troubles derail the celebrations. But any hopes of enjoying the fun were spoiled by the half an hour he spent queuing for ice cream. Typical Sheffield, he thought, ruining what should have been a memorable evening with such incompetence. Afterwards, Cook wrote to the venue's manager in typically forceful terms to complain about the Mickey Mouse nature of the catering arrangements.

On Monday morning, the first class carriage of the Master Cutler train from Sheffield to London was filled as usual with civil servants, men and women on the public payroll staffing the new development corporations and agencies tasked with regenerating the former industrial heartlands and heading down to Whitehall for their endless meetings with other civil servants. Cook ignored the bureaucrats and found his way to a seat. At a glance, he saw the morning's papers carried reports of plans to enlarge the European Union to central and eastern Europe, a week-long strike by truck drivers in France and the unveiling of the world's smallest and lightest computer at a trade show in Las Vegas. At six by three inches, the LG Electronics device was small enough to put in your pocket. Cook raised an eyebrow and opened his briefcase. He spent the journey working through the numbers to calculate the break-up value of William Cook plc – in other words, the sum of its seven foundries and related operations. By the time the train pulled into St Pancras, he had arrived at £200m, well above the £58.4m value proposed by the Triplex bid. Cook started to feel a little more confident.

It was a bitterly cold morning and the rain was turning to snow but in the City it never settled. Cook hailed a taxi and headed to 135 Bishopsgate for a meeting with his defence team at NatWest Markets to work on the defence document. Entering the room, he nodded a greeting to the crowd of advisors and noticed a new face among them. It was the lawyer Nigel Campion-Smith, a partner at Travers Smith who had acted for Cook previously when he was on the acquisition trail. He was a quiet and thoughtful Cambridge graduate who had joined the City law firm in 1978 and risen to become one of its most prominent figures. He had impressed Cook with his advice on previous matters and was mild mannered, strait-laced and law abiding to a tee. Campion-Smith took a seat next to the bankers Simon Metcalf and Margaret Young and explained why he had joined the meeting.

"It's these comments you made to that chap from the *FT*," said the lawyer, who Cook noticed had put on weight since they had last met. All those expense account lunches, he thought. "They are rather upbeat and have been construed as profit forecasts under the Takeover Code and, as you will know, these things have to be done the proper way. They are quite taboo unless backed up with all the correct documentation from your reporting accountants and financial advisers showing it has been properly compiled in a consistent way."

"Yes, thank you Nigel, I know that," said Cook, the trained barrister. "But with respect you are not the one fighting for your life here. I am and I am not going to let any rules stand in my way. I shall defend myself with everything I have got. The press is a medium in this battle and I am determined to get my message across that Triplex Lloyd and the City are seriously undervaluing William Cook and if they think they can buy this company on the cheap, they have another thing coming. As far as I am concerned, there is one rule that counts – winning is everything. And yes, I know our interim statement before the bid was rather downbeat but I will find a way to explain that away. Remember this is just a job for you and you will get paid your fees regardless, but for me, this is a matter of defending my life's work."

Margaret spoke out. "Andrew, this is serious. We understand what you are saying but it will not hold up with the Takeover Panel. Remember Blue Arrow?"

He did and some of the people involved were still around. Indeed, some were sitting in the room with him. In 1987, the ambitious UK recruitment company launched a takeover bid for US giant Manpower, the world's largest employment agency, and announced a record-breaking £837m rights issue of new shares to pay for the colossal acquisition. Blue Arrow's investment bank County NatWest – the forerunner to NatWest Markets – and stockbroker UBS Phillips and Drew – a sister company of PDFM no less – failed to find enough buyers for the shares and hid a sizeable stake in subsidiary companies, avoiding a legal requirement to disclose holdings above five per cent to the stock exchange. The October 1987 crash exposed County NatWest's stake and led to one of the longest and costliest criminal trials in British legal history, with fraud charges brought against 11 executives from County NatWest, UBS Phillips and Drew and legal advisors Travers Smith. Four were convicted of misleading the financial markets but subsequently cleared on appeal. Cook could see why Margaret was jumpy. Campion-Smith too. Their higher-ups had been implicated. Still, that was their problem, not his; he had to keep his nerve and back his own judgment, thought Cook as he said his farewells and headed off to meet his defence lawyer David Cheyne.

Linklaters was based at Barrington House, a commanding eight-story building in Gresham Street named after a former chairman of Legal and General, one of the City's most powerful investment managers, and built on the site of The Swan with Two Necks, an old coaching inn which dated back to 1500 and a principal staging post for travel to the North of England. Linklaters was an elite London law firm and treated its partners like princelings – each had their own large, well-appointed office with a secretary stationed outside and enjoyed access to the very best facilities, all paid for by eye-watering hourly fees charged to clients. At least Cheyne was good for his money;

in fact, he was one of the best. After the smallest of small talk, Cook and Cheyne got down to business.

"Andrew, I am concerned about this matter of the corporate plane you are in the process of buying. It should be disclosed in your defence document. I am sure you don't need your PR advisors to tell you how this will play with the other side and their fat-cat line of attack. They will have a field day with this."

Cook knew Cheyne was right. The lawyer was a man of intelligence and experience who saw things for what they were and did not slant his opinions. Cook felt he was on his side, unlike some of his paid advisors. Still, the matter irked him. "Only in the UK could such a song and dance be made about a corporate plane costing no more than an average medium-sized machine tool. There is no glamour in travel, just stress, tedium and delay and it wastes a huge amount of time. If I am going to do my job to the best of my ability, which is to keep alive a strategic British industry, I need to be able to make the best use of my time. Anyway, my agreement with the plane manufacturer does not amount to a contract and so would not be disclosable in the defence document." The trained barrister, again. "Problem solved, yet you, Margaret and Simon seem to be looking down your noses at me as if I have done something wrong, like I had my hand in the till or something."

Cheyne shook his head and then smiled. He said: "You know how it is with the City when money is at stake. These people will do anything to win. You are on the back foot over corporate governance, which you clearly make no attempt to take seriously in spite of the prevailing attitudes and the required rituals, and they will use examples like your intended purchase of this plane to undermine your position and take control of

William Cook. Your company's last formal statement to the City was downbeat in outlook and now you are telling the *Financial Times* that the opposite is true. Your interview looks like it was in breach of the Takeover Code, another matter we will have to deal with. My advice is don't give the other side any more ammunition than is absolutely necessary and please be more careful in your comments to the press. It looks like they have it in for you."

"That's good advice David, thank you," said Cook. He packed up his briefcase, donned his coat and left the well-appointed Linklaters meeting room for his final meeting of the day before heading back north. It was with Jonathan de Courcy-Ireland, a quiet, reserved individual with an aura of calm and the good manners of his upper middle class and public school background. He was a follower rather than a leader and the third string at UBS. They met at a coffee shop at Liverpool Street station, which was starting to fill with City workers travelling home to Essex and beyond. Unbelievably to Cook, he was still smarting about his firm losing out on the opportunity to act as joint defence advisor to William Cook. Cook was not particularly impressed with the senior management at UBS, however amiable and affable they were. They seemed more concerned with City point-scoring than the interests of their client, but Cook needed all the help he could get. PDFM, his biggest shareholder and a UBS subsidiary, was inscrutable. It would be key to the whole battle and had recently bought into Triplex Lloyd as well. Cook did not trust PDFM and felt in his stomach that something was up.

"Jonathan, UBS cannot be joint defence advisor because there has to be one single outfit in charge of our defence. UBS is paid to be the broker and do the broking side of the job, which is to keep in touch with the company shareholders and feed back what they are thinking and saying. I am at a loss to what PDFM is going to do. Since PDFM is the fund management arm of UBS, I would hope you can shed some light on the matter. I know you are supposed to have Chinese walls between your organisations, but still…"

The young stockbroker made the right noises to humour his client before moving the conversation deftly onto the issue of fees. "We think about £650,000 and a further £100,000 if William Cook wins, or the bid lapses," said de Courcy-Ireland.

The number was about twice what Cook had expected to pay and double what UBS deserved. It was in the magical realms of Mickey Mouse. A hostile takeover bid could be the greatest show on earth for the corporate finance advisors of the City and five-star entertainment for the financial hacks of Fleet Street. But someone always had to foot the bill. Cook thought twice about arguing the point and shook hands with de Courcy-Ireland. He saw it as protection money and had recalled his maxim: pay out the line and do not economise on the bait because you can always get tough when they are on the hook. Things were going to get very tough indeed.

CHAPTER 13

Necessity is the mother of pretension

Tony Langley was a big man. At 6ft 5in, he towered above most people, even Andrew Cook. He was also a self-made man, who had few formal qualifications and had taught himself engineering at the beginning of an entrepreneurial career that would make him a manufacturing millionaire, many times over. Unlike many in the corporate world, Langley was not a fan of cashing out. Instead, he preferred the long-term approach to building up a business and was an admirer of Germany's Mittelstand, the medium-sized, multi-generational family-ly-owned companies that had established themselves as the world leaders in their niche areas. His success brought him many freedoms, including the ability to stay above the fray of Britain's motorway network. The industrialist piloted his own two-seater helicopter around the UK manufacturing plants of Langley Holdings and on Tuesday, November 26, was due to drop in to see his friend Cook for a pre-arranged lunch in Sheffield, something that had been in the diary before the hostile bid blew up.

Cook heard the helicopter approach and looked up from his desk to see it circle overhead before landing at William Cook's helipad. Langley was a skilled pilot and a loyal friend and Cook was pleased to see his familiar face as the bear of a man climbed out of the cockpit and strode towards the office. In some ways, they were kindred spirits. Like Cook, Langley had rescued a failing family business and transformed it into a world-class enterprise. But unlike Cook, he owned the company outright and had no external shareholders to worry about and keep happy. Langley greeted Cook warmly and the pair settled down to lunch, an unfussy plate of sandwiches and fruit. After enquiries about their respective families, talk turned to the Triplex business. Cook tried to explain his predicament and his problems with the City but did not really know where to begin. It was complicated to an outsider and after returning from London the night before he was feeling tired and weighed down by the immensity of it all. Conversation was desultory at best. After lunch, they agreed to keep in touch. Before leaving, Langley reminded Cook he always had an open door.

Cook returned to his desk after Langley's departure. He picked up the bundle of press cuttings faxed through by his PR advisors Dewe Rogerson. *The Independent* was on top. It had been following the bid closely through reporter Patrick Tooher, a bright young Mancunian, another Oxford graduate and new recruit to its City desk. Under the headline, 'William Cook backs down on chief's claims', the newspaper reported how the bid battle had taken an "unusual turn" and the company was "unable to confirm" media reports containing statements attributed to its chairman Andrew Cook. He felt his stomach tighten.

The Independent went on: "In a series of interviews over the weekend, Mr Cook referred to his company's sales and profits in the current half-year compared to previous periods. He also highlighted improvements in efficiency and indicated big shareholders were not prepared to accept the bid from Triplex Lloyd. Last night, Mr Cook's gaffe was being put down to inexperience. 'It's the first time he has received an offer for his company and naturally he is very keen to get his message over,' said a source familiar with the bid. 'But there are established procedures for getting that information to the market'."

Gaffe, thought Cook, his anger rising. He was fighting for his life here. He could not stand by and let the other side run away with everything he had worked so hard for. And yet, here was his company, the business he had saved from certain death, distancing itself from comments he had made in its defence. It had PR man Tony Carlisle's fingerprints all over it, he thought, the whole of his defence team, Margaret, Metcalf and even Cheyne, showing their commitment to the City club, so frightened were they of upsetting the establishment by not playing the game according to the rules. This was just another job for them, and a well-paid one too.

Cook saw the note from Carlisle accompanying the cuttings, suggesting the coverage should head off any trouble that his comments to the *FT* might cause under the Takeover Code. The ends always justify the means for these people, thought Cook, who felt distinctly uneasy at seeing his company disassociating from him in print, whatever the intended outcome. Was it a portent of things to come and who was really in charge here? The questions troubled him.

That evening, the Cooks entertained guests at home at the Manor House. The Kernlands, an international foundry consultant and his wife, had been at an event in Birmingham and had previously arranged to stay over at the Manor House.

Cook was feeling the strain but managed to play the gracious host. His friends had read about the takeover bid in the news – who hadn't? – and were concerned at what was happening. He looked so tired and drawn.

Cook tried to explain the background. "For some time, it has gnawed at me that all the work I have done, all the sacrifices I have made, will be to the benefit almost exclusively of outside shareholders. In the Eighties, I missed two good opportunities to take the company private when the shares were low enough. Earlier this year, when we completed the rationalisation of the group, I resolved to have another go at taking the company private while the shares were still relatively cheap. I have had enough of the City and its charade of corporate governance and accounting for growth. I started to look at a management buyout but I would have to resign as chairman before making the bid, a very risky move as it would put the company into play and anyone could come in and buy it, without me running the show. So I came upon the idea of the company buying back its shares. This would increase my control of the company, increase the share price and dividends and keep the remaining shareholders onside. I had started the process over the last few months and had been canvassing the views of our major share-holders about further buy-ins, including a long-term incentive plan to buy shares for our senior employees. I had even lined up some banks to help with the funding. We were on the verge of approving this incentive plan when the Triplex bid broke.

"Looking back, it had all seemed too quiet. It appears there was some kind of conspiracy but I cannot quite put my finger on it. I was trying to increase my control over the company founded by my forefathers but it seems some powerful people had other ideas and have set something big in motion. Now, I am on the verge of losing everything."

The Kernlands looked worried. "It's all so difficult to understand, Andrew, especially after everything you have done to save your company and put the steel castings industry on a sound footing," said the wife. Her husband was in agreement. "Anything we can do to help, please just let us know Andrew," he said, trying to sound reassuring. That night in bed, as he struggled to sleep, Cook felt very alone. He had checked on the children and they were sleeping soundly. He wanted nothing to disturb their world. It was becoming a frightening and upsetting time for them. They knew someone was trying to take the family company.

He slipped into another fitful sleep, the next day's appointments and any number of potential ramifications looming large in his unsettled mind.

Lunch the next day was at Dewe Rogerson's palatial offices at London Wall. The Romans had built the wall to defend their Londinium against invasion from the barbarians at the gate. Cook could do with some protection now, he thought as he entered the grand building at number three. The company spared no expense on its lavish facilities and business was good, the benefit of being known as one of the City's best financial PR firms. On the question of fees, Roddy Dewe, the Oxford-educated co-founder, once quipped that "whatever you think of charging, double it. The more you ask for, the more talented and in demand a client will assume you must be". The tactic clearly worked and the company generated a fortune in fees during the Eighties, advising the Conservative government on its £60bn privatisation campaign – remember Tell Sid – and establishing the reputation of slick spinners such as Tony Carlisle.

At 1pm, the aforementioned was holding court in a private dining room with Cook to one side and two journalists to the other. Richard Wachman was the newly appointed City editor of the *Birmingham Post* and Eric Barkas the City editor of *The Yorkshire Post*, two of Britain's most respected regional daily newspapers. On the day, Cook found them sceptical, even hostile. The journalists waded into the food and wine on offer, pausing only to scribble down notes as Triplex's quarry mounted his defence. He told them about the anonymous mail he had received days before the bid became public. "Letters ripped from a book or something were stuck together on a bit of paper which indicated something was in the offing. But it looked like a hoax and I decided not to take it further," he said, adding he was not totally surprised when Triplex chairman Colin Cooke phoned him on the morning of November 15 to announce his company's hostile intentions. Such a needlessly aggressive move, he thought. What kind of person did that? And what kind of system encouraged such behaviour?

The topic of conversation turned to the issue of fees with Cook venturing there should be a law against such bids unless the bidder is willing to pay the defence costs as well as its own. He told them: "I think it's akin to paying the police to come to your house when you're mugged in the street." In response, Barkas suggested he sounded bitter and reached for the wine. "You bet," Cook said. "You'd be bitter too if somebody was trying to steal your life's work." In spite of the worsening atmosphere in the room, Cook did his best to put his message across, acknowledging that William Cook's shares were "momentarily weak" because he had failed to keep the City informed about his major investment in the business. "I hadn't done an analysts' roadshow. That was my mistake, with hindsight, when other people, notably Triplex Lloyd, plugged their companies. I've been concentrating on running the business and talking to customers. I've made no attempt to attract new investors to the company." He also defended his lack of recent acquisitions, the programme of buying back shares – "better than splurging it away" on buying businesses – and his remuneration package. "I think I earn every penny. Don't forget, I've built this company up and I've made a lot of shareholders a lot of money, for which I've received precious little thanks – all I get is flak."

The lunch was hardly the love-in that Carlisle might have hoped for. Barkas skewered his subject in his write-up for *The Yorkshire Post*: "When they made Andrew Cook, they threw away the mould. When it comes to patrician demeanour and a haughty disdain, he could teach Lord Snooty a thing or two. Who would have thought he was a metal basher? And who would have expected to see him glad-handing in the City, rubbing shoulders with people he would normally swim the Don to avoid? Necessity is the mother of pretension. And Cook needs as much support as he can get in the Square Mile… The awkward facts of life, however, are that you tend to get out what you put in. For years Cook has been running his business like a personal fiefdom. Now when he needs favours, there may not be too many to call in."

Cook felt some indigestion after the less-than-successful lunch. He crossed the City by taxi and exchanged pleasantries with the driver, a relief after the tension of the meeting with the two journalists. He much preferred the company of working men to City types and was at his happiest on the shop floor in one of his foundries, solving engineering problems alongside his loyal staff. The Hackney carriage stopped off at Bishopsgate and he tipped the cabbie handsomely from his own pocket.

The next meeting was at MeesPierson, a Dutch merchant bank and long-term lender to William Cook, albeit on minor terms. The institution dated back to the 18th century and was known for being bankers to the Dutch royal family. There was no royal treatment for Cook on this occasion though – the man and woman from the bank very apologetically explained they would be pulling out of the financing for the company's proposed buy-in of shares. The pair were scrupulously courteous and very sorry of course but nothing could be done. Something to do with the higher-ups, they suggested. Cook was left feeling increasingly abandoned by his business allies, even long-standing ones. This is what happens when you are seen as being on the losing side.

CHAPTER 14

Either him or me

Andrew Cook's father McTurk had left a number of messages at home and at the office. Cook was busy and felt harassed and the last thing he wanted was another confrontation with his father. Eventually, the two met face to face at the company boardroom in Sheffield.

"Andrew, this business with Triplex," said McTurk, who seemed quite cheerful. "You know I can help, don't you?"

Cook said nothing, waiting for him to continue.

"You need to find people to buy paper in the company, invest in the shares, which will drive the price up and force the other side to increase their bid. I know people in the City who might be able to assist. Let me help, Andrew."

Cook bridled at the suggestion. He knew his father was basically right – of course any increase in the share price would put pressure on Triplex to put up or shut up – but it was hardly a revelation. And he doubted, too, whether his father's supposed contacts would have the influence required to make a meaningful difference. He noticed his father was smiling. McTurk seemed to be enjoying all of this trouble. Maybe he thought his son was getting a long overdue comeuppance.

"I will consider your offer of help," said Cook, thinking

anything was worth a try at this stage. "Is there anything else?"

"Do that, Andrew. You look like you are in need of some support. You haven't got all the answers, you know. We don't want the family firm falling into someone else's hands now, do we?"

Cook seethed. If it wasn't for him, the company would have closed 15 years earlier. It was only through his perseverance and determination that William Cook was still in existence and capable of paying the bill for his father's lavish retirement. He saved the company from certain death and had no choice but to fight and doubted whether his father or his saloon-bar friends in the City would be of any assistance whatsoever.

His father blathered on, saying how well respected he was in the City and how he had connections and how he knew people who knew people who could pull some strings. Cook held him responsible for his plight, having sold the family's majority shareholding back in 1956.

"Frankly, Andrew this whole show is an embarrassment to me and to the family name. Goodness knows what they are saying at the club," added McTurk. "Anyway, if you had done a better job of keeping your shareholders on side, you wouldn't be in this mess. This is all of your own making, boy. Don't say I haven't tried to help."

He turned his back and left, leaving Cook in a state of advanced agitation. His father had never supported or encouraged him. He hadn't even wanted him to join the company. In fact, it was his father who had wanted to shut up shop.

In 1980, British industry was on its backside and struggling to survive under the weight of rising costs, overcapacity, union strife and management incompetence. After the social and economic malaise of the Seventies, the nation's factories were wholly uncompetitive and orders were evaporating. The new prime minister Margaret Thatcher was administering her medicine to the sick patient – "there is no alternative" – to drive down rampant inflation. Her policy of high interest rates and spending cuts succeeded in taming the beast but led to a deep fall in manufacturing output and lower cost, higher value rivals from overseas were stealing the nation's lunch. The problem was particularly acute in the steel castings sector, which was operating at 50 per cent or less of capacity. Lame ducks were everywhere. Still, it is an ill wind that blows nobody any good and merchant bankers in the City had dreamed up a clever piece of financial engineering to rationalise the sector and, in turn, generate a handsome return for their efforts.

Lazard Brothers and Co was a merchant bank which dated back to the 1840s, the same decade that William Cook founded his eponymous company. Five *frères* had emigrated from France to the new world and set up nascent investment banking operations in New Orleans, San Francisco, New York and also Paris and London, cementing Lazard as well-connected, cross-border advisors to business and governments spanning the western world.

Peter Grant, an Oxford-educated Scot and father of five, was Lazard's man in London and a leading light in the City's corporate finance establishment. He and his colleagues conceived a DIY rationalisation scheme to deal with the chronic overcapacity in the steel castings sector: pay and stay or take the money and go. They consulted the Department of Industry and the Bank of England on their proposal and received blessings. The *Financial Times* noted "the choice may appear harsh, but if the scheme is rejected part of the industry will undoubtedly find death by a different route". In 1981, Lazard wrote to industry leaders outlining the plan. Grant told the *FT* that reaction was "on the whole favourable". Indeed, McTurk made it plain he was in favour of taking the money. Rivals put it about that William Cook was to participate in the scheme, leaking the rumour to the press to damage the company's prospects. By 1982, Lazard had successfully secured the involvement of most of the sector with firms representing nearly a quarter of production agreeing to close. The bankers wrote again to William Cook, by now an obvious outlier.

Facing off against the merchant bank and the wishes of his father, Cook told Lazard "it is my firm intention that we not only stay open, but also substantially improve our performance and prosperity". This was easier said than done. But unlike his father who preferred to pursue his leisure interests as a hands-off owner, Cook knew the company's foundries and how they worked, having served a long apprenticeship during the Seventies, winning the respect of the working men through his commitment to solving complex engineering problems, bringing order to the sometimes shambolic nature of the company's operations and seeing through to completion the mammoth project to commission new works at Parkway in Sheffield, which would be key to the company's future. His responsibilities and capabilities grew during that largely unhappy decade and yet his father still asked when he would be returning to the Bar. "You should be a High Court judge," McTurk would say, oblivious to his son's determination to make the company his career and his natural talent for engineering.

Cook entered a tunnel-like existence as he fought to turn the company round. At 32, the board promoted him to managing director, although he was still nominally under the command of the chairman, his father. He became single-minded, purposeful and ruthless as he pursued his goal of reviving the firm founded by his forefathers and creating the finest steel foundry in the world. It was a lonely existence and without experience or anyone to advise or share the burden with him, Cook became bad tempered and intolerant. Feelings of great responsibility and insecurity plagued him.

To survive, Cook knew the company had to cut costs and that could only mean redundancies. Many of the men had served William Cook for their entire working lives as had many of their fathers and grandfathers. It was a difficult task with unpleasant human consequences but Cook did not flinch as he set about reducing the number of workers by a third. He also sacked some of the management, including his father's right-hand man, with whom he clashed repeatedly over his plans to modernise the plant. Cook wanted to replace men with machines to increase efficiency and productivity. For generations, men would do the physical work of pouring and moving around moulds. Cook decided the process should be mechanised and used some of the company's cash pile to invest in the latest Swiss-made industrial equipment, taking advantage of the strong pound. He also bought an annuity for his father, again at a very agreeable rate. And he hired a new production controller, Sue Browne, who would be instrumental in making a success of the new system. The appointment was the final straw for McTurk who turned up at the office to rant and rave at his son. "What the hell are you doing Andrew? Who is this woman? This is madness!"

Another stand-up row ensued. After McTurk had departed in a huff, Cook wrote a letter to his father saying he could no longer tolerate relations with him. "You have done enough damage to my life," he wrote, recalling the abject unhappiness of his childhood. "I never want to see you again." Then he wrote to board director, Sir Charles Hardie, with an ultimatum. "I cannot continue trying to save the company with this unrelenting hostility from my father. It is either him or me. The board must decide."

They met to discuss the situation over dinner at the Hallam Tower, a once-fashionable luxury hotel jutting out of the Broomhill district of Sheffield. Sir Charles had arrived early and was waiting for Cook in reception. He was an accountant by profession who had risen to the top of blue-chip bean counters Dixon, Wilson, Tubbs and Gillet and then embarked on a high-flying career as a chairman and non-executive director, serving on the boards of multiple companies including British Overseas Airways Corporation, Metropolitan Estate and Property Corporation and the merchant bank Hill Samuel. He was so busy he reputedly mapped every year in advance, starting each October, and, according to a *New York Times* profile, ruffled others with his ambition and almost effortless ability. In person, Sir Charles had a friendly, kind and relaxed manner, a tonic to Cook's profound unrest. They sat down for dinner in the Vulcan Room restaurant with its yellow walls and green carpet and ordered the fixed menu, though Cook waved away the wine. Sir Charles listened attentively as the young man unburdened himself. He observed a highly intelligent, extremely capable and intense individual who was clearly tormented by his family background. The elder man could see the son, not the father, was the future of the company and resolved to do what was in his power to set him free and help fulfil his obvious potential. He promised Cook his support and said he would speak to the senior independent director Ronald Pratt the next day and set in train negotiations for McTurk's resignation.

After the fraught tension that had been building for years, the board meeting to confirm the chairman's departure was an anti-climax. McTurk did not even attend in person. The annuity purchased by his son had smoothed his exit, providing a handsome six-figure pension for a very comfortable retirement. McTurk left William Cook with money, shares, cars and the honorific title of president, specially created for him. The company issued a sanitised statement to the City in its 1983 annual report. "At the end of the financial year, Mr A McT Cook retired from the board. In his 35 years as chairman, Mr Cook has presided over the company's development from a small and backward enterprise employing less than 30 men to a steel foundry without superior among its size and type in the world. It was Mr Cook's vision that resulted in the company's introduction of high frequency melting in 1949 and it was through his efforts that the Parkway site on which the main factory now lies was developed."

Generous words, but father and son would not speak for several years.

In the annual report, his first as chairman, Cook said: "However much demand for steel castings may have fallen, it has not evaporated altogether, nor can it if we are to retain any residual engineering industry in this country. There will always be room for one really first class steel casting manufacturer and it is in this future role, at the very least, that I see William Cook."

Over the next decade, Cook would single-mindedly turn this vision into a reality, first saving the company and then the sector. He was unassailable, until the arrival of Triplex Lloyd and its backers in the City.

CHAPTER 15

A company to watch

The Lloyds were a Quaker family of Welsh descent whose distant ancestors were said to be Welsh kings. They were just as powerful in the West Midlands where Sampson Lloyd the Second, a successful iron merchant and the founder of Lloyds Banking Group, established Birmingham's first bank in 1765. They were a fecund lot – Sampson Lloyd the Third had 17 children, his half-brother Charles 14 – and they created alliances through marriage with other Quakers such as the Barclays and the Gurneys, the founding families of Britain's financial services industry and the Black Horse and Blue Eagle banks. The *Punch* journalist EV Lucas wrote: "Too much attention has been paid to the growth of kingdoms: the growth of a bank is equally interesting. Both are equally the story of human ambition and address."

Francis Henry Lloyd was the great-grandson of Sampson Lloyd the Second. By the time he was born in 1844, the Lloyds dynasty had extensive interests in banking, manufacturing and politics.

Francis chose manufacturing over finance and with his family's money bought a disused timber yard in the Black Country in 1879, establishing a small foundry at James Bridge with three forges and a fitting shop and becoming a master of the craft. The company, FH Lloyd, flourished and in 1912 was producing 2,000 tonnes of steel castings a year. It boomed during the Great War, making cast steel shells for the Western Front. Francis was the archetypal well-to-do industrialist, serving on the local school board, sitting as a justice of the peace and co-founding the Wednesbury Society for the Relief of the Indigent Sick. As a pillar of his community, there was great sadness at his untimely demise in what can accurately be described as a slow-motion train crash. In 1916, Francis was crossing a railway line on his way home when he was hit by a locomotive travelling at four miles per hour. He suffered a fractured skull and died from his injuries. The inquest returned a verdict of accidental death.

His son Daniel Charles Lloyd took over and applied his own ideas to the business, installing its first electric furnace and building a new heavy foundry. FH Lloyd grew to become Europe's largest steel foundry and by the end of the Second World War was producing 26,000 tons of castings a year – including turrets for Centurion battle tanks. An advert in *The Engineer* magazine in 1953 introduced readers to "the men who know steel best… who've spent twenty, thirty years and more in steel founding. Pattern-makers, core-makers, fettlers, machine men – the ways of steel are ways of life to these craftsmen of Lloyd's. Delicate laboratory controls, vital though they are, cannot supplant the inborn feeling of these men for their material". Carried by their efforts, FH Lloyd continued to grow during the sixties, acquiring companies and foundries across the Midlands and Wales, but fell on hard times during the industrial malaise of the Seventies and early Eighties, forcing the closure of the once-mighty James Bridge works. FH Lloyd limped on with just one foundry at Burton-on-Trent – later acquired by William Cook plc – and in 1987 merged with the publicly quoted Triplex Foundries Group, a fast-growing conglomerate led by the thrusting chief executive Jim Doel. The newly enlarged entity was named Triplex Lloyd and served the automotive and engineering, building products, power and defence and electrical engineering markets. Its line-drawn logo bore a phoenix rising from the flames.

In 1989, Triplex Lloyd appointed Colin Ivor Cooke, of Bridgend, South Wales, as a non-executive director. Cooke, a balding 49-year-old with hooded eyes, thin lips and inscrutable glare, was a metallurgist by background, though he had swapped his overalls for the double-breasted pinstripe suits of the City. He was in the ascendancy, this being his 10th company directorship. A year later, Triplex Lloyd promoted him to deputy chairman to help oversee the young and vigorous executive team. "Changes of great moment are under way," wrote Doel in the annual report. "Triplex Lloyd is a good company but that is no longer good enough. To succeed in the 1990s we must be an outstanding company." Doel did not live to fulfil his ambition, reportedly suffering a heart attack on a cricket pitch at the age of 46. Four days after his death in July 1991, Cooke was appointed chairman of the board, giving him full control of the company and its manufacturing interests, along with 4,500 employees.

The UK economy was in the grip of another downturn, caused by high interest rates, falling house prices and an over-valued pound, and manufacturing was suffering. Triplex Lloyd reacted by cutting 800 jobs. In an interview, Cooke told *The Guardian* in December 1991: "We are literally pared down to the bone, although our operating performance has proved to be resilient in spite of the fact that the severe recession has placed considerable pressures on us." Keith Harper, the newspaper's industrial editor, described Triplex Lloyd as "the epitome of what came to be affectionately regarded over the years as the backbone of industry. Today it is disregarded by Whitehall". A pugnacious-sounding Cooke said: "We have had a succession of hand-to-hand battles during the past 20 years from the politicians. If it goes on much longer there will be no industry left to fight over." He complained that none of the people in the political parties had any experience of industry. Cooke added: "Mrs Thatcher thought we could survive on service industries alone and we can't."

Those service industries of the City of London, which could trace their roots back to the Quaker banking families of the 18th and 19th centuries, acted as kingmakers in the consolidation of struggling industrial sectors. In Triplex Lloyd, perhaps they saw one of their own. Under Cooke, the company was able to raise tens of millions of pounds from investors to help add more businesses to the group. It caught the eye of appreciative analysts such as Tim Bennett at brokers Albert E Sharp who noted: "This is a company to watch. It has been looking at some sizeable acquisitions." Some commentators were more spiky in their assessment, notably the trade title *Accountancy Age* which observed how Cooke had spent the past few years buying companies and concentrating on accounting. "Now he is going to have to spend some time on actually doing the business," it added. The analysis proved prescient as Triplex Lloyd dived to a pre-tax loss for 1994 – *The Daily Telegraph* warned readers the "track record is patchy" – but recovered, phoenix-like, the following year to unveil stonking profits. Cooke told investors he was "delighted" with the results, adding "it has been a difficult period following the restructuring and rebuilding of the group". *The Independent* noted: "The turnaround at Triplex Lloyd, the former West Midlands metal basher, is all the more remarkable for having been led by the same chairman, Colin Cooke, who presided over the group's recent problems. Now stepping down to the non-executive chair, Mr Cooke can congratulate himself on his achievements." The City liked what it was seeing: the London Stock Exchange Group presented Triplex Lloyd with awards for excellence in financial reporting.

Cooke was in demand. Fenner plc, the listed conveyor belt maker, appointed him non-executive chairman in 1993. He joined the board of Yorkshire Water as a non-executive director in 1995. Although he was stepping down from day-to-day executive duties at Triplex Lloyd, he told investors he would retain a close interest in the group as non-executive chairman. After all, he had amassed a large financial stake in the company. With a fresh management team including new CEO Graham Lockyer and the blessing of the City, Triplex Lloyd was able to survey the horizon for new takeover targets. After setting its sights on William Cook, the board agreed to a hostile approach. Cooke saw potential for a global business serving customers in Europe, North America and Asia and generating millions of pounds in profits in the coming years. In the words of EV Lucas, it was yet another story of "human ambition and address". The enlarged group promised significant scope for further benefits in manufacturing and purchasing and, rather euphemistically, "head office cost savings" – in other words, the sacking of Andrew Cook.

CHAPTER 16

Like Janus, they face both ways

Paul Compton was another man who wanted Andrew Cook sacked. Known as 'Compo' to his friends, the Cambridge engineering graduate was a successful analyst in the City and enjoyed the lifestyle that came with it, living in a multi-million pound house in the leafy south-west London suburb of Richmond, sailing yachts and driving an Aston Martin DB9 with the number plate 007. "He earns his money and likes to spend it," remarked his father Donald.

Cook first met Compton in the late 1980s and had been impressed with his knowledge of the engineering sector. Like William Cook plc, Compo's then employer PDFM was also in the ascendancy under the leadership of Sheffield-raised Tony Dye, an opinionated fund manager with a relentless focus on dividend yield and asset value rather than projected growth and the eye-catching nickname of Dr Doom. In turn, PDFM would become William Cook's biggest shareholder, buying in at a high price in the belief its shares would only rise higher, and Cook and Compton enjoyed good relations as William Cook continued to flourish. But when the company cut the dividend in 1992 following its ill-fated acquisition in the United States, the once-friendly Compton turned against Cook and started agitating for change, issuing research notes that cast Cook in an unfavourable light and suggesting the company's fortunes would improve with a new leader. After Compton's most recent missive, prior to the Triplex Lloyd announcement, Cook had instructed lawyers at Irwin Mitchell to fire off a letter to Compton's employers threatening to sue for libel if their man continued to act in this way. But still he had not given any real credence to the prospect of a hostile takeover bid against his family firm.

It was Saturday, November 30 and Cook and wife Alison were getting ready to go out for a rare social occasion. The pressure of fighting the bid had become all-consuming and there was precious little time for family life. Cook missed his children and it seemed they were growing up out of sight. There was also the impact of the battle on them. Young William was worrying about the family being made destitute if they lost.

The Cooks weren't going far that evening – a short walk across the village of Froggatt with its small cluster of stone houses and narrow lanes to the home of Sarah Grunewald and her husband Richard, a consultant neurologist at Sheffield Teaching Hospitals. Grunewald was a rare thing: a female director in the male-dominated world of corporate finance, heading up NatWest Markets' operations in the North of England and a trusted advisor to companies looking to fundraise and carry out mergers and acquisitions. She was well-connected, energetic, perceptive and popular with clients and a mother of three to boot. The press could not resist drawing parallels with her Oxford contemporary, the high-flying City fund manager and mother-of-six Nicola Horlick. "People I know have likened me to Nicola, but I am no superwoman," Grunewald would tell the *Daily Mail*. "First and foremost, I am a mother. Combining home and work means I am always tired and always guilty – guilty that you are not giving enough time to everything."

The champagne cork popped as Grunewald and her husband greeted their guests. Around the dinner table with the claret in full flow, talk inevitably turned to the takeover battle.

"I think PDFM have set you up here," said Grunewald, cutting straight to the point in her typically direct, no-nonsense style.

"I think you are right," replied Cook, wondering why on earth his highly paid advisors weren't able to state things so clearly. "They had been blowing hot and cold on our plan to buy shares back and are devilishly hard to read. I just don't trust them. They are like Janus, the two-faced Roman god of duality. They face both ways."

"Trust your instinct," said Grunewald. "PDFM were originally shareholders in Triplex Lloyd. They sold out but bought in again recently. It looks pretty clear to me." Grunewald passed the decanter of wine to Cook, who accepted another glass. He wondered aloud whether she would be able to help out by mustering her considerable resources. After all, NatWest had recently refinanced Sheffield Forgemasters, the perennially troubled heavy engineer. Perhaps Forgemasters could ride in as a White Knight and see off Triplex Lloyd and gain a stock market listing. He could run the new show, give it the Cook treatment and provide an exit opportunity for the long-standing CEO Phillip Wright who was said to be looking for a way out after the stresses and strains of the Iraqi supergun scandal that had dogged the company since 1990. Grunewald plainly didn't warm to the idea. Perhaps she was another one who did not rate Cook's chances. He felt his mood begin to drop again. The champagne and claret were wearing off.

He and Alison said their goodbyes and traipsed home to the Manor House. Alison went off to sleep and Cook headed to the study. His PR man Tony Carlisle had faxed through a new article from the *Financial Times* written by Midlands correspondent Richard Wolffe. Aptly named, thought Cook, who felt like he was being hunted. He took a gulp of water to quench his parched throat and read on.

"In the toilet at the head office of William Cook, two crumpled US dollar bills are framed on the wall. The inscription underneath reminds anyone using the facilities that the cash was all that the steel castings group received when it sold its US subsidiary Unitcast in 1992. The US failure – bought for more than \$12m (£7.1m) in 1991 – represents more than just a reminder about flushing money away. Unitcast remains a thorn in the side of William Cook, as one of the key arguments behind the current £58m hostile bid for the company." In his story, Wolffe noted Cook's investment in machinery to replace some of the painstaking work of making patterns for moulds for castings but claimed much of the spending had made little obvious impact on the foundry floor. "From the soot of the moulds to the molten metal of the furnaces, the castings process would probably be recognised by Mr Cook's forefathers, who established the company in the Victorian era," wrote the journalist. Cook rolled his eyes and pictured his predecessors spinning in their graves at the turn of events. He hauled himself off to the bedroom, feeling the old ache from the car crash injury, took a couple of sleeping pills and collapsed into bed. As he lay down, Cook felt a reeling sensation, like he was at the centre of a vortex and being sucked into its depths. The last thing he remembered was the swirling curtains.

Strong north-westerly winds woke Cook from his slumber early the next day, a dark Sunday morning. The gales added to his sense of foreboding, of something greater and more powerful at work. It was December 1 and *Breakfast with Frost* was on in the background. The news contained more woes for John Major, continued talk of EU enlargement and the death of American songwriter Irving Gordon, composer of 'Unforgettable'. This year would be one to forget, thought Cook, who was feeling the groggy after-effects of the champagne, claret and sleeping pills. The children were up and about, the girls playing in a den made with sofa cushions and William driving around the patio in his new electric toy car wearing his father's motorcycle helmet. After tea and toast, Cook returned to the study and resumed work on the defence document. It would be launched this coming week and there was much to do. He was still irritated by the disappearing act his London banking advisors had staged at the end of Friday, handing him a half-complete job and then clearing off for the weekend. Cook had ended up staying on with a couple of juniors to sort out the document, eventually catching the 10pm train home from King's Cross.

Cook's mood lightened when his finance director, the reliable John Caldwell, arrived at the Manor House for 10am prompt and the pair got down to business, sourcing the evidence to back up their claims to counter Triplex Lloyd's lines of attack. The act of work calmed Cook's troubled mind. They were joined in the study by a charming young female lawyer despatched by David Cheyne from Linklaters in London to assist with the legal niceties. She was soon soothing any ruffled feathers. Cheyne was a canny old boy, thought Cook, and with the solicitor's help they completed the verification process without any eruptions, finalising the headline arguments and making sure they included all the correct background information. Cook was not entirely happy with the finished product and recognised it as the compromised work of a committee, but it was the best they could do in the time available and at least it was better than NatWest's risible attempt. It was now ready for launch on the coming Friday, December 6.

Tony Carlisle's offices at London Wall Buildings never failed to impress. The crescent-shaped block was grade II-listed and felt more like a palace than a PR firm. Carlisle and his colleagues with their Oxford PPE degrees truly were the kingmakers in the new capital. If the grand surroundings helped win over the City scribes, it would be worth it, thought Cook as he arrived for the breakfast briefing at 8am. He felt exhausted, the sleeping pills prescribed by the family doctor only providing him with three or four hours at best. He hadn't slept well for three weeks and was getting closer to the edge. Cook was shown to the hall for the event and walked in through the double doors. It was a cavernous room, like a Roman bath, and nearly empty. Carlisle had managed to drag in a couple of analysts and a handful of journalists. The other seats were occupied by the home side and paid to be there. After the regulation coffee and sickly sweet Danish pastries Cook took to the lectern and started his presentation. He felt so tired, his usual fluency deserting him. On he laboured, talking through the slides, highlighting the supposedly superior quality of William Cook, pointing to the bar charts, and trying to explain why he had written off the company's spending against revenue rather than capitalising it instead. Most self-respecting public companies added such expenditure to their balance sheets because overall it tended to flatter their share prices. Financial engineering, in other words. As was the City's way. Cook looked at his audience. One of the analyst's stifled a yawn, the other seemed to be fixated on something in the ornate ceiling.

"William Cook is in better shape than at any time I can remember in the last 25 years," Cook told the near-empty room, his voice echoing back at him. "We have very real long-term prospects for increased growth and prosperity. It is not right that an opportunistic predator should deprive our share-holders of these benefits with this ludicrous bid. The Triplex offer document is highly selective in its information and glosses over the fact that William Cook has seen faster sales growth, a more consistent profit record, higher earnings-per-share growth and consistent cash-flow generation."

Cook brought his talk to a close and invited questions. Silence. Thank God that was over, he thought as he stepped down from the dais and walked towards Carlisle and the pack of journalists at the back. His banker Simon Metcalf strode up alongside and leaned in to Cook. "Andrew, you might want to spend some time brushing up on your presentation skills," he said in a low voice. If he wasn't so bloody exhausted Cook might have reacted, but instead he just groaned and headed off towards the waiting press for the interviews. Alarmingly, the line of questioning was not concerned with Cook's value argu-ments, rather a footnote buried at the back of the document detailing his personal arrangements if the company succumbed to the Triplex bid, namely a compensation package of up to

£1.5m. Cook played the questions with a straight bat, believing honesty was the best policy and vainly tried to steer the topic back to the underlying value of William Cook. The journalists nodded and scribbled away. Cook noticed they were all smiling. After half an hour of questions, he packed up and returned home, wearier than ever. He would take three sleeping pills that night.

The morning's headlines shook him from his slumbers soon enough, zeroing in on his comments about the compensation package. 'Prospective £1.5m payoff "a pittance"', said *The Times*. Cook immediately regretted being so candid as he read his own words: "It's a pretty small price to pay for losing your life's work. I don't think it's excessive at all." One of his favourite Kipling quotes came to mind. Worse was to come in *The Daily Telegraph*. Its reporter Charis Gresser had approached Triplex Lloyd for reaction to the compensation package. CEO Graham Lockyer told the newspaper: "We will be looking closely at this with our legal advisors to understand it and take appropriate action." Lockyer added the William Cook annual report and accounts omitted mention of the chairman's personal arrangements, which would be in breach of the London Stock Exchange's listing requirements. Cook felt his throat tighten and read on. Never knowingly out-punned, the *Daily Mail*'s headline said 'Cook gets hot under the collar'. *The Scotsman* noted Cook "seemed confused". Triplex Lloyd had told the *FT* that Cook's value argument was "entering the land of the stupid". Cook was in crisis, but the journalists appeared to be having a field day with all these insults flying. *The Independent* also sought comment from Lockyer who heaped scorn on the defence document and its dramatically improved profit forecasts coming so soon after the downbeat interim statement to the City prior to the Triplex bid. "The miracle that has occurred in the past six weeks is unbelievable," said Lockyer. "The TV magician Paul Daniels would be proud of him." Cook would need to conjure up something big to get out of this hole.

CHAPTER 17

The typical background for a successful entrepreneur

Andrew Cook did not have many natural allies in the City. His consistent failure to play the game had seen to that. But he did have one in Terry Smith, an iconoclastic stock picker with owlish eyes who had made his name by seeing things as they are and speaking truth to power. Like Cook, he was a grammar school boy and no old school tie network had assisted his rise to the top, just a rare intelligence and the in-built toughness from growing up in poverty in the East End of London. Smith was the son of a lorry driver who died of asbestosis and the nephew of a boxer and he had a simple view on life. "I don't start fights with people but I will finish them," he once told the *Telegraph*. "A lot of people think I am tough, but they also think I am straight."

Smith was the first in his family to go to university, gaining a first in history from Cardiff. He joined Barclays as a graduate trainee and managed branches in Wales and Pall Mall before moving into the finance department, where he came into contact with City analysts and discovered that lo and behold, they were no smarter than he was. Armed with this revelation, he quit and joined W Greenwell and Co, a wealthy stockbroking firm, where he made a name for himself with razor-sharp analysis of corporate balance sheets. UBS Phillips & Drew came calling in 1990, seeking to rebuild its reputation after the Blue Arrow scandal, and hired Smith as its head of UK company research with a brief to reclaim the bank's moral high ground. The straight-talking analyst did just that by exposing the techniques companies used to generate profits without growing their cash position and naming and shaming the guilty parties. Unfortunately for UBS, some of these companies were also paying clients and it put pressure on Smith to stop. He refused and published a book expanding his argument called *Accounting for Growth*. UBS sacked him and then sued; Smith countersued, pitting himself against a global financial institution with unlimited resource. They eventually settled out of court and Smith's book became a best-seller with its underlying message that cash is king.

Smith landed at the embryonic Collins Stewart and built it into one of the City's top stockbroking groups, demonstrating a strong entrepreneurial drive uncommon among the jobbing City population. Sitting at his desk with his mascot, a small statue of himself wearing a rugby shirt from his university days, Smith told *The Daily Telegraph* about his ascent. "To be a successful entrepreneur, you've got to have a number of things," he said, listing off divorced parents, being sent to boarding school, having a near-death experience as a child, losing a parent at an early age or being an only child. "If you have two or three of those, then that's the typical background for a successful entrepreneur. If you get all five, then you're mad. You are completely paranoid." Smith had two of them, as did Cook. With their grammar school backgrounds, they were almost kindred spirits in a financial world dominated by the privately schooled and Oxbridge-educated. Cook had visited Smith at the end of November to seek his support and found him bullish and supportive but left the meeting with the impression there was not much his friend could do, beyond putting out some research notes in favour of William Cook.

It would take more than one man, however influential, to turn the tide in Cook's favour. His press coverage had been predominantly awful. To borrow a phrase from Smith's favourite sport of boxing, Cook was on the ropes. The launch of the defence document was supposed to win over the journalists with his value argument but instead they had focused on details of his prospective payoff buried in the back, leading to disastrous headlines. In spite of the backlash, he couldn't help how he felt: £1.5m would be a pittance for his life's work. And it wasn't just his life either, it was the culmination of his family's work, stretching all the way back to the beginnings of William Cook in the early 19th century. All that sacrifice and toil over all those decades. Now here was Triplex Lloyd and its cheerleaders in the City and Fleet Street prising the company from his grip.

One journalist at least appeared to show a little bit of support. Born in 1934, Christopher Fildes was a veteran financial columnist for *The Daily Telegraph* and author of the long-running City and Suburban column in *The Spectator*. Unlike the vaulting young hacks in Fleet Street, he had already made his name and enjoyed a large following of readers with his erudite commentary. And he was probably the last journalist in Britain in 1996 to wear a bowler hat and button-hole carnation. Along with his colleagues, Fildes was enjoying the spectacle of the increasingly acrimonious battle. But he seemed to have spotted something about Cook the others had missed in their haste to put the boot in. Writing in City and Suburban on Saturday December 7, the day after the disastrous launch of the defence document, Fildes took a more measured view of the situation, even if poking a little fun at Cook's foibles.

"We haven't had a good steel scrap for ages, and Andrew Cook is a scrapper after my own heart. He is chairman and Lord High Everything Else of William Cook, the Sheffield steel founders, now on the receiving end of a £58m takeover bid. He could also claim to be the most incorrect chairman – politically, Cadbuarially, Euromanically – of any British company."

Fildes presented the argument for his case: Cook's outspoken welcome of Britain's withdrawal from the Exchange Rate Mechanism in 1992, his one-man legal battle against Brussels over illegal subsidies for European competitors, his formidable political debating skills ("he took on Sir Edward Heath in front of the cameras, and melted him down") and his stand against the non-mandatory Cadbury and Greenbury codes. "Now, I suppose, all this will be taken down and used in evidence against him," wrote Fildes, who quoted industry veteran Arthur Woods describing Cook as the best thing to have happened to his sector in a generation and William Cook's six foundries as the most profitable steel group in Europe. Woods added: "William Cook is his life. It would be a great shame if he were to be brought down by the accountants of Triplex."

Fildes agreed, telling his readers "it certainly would be a shame if he were brought down for incorrectness", noting that Cook had offered to give up his contract and set up boardroom committees if his investors wanted them. One investor had claimed a more compliant company would be more highly valued by the City and William Cook was a sitting duck because the board was just Andrew Cook. Concluding, Fildes said: "Brokers and investors who could see beyond the covers of their code-books would judge Mr Cook not by his correctness but by his effects." The doyen of financial journalists had spoken, but whether his words would have any sway remained to be seen.

To address the argument that his company was a one-man band, Cook decided to take his executive director to meet investors. Roy Henson was a production stalwart and a barrel-chested man who looked like he was cast from steel himself. Henson had joined William Cook in 1948 and witnessed its transformation from dirty old factory to modern master of the craft, playing a significant role himself in its renaissance under Cook. In a company of hard men, he was a natural leader of the shop floor and workers would lay down their lives for him. Henson was also highly intelligent with a rare gift for communication – if thee could actually understand what he was saying in his strong Sheffield accent. Some found him hard to fathom but he could communicate freely with foundrymen from anywhere in the world.

Cook and Henson arrived at Lazard Brothers above Moorgate station for 2pm on Monday, December 9. The Lazards name conjured an old-world mystique, but the partnership's Sixties-built City headquarters were rather down-at-heel. They were greeted by Richard Smith, a well-regarded fund manager who had been with the firm since 1975, and guided through the rambling and dilapidated corridors to a meeting room. The conversation began. Cook considered Lazard to be his most supportive shareholder or at the very least it seemed to believe the Triplex offer was insufficient and was prepared to say so. Under his polished exterior, Richard Smith was a shrewd operator and did not sell out of William Cook in the share buyback scheme because he knew very well the company was undervalued. The meeting seemed to be going well and Smith was making bullish and upbeat noises. Henson was invited to speak. He stood up, jammed his enormous hands into his pockets and started speaking about production volumes at William Cook's various foundries. He spoke faster and faster, jangling change in his pockets and mangling his words and then launched into the topic of oil quenching for high-tech machinery. Cook quickly rose to his feet and gently touched Henson's arm as a signal to stop. Henson collected his nerves and both sat down again.

"Thank you for your insights, Roy," smiled Smith without any trace of slight. "And don't worry Andrew, we won't be selling you at £3 or anything near. Can we assume your price will begin with a five?"

"It will certainly begin with a four, at the very least," replied Cook.

More meetings followed the next afternoon with shareholders Jupiter and Barings, both camps surprisingly supportive of the undervaluation argument. At 4pm, Cook had his final appointment of the day and the most important since this whole affair began: a meeting with PDFM at Triton Court, a dramatic 10-storey building in Finsbury Square with a statue of Mercury, the God of Financial Gain, standing on a globe on top of its central tower, overlooking all in the streets far below.

CHAPTER 18

The road to hell was paved by committees

Scientific studies have long sought to understand why human beings keep on touching their faces, a habit that appears before we even come to this great stage of fools. Ultrasounds have shown foetuses are more likely to touch their faces when their mothers are feeling stressed. German researchers have speculated that spontaneous facial self-touch helps people to regulate emotions. Zoologists have gained some useful insights from the animal kingdom, noticing that rodents often paw their faces before pouncing on another male in a fight.

Hugh Sergeant, the mild-mannered and softly spoken senior fund manager at PDFM, was covering his face with his hands during the meeting with Andrew Cook. It was the first face-to-face encounter – if you could call it that – between the chairman of William Cook and his biggest institutional share-holder since Triplex Lloyd, another PDFM holding, launched its hostile takeover bid nearly one month earlier. After they exchanged some cursory niceties, Cook tried to scrutinise the bespectacled Sergeant but he could only see his brown eyes peering above his hands.

Sergeant was polished enough in his manner, a product of the Quaker-founded Leighton Park School in Reading, who graduated from the London School of Economics and entered the City via a graduate training scheme at Gartmore Group, an investment management business. His colleague Jerzy Wielechowski was flicking through Cook's defence document in a manner that Cook found desultory. A copy of the Triplex offer document lay on the table. Wielechowski's title was corporate governance director, a reminder that PDFM had declared a policy of actively promoting "best practice" in the boardroom and would take direct action through "a change in company strategy and management if a company consistently fails to meet our expectations". Had Cook fallen foul of their creed? It was difficult to tell because he found them so hard to read. Cook was not naturally the most empathetic person but he did have a powerful ability for quickly and accurately analysing most situations yet here he was feeling a bit stuck. In the summer, when he was lining up his plan to buy back William Cook shares and increase his control over the company, he believed PDFM had indicated it might sell out altogether at the price of £3. But when Cook returned later in the summer to confirm their commitment, PDFM appeared to have backtracked. It did not like Cook's personal share of the proposed long-term incentive plan and further, it did not like his level of remuneration. That was rich, thought Cook, coming from a fund manager which paid its senior people millions of pounds every year in what was arguably other people's money. He was at the coalface, keeping alive a strategically important part of British industry and his biggest shareholder, who he might reasonably expect to be supportive of his efforts, was chipping away at him. After an hour of trying and failing to pin down PDFM to a position, Cook checked the clock on the wall and saw that he would need to be on his way. He bid his farewells, trying to sound as upbeat as possible, and glanced at Sergeant's face in an attempt to gain some kind of understanding about where he stood but it was no use, the man's hands were covering his face again. Was he actually smirking?

On the train back to Sheffield that evening, Cook picked up a copy of *Financial Director* magazine, his attention attracted by the cover story 'Has governance lost its focus?' In the article, Sir Ronald Hampel, the chairman of ICI and the man in charge of yet another committee looking at corporate governance, was quoted as saying "a visitor from Mars would think a new industry had been created, one which was a bonanza for conference organisers, for consultants, for the media and even for the Committee on Corporate Governance". This latest committee followed the recommendations of the earlier Cadbury and Greenbury committees that another committee be created to review the implementation of their committees' findings. Sir Adrian Cadbury's original committee was established in the wake of high-profile failures such as Polly Peck and the Maxwell empire and recommended the splitting of chairman and chief executive functions, the appointment of at least three independent non-executive directors and the creation of audit and remuneration committees to crack down on fraud or bad management. Sir Richard Greenbury's follow-up committee went further, recommending that companies set up an additional committee for remuneration to link executive pay to corporate performance in response to growing concerns about boardroom fat-cattery. The road to hell truly was paved by committees.

Cook felt his eyelids drooping but read on, underlining the

sentences "companies which eschew the recommendations risk being pilloried as second class citizens" and "governance should not be so prescriptive and inflexible that it strangles corporate activity and innovation" and found himself nodding in agreement with Lord Hanson, another Yorkshire-born industrialist, who was quoted as saying "we want hound dogs in our boardrooms, not watchdogs". With that, Cook nodded off, awakening only when the train rolled into Doncaster.

The next morning, Cook was up early again and feeling thick-headed after the sleeping pills. He skipped breakfast as usual and greeted Martin the driver who was waiting in the Bentley on the gravel outside at the Manor House. They picked up the A625 and drove over the moor tops to Sheffield. Cook listened to the mellifluous Radio 4 presenter James Naughtie talking about President Nelson Mandela signing into law a new constitution for South Africa, consigning apartheid to the dustbin of history. Cook glanced through faxes Martin had brought for his attention and read that Triplex Lloyd had secured a new £50m facility with HSBC to help finance its planned acquisition of William Cook. The bank's terms looked quite agreeable. Did everyone else believe this was a done deal?

He peered out of the window as the Bentley swept through the south-west suburbs of Sheffield, along Ecclesall Road and its prosperous row of restaurants and bars, past the down-at-heel Park Hill housing estate and the nondescript office buildings of the city centre and towards Parkway Avenue and the headquarters of William Cook plc, with its blue-overalled foundrymen with strong arms and dirty faces. How he preferred these surroundings to the deceptively clean City of London and its white-collar professionals. Martin dropped Cook off at the semi-circular glass entrance to his office and went off for a full English breakfast at a cafe nearby.

The defence bankers Simon Metcalf and Margaret Young from NatWest Markets were on their way up from London with stockbrokers from UBS Phillips and Drew. They needed to drum up analyst interest in William Cook and its plants to help promote the argument in the City that Triplex Lloyd's bid undervalued the company. The trouble was that few analysts followed William Cook bar Paul Compton of Merrill Lynch and he had been tipping the company for takeover. This lack of analyst coverage was another consequence of Cook's failure to play the game in the City. When he needed favours in the Square Mile, there were few to call in. NatWest had succeeded in dragging a small group of analysts to Sheffield including Sandy Morris from Hoare Govett who had already come out in Triplex's favour, telling the *FT* it was "a very sensible value-adding bid". Cook led them on a tour of Parkway, the site he had personally commissioned in the 1970s, and then Hi-Tec, the foundry which specialised in the manufacture of large high-integrity castings for the power-generating and offshore industries. Cook and his advisors repeated the value argument over and over to the sharp-suited but rather dry analysts who just nodded blankly. They seemed to think Triplex Lloyd was getting a very good deal with this takeover and at just over £3 a share, it was. The tour ended as the day darkened and the men from the City sought refuge on the train home to London.

Cook returned to his office and said hello to his secretary Jane who handed him a batch of correspondence. "I thought you might like to see these Mr Cook," she said. He poured himself a large glass of water and settled down to read the letters. They were from well-wishers. The first was signed Alfred Browne of East Molesey in Surrey. It said: "You may recall my coming up to Sheffield to see you some years ago and the letters we exchanged. I fell into silence after the death of one of my daughters, which hit me hard. She was an engineer by training, graduating top of the list at Southampton. I stopped writing my book – I must have bent your ear some time with my theories about the working of the universe – but I started again last year, with the benefit of some years further thinking while walking the dog, and it now stands complete at 88,000 words. A lot of original ideas, I think, but whether anyone will publish I cannot say. You must be very busy at this time, dealing with what does seem to me an impertinent proposal. I hope you are successful in fighting it off." Browne enclosed a copy of his letter sent to Colin Cooke, chairman of Triplex Lloyd. It was deeply critical. Cook remembered Browne, a decent man, and his letter reminded him there were decent men out there. What grief he must have experienced. The world was cruel in so many ways.

The next letter was in calligraphy, written in green ink, and from Michael Bell, executive chairman at MS International, the defence, forgings and petrol station superstructures engineering group. "I read about the hostile bid for your company and just wanted to wish you well. As you know, I have been there and know too well that the next few weeks will be a time of considerable pressure and harassment as you try to present your case for independence – or at least a much better price – to fund managers and all the many others. That said, I know that you are not one to walk away from a challenge – but remember, in the end it's all down to you and don't rely on the others. Keep your head up, walk tall and emphasise the positives."

The last letter of note was from Bob Kemp of Chard in Somerset, the director of a castings company and an industry acquaintance. Kemp wrote: "I would like to wish you good luck and success in your campaign to resist the unwanted advances of Triplex Lloyd. You have always spoken your mind as an industrialist and are respected for it. There are too few champions of causes, especially when the odds seem to be stacked against the individual by 'the system'. Unfortunately, industry today seems to call for 'followers' when what it needs is 'leaders'. Your stand as an autocratic champion has the merit of honesty and openness which will surely gain all the support you need. Please continue to follow your own beliefs, few are in your position to be able to stand up and be counted to such good effect."

The phone rang, interrupting Cook from his thoughts. It was Terry Smith. "Andrew, this is ridiculous. William Cook is worth twice as much as the bid price. I'm going to put out some research saying as much."

CHAPTER 19

He has spoken a terrible truth

As a first-class student of history, Terry Smith was offered a lectureship at Cardiff University but, as he later told a reporter, he turned it down for "vulgar commercial considerations, like making some money". He proved equally good at that and was able to combine the two talents in his eye-catching notes scrutinising the worth of listed companies. Smith's report on William Cook was a case in point, blending colourful historical anecdote with sharp financial analysis.

The Second World War buff transported his readers back to December 1944 and the last German Army offensive on the Western Front when Panzer tanks under the command of General Lüttwitz mounted an attack through the wooded and hilly terrain of the Ardennes and succeeded in surrounding the American 101st Airborne Division in the Battle of the Bulge. General Lüttwitz called on his US counterpart General McAuliffe to surrender or face total annihilation. He received a single word in response: "Nuts!" At an Allied conference to discuss the grave situation facing the American paratroops, General Patton promised to relieve McAuliffe within 48 hours. "A man that eloquent deserves to be saved," said Old Blood and Guts.

Wrote Smith: "What has this history lesson got to do with current events in the City? Hopefully, without engaging in too much hyperbole, there is a man in the City who deserves to be saved for the same reasons as General McAuliffe. Andrew Cook, the Chairman and Chief Executive of William Cook, the steel castings company based in Sheffield, who is now on the receiving end of a hostile bid from Triplex Lloyd. But why should we concern ourselves about a bid for a small engineering company? To take a leaf out of General Patton's book, Cook is undoubtedly eloquent. He is a barrister. He quotes Benjamin Franklin in his annual report. Only a William Cook annual report is likely to describe the activities of competitors in taking on work at unprofitable margins as 'a severe epidemic of busy fool syndrome'."

Smith noted Cook was short of friends in the Square Mile with the consensus among stockbroking analysts that William Cook would lose its independence. His "unusual eloquence" could be held against him, Cook being a straight talker who did not court institutional support for his shares, preferring to get on with running his business and let the City do its job of valuing shares, added Smith. The author suggested the main reason for Cook's lack of support in the City is that "he is a man who has committed a heinous crime: he has spoken a terrible truth" and the upsurge of interest in corporate governance, brought on by various high-profile corporate disasters, was a classic case of slamming the stable door after the horse had bolted. Smith wrote: "Can anyone name a disaster which has been averted by the action of one of these devices? I can't. But I can name plenty of companies which have gone bust while complying with every rule and regulation of the City and the accounting profession."

The best protection against shareholders losing value in a company, argued Smith, is "surely a management with a confluence of interests with shareholders" and the best way to judge Cook's record in running William Cook was not to examine whether the board structure meets with regulatory approval, but rather to examine the results. He quoted the *Financial Times*, which credited Cook with "saving the steel castings industry, after the recession of the early 1980s almost wiped out domestic demand". Smith then played his hand, stating that William Cook had delivered better sales growth than Triplex Lloyd and had a more consistent profit record, higher growth in earnings and dividends and a better return on capital and cash flow over the past five years. "The numbers speak for themselves," he wrote. "So there you have it. Andrew Cook's only crime is to point out that the regulators who are supposed to protect shareholders are still stark naked, despite the new suit. Whether he survives will be a test of the City's real priorities." As a post-script, the history enthusiast said he was "quite optimistic" because of the fate of General McAuliffe in 1944: Patton kept his promise to relieve him and his troops within 48 hours.

Cook finished reading the note and breathed a deep sigh of relief. Good old Terry, he thought, or should he say Patton? It was an entertaining piece of writing for one thing. For another, Smith was the first independent party of any consequence in the City to point out that William Cook had a far better track record than Triplex Lloyd. But then he remembered the City wasn't so concerned with the truth of the matter, just the appearance of things, and would believe what it wanted to believe even if all the evidence pointed to the contrary. It was like Alice in Wonderland, he thought to himself. His Nokia sounded its sing-song tone. He recognised the number as PR man Tony Carlisle's and answered on the second ring.

"Andrew, it's Tony. Have you seen the wires? Triplex Lloyd has put out a circular to your shareholders. It zeroes in on you and is pretty vicious, I must say. We need to respond. I will fax you a copy and call you back."

Any relief created by the Smith research disappeared in an instant and was replaced by a familiar sinking feeling. Would this never end? The fax machine whirred into life, spewing the latest Triplex screed into the sanctum of his office.

Cook studied the fax. Carlisle was right. The contents took matters to a new level of animosity. The letter from Triplex Lloyd chairman Colin Cooke targeted Cook personally, singling out his £503,000 salary, £1.5m golden parachute, five-year rolling contract, pension arrangements, provision of a Bentley Turbo R and Land Rover Discovery and use of a helicopter. The document criticised the ages of the non-executive directors – 71 and 83 – and that Cook was the only director employed by the company, the others being self-employed consultants. In the accompanying press statement, Triplex Lloyd chief executive Graham Lockyer said: "Andrew Cook's remuneration package has performed much better than your company's share price. Poor corporate governance at William Cook is so extreme that it is not an esoteric debate. It is a monetary issue which has had, and without Triplex Lloyd's offer, will continue to have, an adverse impact on shareholder value. Triplex Lloyd's management is the only one on which William Cook's shareholders can rely."

The letter accused William Cook of making "wholly incon-sistent" claims about its future prospects and questioned why the company did not make its shareholders aware of "the full story" before buying shares for the long-term incentive plan for employees, pointing out the share purchase would have been below the Triplex Lloyd offer price – "a price which William Cook now claims is a 'massive discount' to its real value". In his statement, Lockyer added: "It is about belief and trusting in people."

Cook rang Carlisle and uttered a swear word when asked by the PR man what he thought of the letter. Together they hashed out a statement, which read as follows.

"We are not surprised but we are disappointed that all they can do is rake over issues that have been well aired. We prefer to make considered market value points, not cheap personal points. At the end of the day, the bid is about shareholder value. We have made it very clear that we are committed to shareholder value and that the offer values the company at a ludicrously low price. This document is a complete irrelevance. It fails to address the issue of value. We have made our position plain. If Triplex Lloyd has difficulty in understanding those statements, we invite them to read them again."

The final version was sent off to Fleet Street's City desks, which were relishing this increasingly bitter battle. Richard Wolffe of the *Financial Times* was one of the first on the phone to Cook to ask for further comment. Cook told him: "If the shareholders tell me to pay myself less so that they will stay with me, then I would have to look at that pretty seriously. But I reckon that shareholders get better value out of each pound they pay me than out of each pound paid to Mr Colin Cooke.

When our shares were at 9p, some 12 or 13 years ago, I had a Ford Escort, my pay was £20,000 a year and I slept on a camp bed in the office. I have paid myself only what the company and the shareholders can afford."

Cook left the office late and headed home in the dark. He had barely seen any daylight. It was Friday 13th, he noticed.

CHAPTER 20

Holed below the waterline

The Pratt and Whitney engines on the Super King Air 200 roared into life and the aircraft taxied to the runway at East Midlands Airport, preparing for take-off. A professional pilot was behind the controls in the cockpit and Cook, his wife Alison, their four children and Cherry the nanny buckled up in the comfortable leather-bound cabin. The air traffic controller gave the all-clear and the twin-turboprop plane took off into the overcast sky, course set south for the northern coast of Spain. The Cooks were going away for the weekend at Alison's behest in an attempt to provide some much-needed relief from the stresses and strains of the last month, which were starting to show on her husband. For the first time in weeks, Cook felt free. It was only when travelling that he managed to achieve any sense of ease, gaining comfort from the idea of being protected from the world outside the window of the plane, train, car or boat. Cook felt fortunate at the freedom afforded by being the boss of a successful business, which enabled him to charter a plane at the company's expense, in this case costing £5,000.

Two hours later, the King Air broke cloud and began its descent towards San Sebastian, the runway beyond the headland stretching like a spit of land along the Bidasoa river. Safely on *terra firma,* the plane pulled up to the sole terminal at the small, largely deserted airport. Cook flicked some switches and opened the cabin door, its air stairs extending down to the tarmac.

"Bienvenido Andrew!" It was Enrique and Lola Lartundo, waiting for them on the apron. The Cooks disembarked, the children swarming excitedly around 'Uncle Henry' and his kindly, elegant wife. The airport manager unloaded the baggage with the help of Lartundo's chauffeur and led the Cooks through the arrivals hall, the few airport staff on duty greeting the Cooks and their hosts like minor royalty. Lartundo was well known in the Basque Country, the 70-year-old industrialist a local dignitary and a personable, friendly man with a knack for putting people at ease.

The waiting vehicle took the Cooks along the lush coast and through winding roads up to the clifftops and past big wooden gates to where the Lartundos lived in a villa overlooking the Bay of Biscay. The property was magnificent, equipped with indoor swimming pool, games room and probably the best private wine collection Cook had ever seen. They arrived in time for lunch, served with vintage champagne and the type of magical Rioja that was far too good for export. Lunch was followed by perfectly wrapped presents for the children. The Lartundos were marvellous with the little ones; they had no offspring of their own, a sadness they masked by lavishing attention on their friends' children. A glass of Coca Cola spilt on the billiard table? It is no problem that our cleaner cannot fix, *pequeña querida.*

Cook had become firm friends with Lartundo during his attempts to create a European network of steel castings producers and admired his Spanish counterpart's success in a difficult industry, distorted by state subsidies across the Continent. Like Cook, Lartundo had made a fortune through the modern mastery of ancient methods, starting out buying a bankrupt foundry and transforming it into a highly profitable venture, establishing a niche in the market, helped no doubt by his easy charm. A generation older than Cook, he liked to regale his friend with stories of his colourful life, such as the time when he persuaded Sir Donald Stokes, the head of British Leyland, to supply him with one of the first Triumph TR3 roadsters from the production line, British sports cars being highly coveted and extremely rare in Franco's Spain during the Fifties. Lartundo had travelled extensively too, seeking business in the United States and making multiple transatlantic voyages aboard the SS Raffaello, the futuristic Italian luxury ocean liner. Lartundo retained full ownership of his business, meaning there was no chance of any hostile takeover bids, although his flamboyant lifestyle attracted the attention of ETA, the Basque separatist movement which issued a death sentence against him for sacking a group of striking workers from his foundry. The threat to his life forced Lartundo to flee to Paris, where he lived for a couple of years, making covert returns to his homeland whenever he dared on board the Sud Express, the luxury train linking Lisbon and London and stopping at Hendaye, just across the French border from San Sebastian. He eventually paid a large ransom in cash to commute the sentence.

After lunch, Cook confided in his sympathetic friend about his own troubles and the Sword of Damocles he felt hanging over his head. He asked Lartundo outright whether he would invest some of his own money in William Cook, which would have the effect of lifting the value of its shares beyond Triplex Lloyd's offer price. Lartundo, a man of emotional intelligence, responded by expressing anxiety and concern for his friend's predicament but added truthfully he did not consider foundries to be good investments and he did not understand how his was performing so well, especially as he had spent so little money of late on new plant and machinery. In any event, he was not sure how he would make such an investment in a listed company. Cook responded by saying Lartundo's financial advisors would surely know the mechanics, but he could see from his friend's face that he was not winning the argument and rather than push his case any further, he left it and smiled ruefully, gazing out of the window towards the ocean horizon. Lartundo said: "Andrew, *mi amigo*, a good heart breaks bad fortune, as we like to say." The two friends retired to freshen up for dinner that evening.

The family-owned Arzak restaurant dates back to 1897, when its founders opened a wine shop and tavern on the eastern side of San Sebastian. Grandson Juan Mari Arzak took over the restaurant in the 1960s and won international acclaim for his traditional Basque dishes with a gourmet twist, earning three Michelin stars and plaudits from food critics such as AA Gill who would "grow tearful and speechless when trying to recount the bliss of his menu". The room was packed with people enjoying some of the best food in Europe when the party arrived for 9pm, the children back at the villa with their nanny for an early night. After more champagne and the first of many exquisite fish dishes, Cook could feel his mask begin to slip. He could not hide his fears any longer. He could not shake the thought that he was losing the fight and it was just a matter of time before Triplex Lloyd upped its bid and won the day. Weary and feeling the effects of alcohol, anxiety, stress and fatigue, he launched into a rambling anecdote about his predicament, comparing himself to the designer of the Titanic because he had failed to secure enough bank borrowings to ward off the bid and lacking the necessary finance, he was sunk. Voice trembling, Cook said: "I'm holed below the waterline." With that, he burst into tears and sobbed loudly as the enormity of this realisation set in. Cook checked himself, bracing for disapproving looks, but saw the other diners paid him no mind. They were more used to displays of heightened emotion here, the land of *duende*. The act of crying had a calming effect, the release of endorphins easing his overwrought condition. Meltdown over, Lartundo insisted on settling the party's bill and they headed back to the villa and to bed, where Cook lay awake, listening to the sounds of the Atlantic outside the window.

The King Air landed at East Midlands Airport on Sunday evening, safely touching down on the runway at the former RAF Castle Donington. As the plane taxied to the apron, Cook reflected to himself it might well be the last time he would be able to travel with such freedom. Peter, the friendly handling man for Cook and other private flyers, was waiting for them, helping Alison, the children and nanny off the plane and through the terminal to their car for the 45-mile drive home. "Thank you, Peter," said Cook gratefully, handing the man a large cash tip and wishing him a happy Christmas, which was just 10 days' away. The travel had put him in reflective mood. He supported a number of people's livelihoods. What would happen to them if Triplex Lloyd won the day?

CHAPTER 21

A friend of liberty in evil times

The grey men with their grey hair and grey suits peered up from their daily papers as the distinctive-looking individual entered the first-class carriage and found his seat aboard the early Monday morning Master Cutler train, bound for the capital. Andrew Cook shook open his copy of the *Financial Times* and saw its lupine correspondent Richard Wolffe had been busy writing about his travails again. Wolffe had sought reaction from the other side about stock-picker Terry Smith's analysis of the companies and their contrasting prospects. Smith had described Triplex Lloyd's bid as a "gross under-valuation" of its target and raised questions about the predator's ability to maintain the momentum of its cash-flow after a strong start to the year. CEO Graham Lockyer was having none of it, telling the *FT*: "I believe it is totally sustainable at that level." Sandy Morris, the analyst at Hoare Govett also pitched in with support for Triplex Lloyd. "The word growth does not figure large enough or often enough at William Cook and it is a major sticking point," he sniped. "If your capital employed is not growing – and you show no signs of growing it – then you stand at a big discount to the market. It is only because Cook is static that the company is generating its current levels of cash." Cook put the newspaper down and took a deep breath as he gazed out of the window at the cold and foggy world flashing by.

Courtesy of a chatty East End taxi driver, Cook arrived at 135 Bishopsgate at 10am to meet with his defence team at NatWest Markets. He sensed an atmosphere as soon as he walked into the meeting room and found Margaret Young and Simon Metcalf waiting for him, serious expressions on their faces. "It's Triplex Lloyd," said Margaret before he had even sat down. "They have published the level of acceptances from your shareholders to their offer and it is above five per cent, which is unprecedentedly high at this stage of the process. Frankly, it's a disaster." She handed him the Triplex Lloyd announcement from the wires, which confirmed the news and trumpeted the level of acceptances was typically one per cent for opening offers in hostile takeover bids. The bidder had also extended its offer to December 31, buying more time to win over the City. William Cook's shares had increased sharply on the news, as investors considered a larger bid increasingly likely given the evident appetite for change at the company among existing shareholders. Cook quietly considered what it all meant and started to speak. "I think there must have been some kind of cock-up," he said. "Or a conspiracy. Who is the investment banking advisor to Triplex Lloyd? It is Schroders, which has a fund management arm, which is a big shareholder in William Cook. Have the investment bankers put the fund managers up to making the acceptance?"

Young shook her head. "That's highly unlikely and totally against the City rules on Chinese walls, which are supposed to block the exchange of information between different departments if it might encourage behaviour that is legally or ethically questionable," she said. Legally and ethically questionable just about sums up the City, thought Cook. Young went on: "Anyway, fund managers never show their hands until the last minute. I really don't think this is a cock-up or a conspiracy. I think it is reflective of a genuine concern among your shareholders about corporate governance, which is the new creed of the City. We think you need to get serious about hiring a chairman to dispel the notion once and for all that William Cook is just the Andrew Cook show." Cook looked across at Metcalf, who nodded in agreement. "We have just the person in mind," she added. "His name is Doug Rogers and he is the former chairman of a respectable engineering outfit called Newman Tonks which makes door knobs, locks and handles and we think you should meet him."

Cook had never heard of Doug Rogers or Newman Tonks and found the names faintly ridiculous but agreed to see the man, if only to maintain his policy of trying all options to see off this cursed bid. With that, he left the bankers and headed off to his next appointment – a meeting at the Office of Fair Trading, the quango responsible for enforcing competition law, to plead his case that Triplex Lloyd's move should be referred for a market investigation on public interest grounds. The head office was at Fleetbank House, a grey slab of a building in Salisbury Square off Fleet Street. At the centre of the square stands an obelisk dedicated to Robert Waithman, an early 19th century Lord Mayor of the City of London. Walking past, Cook observed the inscription, describing the draper turned politician as "a friend of liberty in evil times". Inside the offices, Cook met with a competition lawyer from Linklaters – a colleague of David Cheyne's – and together they presented their argument to a collective noun of civil servants.

In essence, without steel castings, Britain's engineering industry would not exist. Cook had succeeded in saving Britain's castings industry, transforming it into a profitable, modern and efficient operation. By contrast, Triplex Lloyd had no track record in any industry in which it had been involved, growing out of financial engineering and coming to be involved with foundries by accident. It had no understanding of Cook's products and markets and had no involvement with them, but was hell-bent on acquiring his company as yet another piece of financial engineering, aimed at buying a high quality business on the cheap and then harvesting the proceeds for the benefit of its City shareholders. Triplex Lloyd would sack Cook and destroy many customer relationships in the process. William Cook would suffer under the new ownership, with negative consequences for its British customers and by extension British industry. This could not be in the public interest, concluded Cook. His audience seemed unmoved. The lawyer did his best but was a bit wooden for Cook's liking, especially considering his handsome hourly rates. The civil servants politely thanked them for their time and promised to respond in due course.

Worth a try, thought Cook as he headed back to King's Cross for the train north and a digest of the day's paperwork. An article in the *Birmingham Post* grabbed his attention. These regional newspapers often provided a different perspective from the groupthink found in Fleet Street. In his City View column, Andrew Turpin wrote that Triplex Lloyd had one major advantage in its takeover battle – there was no sign of a rival bidder coming forward. It meant that while it would probably have to increase its shares and cash offer from about 310p per share, it certainly would not have to go overboard to woo shareholders.

Turpin added: "There's no doubt that William Cook probably has been undervalued by the stock market for the last couple of years, but not by a vast amount. It also sounds as though controversial chairman Mr Andrew Cook has hardly helped his own cause and his company's share price, according to many City observers, by making little effort to keep in touch with analysts. This incidentally is a problem encountered by many provincial companies who find it difficult to get on the City's wavelength. Earlier this year, the shares were so cheap that Cook was buying them back. One City cynic said yesterday: 'It almost seemed as though they were trying to take it private again rather than tell their story to the City and talk the price up.' The perception was hardly helped by what amounted to a profits warning earlier in the year, which stands in contrast to the bullish noises emerging from behind the circle of wagons at Cook's Sheffield stronghold."

Turpin pointed out that Cook shares had increased by nearly 50 per cent since the launch of the takeover bid and signed off with a prediction that Triplex Lloyd would return with a higher price of 330p per share. Cook blanched – it was still ludicrously cheap and would be a highway robbery at this price, leaving him swinging in the wind. Why won't the commentariat recognise the underlying value of his company? The train hurtled on towards its destination.

Cook's question was answered in a fashion the following day. Brian Cooke was the chief executive and chairman of Castings plc, a manufacturer of iron automotive parts which dated back to a maker of metal items for the saddlery trade in 1885. Cooke (no relation to either) had followed his father into the family firm as an engineering apprentice in 1960, the year it sacrificed independence and floated on the London Stock Exchange, and worked his way through the ranks to become a director by 1966. Cooke had developed a withering view of City analysts and advisors, which he shared with Andrew Cook over tea and biscuits in his modest, cramped office at Brownhills, a former coal-mining town in the West Midlands that had seen better days. In spite of Cooke's forthright opinions about the Square Mile, shareholders seemed to love his company. After exchanging pleasantries, Cook asked his friend why he and his company were so highly regarded.

"It's all down to pay and rations," said Cooke, in his deliberate style. "They're jealous, Andrew. You pay yourself more than they think you ought to. I don't. I am happy with my lot in life. I pay myself about £150,000 a year, drive a Saab, work in this modest office and make a point of talking to analysts. They like that. I treat them as equals while you treat them with barely disguised contempt. I know you don't actually, but at least that is the way they see it."

"You are quite right Brian," replied Cook. "I don't like speaking to analysts. I prefer speaking to customers. Consequently, shareholders are not so clear on what William Cook has been achieving and how undervalued our shares are. Triplex Lloyd, meanwhile, is a basket case of disparate businesses devoid of cohesion, strategy and objectives, which needs acquisitions to keep producing the results it has told investors to expect." Cook took a gulp of water and continued. "I need to nail this lie about corporate governance at William Cook. Would you become a non-executive director? You know how to play the game in the City. Your good name would help see off these concerns. It need only be a day a month at most."

Cooke smiled and thanked him for the offer, which he said he would consider in the fullness of time. Cook pressed his friend a little further, knowing what was at stake here. "Okay then Andrew, seeing as it is you. I agree to become a non-executive director at William Cook if the bid lapses." They shook hands. "You're a good man Brian," said Cook, thankful for the show of support. He needed all the help he could get from the few friends he had.

Martin the driver was waiting patiently outside in the car park. Cook got into the front passenger seat and they left Brownhills for his next appointment, with the chairman providing navigational directions to the driver, as was his habit. He noticed most of the high street shops seemed to be boarded up. What would become of places like these without employers like Castings plc? The Bentley accelerated out of town along the A38 towards Burton-on-Trent and an appointment with the aforementioned Doug Rogers of Newman Tonks.

They met at Lloyds Burton, the foundry William Cook acquired from Triplex Lloyd in 1990. Rogers was waiting for him in the reception. Cook looked his guest up and down, assessing his potential. Rogers wore large, square-rimmed glasses and his hair brushed back, accentuating his bushy eyebrows. The pair settled into a meeting room and started talking. Rogers' early years showed he had something about him, leaving school at 15 after the death of his father and his mother's cancer diagnosis, and attending night classes to qualify as an engineer. He joined Newman Tonks as a young man and worked his way up to become chief executive and then non-executive chairman, a role he relinquished earlier in the year. He now held a number of other chairmanships. His track record was solid enough and he was a personable chap but he hardly struck Cook as a stellar individual, rather someone who had been in the right place at the right time. Inevitably, the talk turned to money. Rogers considered £60,000 per year a straightforward salary for a non-executive chairman. "I don't want to be rich, I just expect to be properly paid," he said. Cook thought it a bit steep. In a subtle power-play, Rogers switched the discussion to Cook's pay and perks, a subject of much contention in the takeover bid. "We must make sure you are a happy chappy," he said. Cook, who was used to ruling the roost, could not help but find the tone patronising and made non-committal noises. They parted amicably, Cook waving off Rogers and saying to himself, "sorry Margaret, your Doug Rogers is not for me". Ever the loner.

CHAPTER 22

A deucedly awkward situation

Cook was in combative mood as he headed to the Stock Exchange Building at 125 Old Broad Street, a 27-storey tower opposite the Royal Exchange and overlooking the Bank of England, for an appointment with the Takeover Panel, the regulatory body designed to ensure good business standards and fairness to shareholders in the City of London. Selected by the central bank, the panel consisted of City grandees, the great and the good of the Square Mile led by chairman Sir David Calcutt, former chairman of the Bar, and deputy John Hull, former chairman of Schroders. Cook was expecting a row over his comments to the *Financial Times* the previous month, which were construed as a profit forecast and in contravention of the Takeover Code. Spoiling for a fight, he arrived early and waited in reception, watching *Sky News* report on the formal election of Bill Clinton to a second term as US president and China's censorship of western media sites on the so-called Information Superhighway. Cook was promptly joined by Margaret Young from NatWest Markets. He wished her good morning and could sense she was tense, the Panel representing her employer's highest authority.

Peter Lee, the genial deputy director general, entered

reception and welcomed his guests, leading them to a meeting room where his assistant, Angus Pottinger, was waiting. Lee had joined the Takeover Panel in 1971 on secondment from law firm Messrs Herbert Oppenheimer, Nathan and Vandyk and had never left, gaining an encyclopaedic knowledge of the code and its precedents. The panel was formed in 1968 in response to growing concern about unfair practices in mergers and acquisitions in the City and the rise of corporate raiders, a ruthless new breed of investors who targeted undervalued companies and launched hostile takeover bids to seize control and strip their assets for a mighty profit. In contrast to the red-blooded capitalists he was supposedly policing, Lee was a mild-mannered and courteous individual. He offered teas and coffees in an attempt to lighten the mood in the room, which had the feeling of a stand-off. Young was deferential to her erstwhile governor while Cook sized up Pottinger, a chubby-cheeked young man who was wielding the offending *FT* article and a copy of the code of conduct.

Lee started the meeting proper, referring Cook to the code and his roles and responsibilities as a company director during the course of an offer. Pottinger took over, pointing Cook to the principal sources of the rules governing the code, including the Criminal Justice Act, the Financial Services Act, the Companies Act and the Listing Rules, and the gravity of the situation. Cook felt his fists tighten. "All statements made should be prepared to the highest standards of care," said Pottinger, eyeing Cook. "Information must be adequately and fairly presented in sufficient time for the company's shareholders to reach a properly informed decision. May I remind you that directors must not, without shareholders' consent, take action which might frustrate a bid." Young interjected, replying that her client understood such matters and any breaches which were entirely unintentional. Pottinger went on: "It is very difficult after publication to alter an impression given or a view or remark attributed to a particular person. The code places the responsibility on the person concerned. And in this case, that is you, Mr Cook."

Cook ignored Pottinger, turned to Lee and began to speak. In the corner of his vision, he could see Young shifting uncomfortably. "I am the chairman and chief executive of William Cook plc. This company would not exist without me. William Cook is a strategic supplier to what remains of the British engineering industry. We have between 60-70 per cent of the UK steel castings sector and a dominant position in the defence, construction equipment, mining and quarrying plants, forklifts and valves markets and a strong one in the power generation, railway and heavy trucks markets. Many important British companies rely on William Cook for critical components. Without us, they would be forced to look overseas for inferior substitutes, which would have a detrimental effect on the national interest." His face hardened. "This is my life's work and I will do whatever it takes to protect my company from this hostile takeover bid. Whatever it takes."

Pottinger reddened and was about to respond when his boss jumped in and thanked Cook very much for his time and his comments and requested that he bear in mind the code and invited him to get in touch if he had any further concerns about the bid and that if he did, he would be very happy to look into them. The last thing the mannerly Lee wanted was a kerfuffle in the Stock Exchange Building, the heart of the world's pre-eminent capital market. It wouldn't be the done thing. He quickly and politely ushered Cook and Young out of the meeting room and back along the corridor to reception and bid them farewell. The whole episode was over in minutes. Young's face looked drawn. Never mind her paying clients, it was the Panel that held dominion over bankers, at least when they were in its spotlight. Cook felt strangely upbeat and amused himself with a historical anecdote, recalling a reply from the Duke of Wellington to one of the many supplicants who wrote to him seeking advice after he became a national hero at the Battle of Waterloo. "Sir, you have got yourself into a deucedly awkward situation," wrote one of the last great Englishmen. "And you had better get yourself out of it as best you can."

Later that evening, Cook was back in his wood-panelled study at the Manor House and speaking to Terry Smith on the phone, repeating his fears that while he believed William Cook was worth £6 a share, it could be sold for half that amount. Cook knew that PDFM would determine the outcome of the bid and decide the company's ultimate value. The decision rested with Hugh Sergeant, the deucedly hard-to-read fund manager who could not look Cook in the eye without covering his face. In a moment of clarity, Cook said: "I ought to be having a go at this, Terry, if I can get someone to back me."

The next day, Cook was in London again for a meeting with banker Simon Metcalf at NatWest Markets for the publication of William Cook's latest profit forecast. It confidently told investors to expect a £10.7m profit in the coming year, an increase of 26 per cent thanks to the completion of a £2m modernisation programme, and a 43 per cent hike in the final dividend. On paper, Cook considered the value argument for his company to be overwhelming, but the City clearly had other ideas: the share price did not move a penny. It had been stuck at around £3.50 since the start of the bid in spite of his strenuous efforts. Metcalf called in for some much-needed coffee.

Cook was in reflective mood. He had known Metcalf for more than a decade and could speak freely in his presence. "Do you remember when we first met, Simon? It was 1985 and you were working at County Bank and I was on the acquisition trail at William Cook. Robert Hyde and Sons, my mortal competitor, was up for sale and we put in a bid, but it wasn't enough to win over the shareholders. If we had increased our offer, we would have succeeded. I have been saying 'if only' to myself ever since. That failure tormented me. I remember you saying to me that if the shareholders didn't want to sell to me, there was no power on earth that would make them. But I have learned there is such a power. It is money. I have got the same feeling now. If I don't have a go at buying William Cook myself, I will never get the chance again and I will probably lose because the City just isn't buying into our defence argument." Metcalf listened quietly and, after a pause, replied: "You have a fine sense of history Andrew. All right, I won't stand in your way."

On the last train home, Cook recognised the friendly face and military bearing of Jonathan Hunt, a partner at Wake Smith law firm and a well-known professional in the Sheffield business community. The lawyer and army reservist asked Cook how he was doing; he and his colleagues had been following the media coverage of the bid with interest. "Bearing up Jonathan, thank you. We shall see what happens. But one thing's for certain. If nobody else gets £4 per share on the table, I will," said Cook, floating the idea of a buyout. The train pulled into Chesterfield and Cook hurriedly gathered his belongings, said goodnight to Hunt and stepped out of the carriage into the freezing night air. "To blazes with the Panel and its rules," he thought to himself. If the other side was going to spread some rumours, so would he.

He woke early the following morning to a heavy frost. It was December 20. The house was fully decked out for Christmas, decorations everywhere and presents of all shapes and sizes wrapped beneath the tree. Cook was so engrossed with fending off the takeover bid he had barely registered what time of year it was, but now he felt a deep pang for his children that wrenched his heart. How he missed them. His life revolved around them and the company. There was nothing else that mattered. After a cup of strong tea, he dragged himself into the study and heard the familiar whirr and click from the fax machine as it relayed the latest press cuttings. Britain's biggest building society, the Halifax, was converting to a bank and floating on the stock exchange. Partners at Goldman Sachs were in line for year-end bonuses of $1m after a bumper fourth quarter with earnings up 69 per cent. Corporate UK was back on the takeover trail, according to the *Financial Times*. Didn't he know it. The *FT* said aggressive fast-growth companies are targeting "weaker brethren" left behind by the past year's surge in market values, quoting figures from the Takeover Panel that the number of bids had nearly doubled since 1995. "And after years of discreet, friendly approaches, often rebuffed, companies have taken to launching hostile bids," said the *FT.* There was Peter Lee, telling the paper it was probably the highest level of hostile bid activity he had seen in the decade. Cook allowed himself a wry smile that Newman Tonks had found itself on the receiving end of an unwanted takeover attempt. John Dean, the analyst at Albert E Sharp, said: "There are a lot of businesses that are undervalued but many of them are not of the best quality." He added that companies were seeking out targets that were poorly rated by the market but whose activities were highly complementary to their own. Mr Dean said: "If we see some of these bids succeeding at half-way reasonable prices, that will encourage other companies to consider taking what is normally a very risky step – launching a hostile bid."

The papers had covered William Cook's profit forecast matter of factly but most gave the last word to Graham Lockyer, chief executive of Triplex Lloyd, who described the figures as "totally implausible". "Before we bid, they were downbeat about prospects," he said. "These profit forecasts are short term, not sustainable under current management." The *Birmingham Post* noted that in October, Cook's own broker UBS had forecast a rise of less than five per cent. There was more nonsense about this non-existent helicopter and it seemed to be landing. In the *Investors Chronicle*, the Dutch journalist Peter Thal Larsen wrote: "During hostile bids small details sometimes take on great importance. In Granada's campaign to acquire Forte, the target company's corporate jet symbolised all that Granada thought was wrong with the hotel group. Triplex Lloyd's £58m bid for rival castings group William Cook is on a much smaller scale. But by drawing attention to the fact that William Cook keeps a corporate helicopter, even though its businesses are all close to Sheffield, Triplex is aiming for a similar effect." This was getting ridiculous, thought Cook. The company did not own a helicopter and nor had it ever owned a helicopter or any other type of aircraft. Yet the truth of the matter did not seem to make much difference when it came to the City and its co-conspirators. To offset his growing anxiety, he dashed off a letter to Peter Lee at the Takeover Panel to complain about Triplex Lloyd's "distorted and groundless" mud-slinging. Again, the act of doing something rather than nothing had a soothing effect. Once the letter was finished, he picked up a message from Terry Smith. It contained the names of two venture capitalists which might be interested in backing a management buyout: Candover, a leading name in European private equity, and Electra Fleming, an altogether different proposition.

CHAPTER 23

I've been expecting you

Towards the end of his life, Robert Fleming would have simple advice for young men entering the world of high finance: "Lairn to say no, laddie. Lairn to say no." The Scottish banker made his fortune selling sandbags to both sides during the American civil war, founded one of the City of London's most enigmatic merchant banks and arguably set his grandson, Ian Fleming, on course to become a world-famous novelist.

Born in 1845 and brought up in a tough Dundee slum, Fleming left school at 14 with a head for numbers and joined Baxter Brothers at its imposing jute mill on the Tayside seaboard. The company was mightily ambitious, its bell tower modelled on the Santa Maria della Salute in Venice, and would become one of the world's largest linen manufacturers. By 21, the tall, physically strong young man had risen to the role of private clerk to the owner Edward Baxter, a transatlantic merchant with strong connections in the United States. "Sent to the US to represent his firm, he immediately appreciated, with the precision of a mathematician and the assurance of a young man on the make, the investment possibilities which the New World was offering the Old," wrote biographer John Pearson. Fleming first sold sackcloth to the Americans and then co-founded the Scottish American Investment trust by public subscription to supply the capital that America needed to build its railroads. With this vehicle, he helped pioneer popular capitalism, enabling small investors to take part in companies' growth. Fleming became one of the pre-eminent money men of his age, competing on equal terms with Wall Street barons J Pierpoint Morgan, Jacob Schiff and the Warburgs with their eponymous merchant bank.

His name was sufficiently famous that *The New York Times* announced his passing in 1933 under the headline 'Robert Fleming, Financier, Dead'. He left his fortune to his widow with instructions that it should pass to his surviving children. His grandson Ian, whose father Valentine had been killed by German shells on the Western Front in 1917, received nothing and had to earn his way in the world. After stints as a Reuters journalist and City stockbroker, he served in naval intelligence during the Second World War and then turned his hand to writing spy fiction. His James Bond novels have sold more than 100 million copies and half of the world's population has watched a James Bond film, the family name immortalised on page and screen.

Robert Fleming and Company remained in the clan's hands through the generations and retained its distinct Scottishness, a bagpipe player greeting guests at its City headquarters at 8 Crosby Square. It also amassed one of the biggest private collections of Scottish art in existence, including works such as Lochaber No More, John Watson Nichol's iconic image of the Highland Clearances. The *Financial Times* noted the company "differed radically from other merchant banks" and was "something of an enigma" but also the "boldest and most far-sighted of any institution in the Square Mile". It was reputed to have links to the British military and intelligence services, helped no doubt by the 007 connection, and certainly had international reach with offices in the Middle East and Far East through its Jardine Fleming joint venture with another influential Scottish family, the Keswicks.

Robert Fleming and Company used its golden touch to diversify beyond merchant banking into wealth management, looking after the fortunes of some of the world's richest families, and private equity to invest in management buyouts, backing executives in the acquisition of the companies they manage. In 1995, the bank took a 50 per cent stake in Electra Fleming, a venture capital trust founded by Marlborough-educated City grandee Michael Stoddart, to find and fund deals. The new company's directors included Tim Syder, a chartered accountant and private equity specialist with a taste for horse-racing.

It was Syder who picked up the phone to Andrew Cook's call. "I have been expecting you, Mr Cook," said Syder, in his polished way. Cook got down to business. William Cook was unloved and undervalued by the City and there was a real and present danger that Triplex Lloyd would buy it on the cheap. The City view seemed to be that it was just a matter of time before Triplex upped its bid by a few pennies per share and won the day. The conventional defence was failing, the powerful institutions of the Square Mile and Fleet Street unmoved by his arguments, and he was running out of time and options. His epiphany had come in conversations with Terry Smith and Simon Metcalf, among the only people he trusted in the City. If he could raise enough money to fund a management buyout, he could top the Triplex bid and take William Cook private. Any new investors would benefit handsomely. As the latest profit forecast had shown, the prospects for the company were looking up. And, Cook thought to himself, he would be rid of the City forever, an association lasting four decades, a union started by his father's decision to relinquish the family's majority ownership and control in 1956.

Syder listened carefully, weighing up the words of the unknown entity at the other end of the telephone. After a pause, his reply was noncommittal and matter of fact. "I know Simon Metcalf from my time at County Bank. If he thinks a management buyout could be used as part of the defence, then I will consider it." Cook thanked him for his time, promised to send more information on William Cook and said Metcalf would be in touch to confirm the possibility of a buyout. Cook's next call was to Candover, another name put forward as a potential backer and a leading light in European private equity. Founded in 1980 by former Foreign Office diplomat Roger Brooke after a meeting with US buyout tycoon Henry Kravis, the firm had blazed a trail through British industry and backed more than 100 buyouts from Goldcrest Films to Greggs the baker but the prospect of adding William Cook to its portfolio seemed unlikely after the initial call, which was lukewarm. Its man was circumspect but Cook agreed to send over information nonetheless, believing in exhausting all options. He felt exhausted himself as he finished his last task of the working week, assigning end-of-year bonuses to staff across the company's seven foundries and head office. He was a demanding, exacting boss with little tolerance for fools but generous in return and even more so than usual this Christmas, bearing in mind it could be his last one as chairman.

It was a bitterly cold weekend but the press was full of speculation about the market for deals hotting up. The newspapers were relishing the hostility. "If there ain't a row, there ain't a story," news editors would bark at young reporters. Doug Morrison of *The Sunday Telegraph* duly obliged, informing his retired readers in the Home Counties that the engineering sector was again a hostile environment; a decade after the frenzy that marked the rise of the conglomerate, a wave of takeover activity was threatening to shake up Britain's industrial heartland. The article, headlined Metal Bashing, was accompanied by a picture of Charlie Chaplin straddling a giant cog in the 1936 film, Modern Times, in which his Little Tramp character struggles to survive in the modern, industrialised world.

"Christmas has come early for City advisors," wrote Morrison, adding the return of the hostile bid to the staid world of engineering was long overdue. Triplex Lloyd had set the tone for this unseasonal acrimony with its bid for William Cook laying the ground for engineers FKI and Fairey Group to launch hostile bids for Newman Tonks and measuring instruments manufacturer Burnfield respectively. All three bids bore the same hallmark, said *The Sunday Telegraph*. Three powerful, fast-growing engineering groups were exploiting the vulnerability of smaller, poorly rated rivals for whom time has run out, the prey desperately maintaining the offers failed to reflect the value of their businesses, potential or otherwise. That was the narrative. Brian McGowan, chairman of bid target Burnfield, told the newspaper: "I don't know if this is the return of the hostile bid but when you have highly priced paper and the stock market is high, people fancy their chances to do deals." He would know, having built W Williams, a small Welsh engineering business, into one of the UK's largest conglomer-ates alongside his business partner Nigel Rudd, later dubbed the 'man who sold Britain'. *The Sunday Telegraph* predicted that all three companies would succumb, signalling further consolidation among scores of industry laggards. Hamming it up further, the newspaper added that anticipation among fund managers had reached a level not seen since the 1980s and the institutions which kept faith with independent manufacturers and engineers through the recession of the early 1990s were losing patience. The wider industry was forecasting growth and yet there was still a raft of poorly performing engineers promising jam tomorrow, the article concluded.

Cook read the report silently over coffee, alone again in his study at the Manor House. He did not like the role that was being cast for him. He could hear the children playing else-where in the house, their excitement mounting with Christmas nearly upon them. For hundreds of other business leaders, this would be the time when they could step off the corporate merry-go-round, if only for a few days, and enjoy the fruits of their labour with their families. Not Cook, though, who had work to do. *The Sunday Times* had taken up the story, describ-ing the wave of hostile takeover activity as "a new and much bolder phase of investor activism".

The reporter John Waples was a rising star on the business desk who had honed his story-getting craft on the beat for local and trade titles. In dramatic style, he told readers that in a low-growth, low-inflation environment, even the most passive fund managers were being forced to step up pressure on poorly performing companies. Waples reported that M&G, for many years the UK's largest fund manager, had broken ranks with tradition and publicly backed a hostile takeover against the aforementioned Newman Tonks. So much for Margaret Young's recommendation, thought Cook. He read on. "In another example that emerged last week, PDFM is understood to have used its 19 per cent stake in William Cook, the Sheffield castings group, to encourage a takeover approach by Triplex, where it is also a big investor. William Cook, like Newman Tonks, has produced poor returns for its long-term investors." Cook read the paragraph again. There it was, in black and white. Cook underlined the sentence, twice. Was PDFM calling the shots?

Waples went on, adding the past year had seen a sharp rise in investor activism as fund managers had come under pressure to boost returns for clients and though the aggression had not yet reached American proportions, Wall Street was an example for the City with fund managers aware that if they made trouble for companies they could improve their performance. One financier told the newspaper: "More institutions are standing up and saying, 'for God's sake, board, start getting it right or we will make some changes'." The newspaper suggested the flurry of bid battles was driven in part by big investors looking to recover money from poorly-performing companies and also the very real prospect of a new Labour administration the following year. The opposition, which had all the appearance of a government in waiting, had made it clear that any company making a hostile bid would have to prove it was not against the public interest. Waples said the knowledge that hitherto loyal institutions were prepared to pledge shares to hostile bidders was bound to create further excitement and M&G had sent out a signal to other companies in which it holds stakes that if directors did not deliver performance, they would find themselves out of their jobs. Waples was very well informed, thought Cook, wondering who was whispering in the journalist's ear, and why.

Next, he signed off a draft press release prepared by PR man Tony Carlisle to hit back at Triplex Lloyd's scurrilous attempt to undermine William Cook's profit forecast with what he saw as a series of cheap jibes. The response included supporting statements from his bankers NatWest Markets and accountants KPMG, claiming the forecast complied with the City code and was consistent with usual accounting policies. Cook added a line from himself, stating that Triplex Lloyd was becoming increasingly desperate to divert attention away from his company's real level of profitability. He faxed over the approved version to Carlisle with instructions to distribute to the City news desks, normally quiet places on Sundays, especially so at this time of year. At the *FT*'s newsroom at Southwark Bridge, the journalist Tim Burt was on Sunday-for-Monday duty when the press release from William Cook whirred through the fax machine. This story really was the gift that kept giving, thought Burt as he read through the release. He picked up the phone to Ginny Pulbrook, the PR advisor to Triplex Lloyd, to seek reaction from the other side. Pulbrook was the co-founder of Citigate, one of the City's most successful PR firms with a large roster of influential clients, and had the in-built confidence you might expect of a former captain of St Swithun's tennis and swimming teams. She was well-connected and knew how the City worked, starting her career in corporate finance at NM Rothschild, the storied merchant bank. Citigate came up with the goods in time for Burt's deadline with a comment from no less than the chairman Colin Cooke. He laid down a challenge for his counterpart: "If William Cook really believes it is worth very substantially in excess of Triplex Lloyd's offer, it should set about finding someone who is prepared to pay that price because it does not appear able to deliver this value on its own."

Reading the remarks the following morning, Cook resolved to do just that and would not take no for an answer.

CHAPTER 24

Lang may yer lum reek

The heating was broken in the first-class carriage on the cross-country train from Sheffield to Bristol and Andrew Cook and his finance director John Caldwell were starting to freeze. By the time they got to Derby, the pair had decamped to a much more comfortable second-class carriage. When the ticket inspector arrived at their seats, Cook politely but firmly requested that he endorse their tickets so they could claim a refund. This might have been his company's money, but he was determined to look after every penny, knowing how hard it was to earn in this game.

They arrived at Imperial Tobacco's head office at the redbrick Regent House for 10.30am for a meeting with pension fund manager Peter Dunscombe whose welcome was more detached than usual, given the long and profitable association between the industrial giant and William Cook. The union had started in 1956 when the fund bought into the company in its stock market flotation. Unlike its staid peers, Imperial had invested in hundreds of smaller British companies during the 1950s under the influence of its fund manager George Ross-Goobey, an intellectual loner who went against convention by persuading trustees to put money into equities rather than government bonds, or gilts. The policy paid off with Imperial pensioners enjoying market-leading returns year after year, at least until the industrial slump of the 1970s. "Ross-Goobey was the only truly revolutionary figure in the post-war history of British fund management," said the journalist Nicholas Faith.

Dunscombe was a mild-mannered man who had helped manage the £2bn-plus fund since the Seventies. Imperial's pensioners and the people paid to look after their money had done very well out of William Cook over the years. Dunscombe was normally very nice to Cook but was distinctly cool from the outset, pointing out an alleged mis-spelling on the cover of the defence document. ("It should be 'focused', not 'focussed', he said.) He was concerned about what he was reading in the papers, particularly about the perception Cook was running the company apparently for his own benefit. He was concerned about the lack of corporate governance. And he was concerned about the timing of share purchases by Cook and the non-executive director Robert Pickford.

Cook dealt with the points, one by one. The company's prospects were good, he began, and shareholders who stuck with him and his management team would benefit. Triplex Lloyd had behaved outrageously, slinging a lot of mud about him in the press, most of it totally untrue, and he had complained about their behaviour to the Takeover Panel. On pay and perks, he said he was fairly rewarded for his efforts – after all, he had saved an important part of British industry from collapse and without him, what was left of British engineering would have to buy castings of dubious quality from abroad. On the share purchases, he had always been assiduously careful to avoid falling foul of the rules on insider dealing and had instructed directors to do the same. As for corporate governance, he said he absolutely refused to bow to the latest City fashion. It was an irrelevant sideshow and he should be judged by his track record of providing returns by rationalising the industry, which had created excellent value and would continue to do so. Dunscombe listened politely and thanked Cook for his comments. The meeting had lasted more than two hours yet Cook was no clearer on whether he could count on Imperial's support. It was just a feeling, but he was doubtful.

It was a clear, bright but bitterly cold day in Bristol. As Cook and his finance director walked the 35 minutes from Regent House to Temple Meads train station, taking in the city's Byzantine and Brutalist architecture and avoiding the Christmas shoppers, he was able to reflect with clarity. He was becoming convinced that a buyout was the only way forward. If he did not have the support of backers like Imperial Tobacco, which had been shareholders for four decades, he would have to find new ones.

Back at the Manor House the following day, Christmas Eve, the children were beyond excited, the presents beneath the tree would be theirs for the opening in just a few hours' time. Cook remained in his study for most of the morning, finishing the information packs for Electra Fleming and Candover, writing a one-page covering letter in long hand for each. Once completed, his wife Alison took the correspondence to the post office in Calver, the neighbouring village on the border between the White Peak and the Dark Peak. "Send them recorded delivery," said Cook, mindful of their importance. In the afternoon, he drove into Sheffield to pick up some cash for the family's annual post-Christmas trip to Switzerland. At Barclays in

Pinstone Street, the friendly branch manager Adrian Belton recognised the distinctive-looking individual in the banking hall and approached him to say hello and ask how he was. Cook saw the same opportunity he had with the Sheffield lawyer Jonathan Hunt on the late-night train a few days earlier. Sheffield had a close-knit and sociable business community, centred around the Company of Cutlers in Hallamshire, a historic livery company for local manufacturers fond of pomp and circumstance. All the professionals knew each other and they traded in gossip. Cook calculated that hinting at his plans to Belton could help his cause. "Things are looking up," he said. "People are talking about this company going for £4 but if nobody else gets £4 onto the table, I certainly will." Belton smiled and winked. "A very merry Christmas to you, Andrew, and best of luck for the new year," he replied. Cash in hand, Cook returned home to the Manor House, his last chore completed. He walked into the hall, locked the door behind him and the children ran into his arms. In the event, Christmas was a peaceful day, the gnawing anxiety that had dogged him for the last six weeks seemed to lift and he felt a strange sense of certainty and calm determination. In the background, the Queen gave her annual televised address. In a difficult year of "discord, sickness, bereavement, even tragedy", the horror of the Dunblane school massacre and the threat of violence returning to Northern Ireland, the theme of her message at the end of 1996 was hope for the future.

At 6am on December 27, Cook was up and out of the house with Martin the driver, collecting finance director John Caldwell from his home in Ecclesall, a leafy suburb of Sheffield, and heading to Manchester Airport through the torturous cross-country route via Whaley Bridge and Pott Shrigley. BBC Radio 4 carried reports of a British nurse charged with murder in Saudi Arabia and another England batting collapse in Zimbabwe. Cook, who didn't care for ball sports, switched over to Classic FM. They arrived at Manchester Airport in good time for Cook's flight to Scotland where he was due to visit Baillie Gifford, a significant shareholder in William Cook. The historical fund manager had a long track record of backing winners, stretching back to its formation in 1908 when it financed rubber planters in Malaya and Ceylon. Its funds under management included the Scottish American Investment Trust, co-founded by the financier Robert Fleming.

At Edinburgh Airport, Cook met the banker Margaret Young who did not seem to be in the best of spirits, complaining that she was suffering from flu and had spent Christmas Day in bed and should probably still be there. Being in unusually good spirits, Cook resisted the urge to remind her who was the paying client. Jonathan de Courcy-Ireland of UBS turned up as well and the four of them squeezed into a taxi for the meeting with Guy Cameron, a partner who headed Baillie Gifford's UK mid and small cap team. Cameron was pleased to see his visitors and in good spirits, ahead of the Hogmanay celebrations in just a few days' time. Cook went through the pitch and his well-oiled argument that William Cook was undervalued by the City. Caldwell did the numbers. Cameron nodded along in agreement, needing no convincing that Cook was right and that Triplex Lloyd would have to increase its offer by a seriously large amount of money if it was to stand a chance with its takeover. The meeting was over in half an hour, job done. "Happy new year Andrew," said Cameron. "Lang may yer lum reek, as your Scottish forefathers might have said."

The party hailed a taxi for their next destination, an appointment with potential investors Aberforth Partners at a handsome Georgian townhouse in the New Town. Cook had a vague recollection of the building but no memory at all of the man who greeted him or their previous meeting. He really should have tried harder with investor relations. The fund manager was a little brusque in manner, the reason why becoming clear as he recounted their last conversation. Aberforth had liked the look of the company and was ready to invest but was deterred by Cook's downbeat mood during the discussion. Now the shares had risen as a result of the hostile bid, the fund had missed out on a big gain and its manager was annoyed, understandably so. It was a wasted meeting. "When it comes to investor relations, this is me to a tee," thought Cook afterwards, in the taxi on the way back to the airport. "Not properly taking in the people I meet or the surroundings I meet them in. No wonder I have so few allies in the City."

From Edinburgh, Cook caught a plane to Heathrow and a connection to Geneva where he hired a car for the last leg of the journey, a two-hour drive to Champéry, a picturesque village in the shadow of the Dents du Midi range, the "Teeth of the South" in French. Cook felt protected by the mountains, reassured by the power of nature and its ability to render human affairs quite meaningless. He arrived at the chalet at 11pm, the children still awake and delighted to see their father. It had been a long day, a long year even, and he fell fast asleep.

CHAPTER 25

Essentially faceless

Marked by mass beheadings and the terrible torture of *bastinado*, the Siege of Malta in 1565 was an extraordinarily brutal battle, a great clash of civilisations as 500 Knights of St John and 6,000 foot soldiers repelled a four-month assault by an army of 40,000 Turks in one of the most famous military defeats of the ages and a turning point in Europe's history. As a youth, Andrew Cook had devoured 'The Great Siege', the British historian Ernle Bradford's 1962 account of the battle between the Holy Roman Empire and the Ottoman Empire. A teenage visit to the small but strategically important Mediterranean island made an indelible impression on Cook, with his acute sense of drama.

He lay awake in the chalet at Champéry, his family asleep, his mind casting back to Malta, his overactive imagination bringing to life the horror of warfare as the defenders fought back their assailants, the cries of men fighting men with sharpened metal, the hacking of flesh and bone and the spraying of blood. Heaven help those taken prisoner. He thought of his own assailants at Triplex Lloyd and the unfairness of their attack against his company, his family and his work, outnumbering him with their supporters in the outwardly respectable institutions of the City of London and Fleet Street, their inner baseness masked by polished accents, good manners and pin-striped suits. The enormity of his task seemed almost overwhelming but he felt calmly determined and did not contemplate defeat. If he contemplated defeat, he believed it would lead to defeat. Nor did he contemplate victory. He resolved to fight on, day by day, and keep on fighting until the battle was won.

After a weekend's skiing, Cook left the chalet at 5am on Monday, December 30, for Geneva airport and a flight back to London and his make-or-break meetings with the buyout firms Candover and Electra Fleming. The 7.20am Crossair flight to London City Airport was virtually empty. On arrival, he bought a bundle of newspapers and flicked through the business pages as a taxi driver took him from the Docklands to his meeting at Candover at its office at 20 Old Bailey. *The Guardian* carried a report headlined 'Steel firm hits out in take-over row' by Ian King, a former HSBC analyst turned financial journalist, an ambitious young hack who was covering the City desk during the festive lull. He informed his left-leaning readers that William Cook had complained to the Takeover Panel after Triplex Lloyd questioned the accuracy of its profit forecasts. The row, wrote King, was part of one of the most contested takeover fights for some time. King quoted Cook as saying he had nearly issued libel proceedings against his foes for questioning the veracity of his statements and had written to the panel about their behaviour, predicting they would come to regret making the claims. The complaint would keep the spotlight on the panel, commented King. Arriving at his destination in the shadow of the Central Criminal Court, Cook looked up to the female statue of Justice, sword in one hand and scales in the other, the dark gold shimmering against the dawn sky.

Cook walked into the reception area, which was undergoing some extensive renovation work. It was deserted apart from a solitary, yawning security guard. Another man, wearing a black wax jacket and polka-dot scarf, walked in and headed straight upstairs, weaving around some paint pots. Cook guessed this was the man he was supposed to be meeting. The finance director John Caldwell arrived. Terry Smith joined them, his wiry frame wrapped up in a long wool overcoat. Cook smiled at his friend with the owlish eyebrows – General Patton and the reinforcements had arrived. The guard gestured towards the stairs with a nod. The trio ascended and were met at the top by the man from reception and ushered into a meeting room and offered coffee. On the table was the A4 envelope marked 'recorded delivery' sent by Alison on Christmas Eve. It was unopened. The man sliced it open with a letter knife before them and idly flicked through the pages while Cook and Caldwell started their presentation. Cook tried his best but was disheartened by the man's apparent lack of preparation. What happened to appraising oneself beforehand? He would have done so if he was looking at a serious investment proposition. Cook did not feel confident. They left after an hour and stopped in one of those tiny cafés in a side street that seem to survive from the custom of passing London tradesmen. They squeezed around a table and had a cup of tea before Smith bid farewell and returned to his office near Bishopsgate. Cook and Caldwell headed to their next meeting, an appointment with Legal & General.

Founded in 1836 by a group of lawyers in a Chancery Lane coffee shop, L&G started out providing an umbrella of life insurance protection to the legal profession in London and expanded by financing railways, canals and property development in Victorian England. In the 1980s, the company had extended its reach across the world, buying life insurance companies in New York and establishing operations in Europe. By the 1990s, L&G was one of the largest investment managers in the world and, in the context of this story, a middle-ranking institutional shareholder in William Cook plc. The two men representing L&G that morning were friendly enough. Cook quickly established they weren't sellers at £3 a share but sellers they would be at the right price. It was a reminder that ultimately, all these institutions cared about was money. So uniform were they in this respect, the men in front of him were essentially faceless. Cook shook hands and he and Caldwell departed for their meeting with Electra Fleming, which had assumed a greater importance given Candover's lukewarm response.

Electra Fleming was based at 65 Kingsway, a Grade II-listed Art Deco office block built on a prominent island site in 1911 for the Kodak Company, its facade clad in Portland stone on a Norwegian granite base. At 3pm, Cook and Caldwell entered through the marble vestibule and ascended the stairway to the first-floor reception area with its marble columns, mosaic floor and screens made from glass and mahogany. They did not wait long before a tall man in his early forties with dark receding hair entered the room. It was Tim Syder who introduced himself cheerfully and led his guests through the deserted building to a private meeting room, where coffee and biscuits were waiting. Cook's information pack was spread across the table, the sheets laid out and annotated in places. Syder appeared to have done his homework over Christmas. Syder called in a couple of juniors to join the session. The coffee was good and provided a nice little bump for Cook as he cantered through the events to date. The pack included a VHS cassette containing William Cook's corporate video. One of the underlings inserted the tape into the room's video machine with a click and pressed play, the large screen mounted on the wall flickering into life.

The film showed the company's plants in action, the visual drama of the molten steel pours, the high-tech of the machine rooms and the gleaming end product, bound for customers in the defence, construction, mining and energy industries. As archive news footage showed the Challenger main battle tanks of the British Army storming across desert battlefields, Major General Patrick Cordingley, Commander of the Desert Rats in the First Gulf War, told the viewer "the tracks were superb". Soundtracked by stirring music, it was undeniably impressive stuff. Cook glanced at Syder and his young colleagues who were watching the spectacle intently.

The film finished and Cook launched into his presentation, his audience asking him a multitude of questions about the company, about him and about his plans. It was dark outside as the group decamped to another room in the office block where a familiar face was awaiting them. It was Chris Kirkness, a director of asset management at Robert Fleming & Co and formerly at UBS, where Cook had met him previously. Cook thanked his good fortune – Kirkness was a former boss of Jonathan de Courcy-Ireland and they had previously discussed Cook's desire to take William Cook private. Kirkness joined the session and the detailed questions about the company and its prospects continued until 8pm when they decided to call it a night. Cook felt they were beginning to warm up to the idea of backing him in a management buyout.

He caught a taxi to the family flat in Sutherland Avenue in Maida Vale, a west London enclave, and walked around the corner to Cafe Rouge, where he had arranged to meet an old friend, Nick Woods, for dinner. Over fillet steak and Burgundy, the two caught up and Cook started to relax in the company of his convivial friend. Woods' father had founded an agency supplying European foundry equipment and was a supplier to William Cook. Woods had inherited the business and enjoyed the lifestyle it afforded him. He was an amusing and educated man and a great conversationalist with a love and knowledge of history and a similar strain of humour. The ideal drinking companion, in other words, at the end of a long day on that evening of December 30.

Early next morning, Cook was up and out of the flat and heading north by train to North Yorkshire and the company's Blackett Hutton foundry at Guisborough, a historic operation which had produced castings for the Humber, Severn and Forth bridges but was in the process of being sold to an American buyer, being deemed surplus to requirements. How he missed the day-to-day running of the company. All the problem solving seemed so simple in comparison to the machinations of the City with its elaborate charades and cast of chancers. Visit complete, Martin the driver took Cook to Newcastle Airport for a flight to Amsterdam's Schiphol Airport and a connection to Geneva and his awaiting family. As he waited in the busy departures lounge, he took a call from Simon Metcalf. The Takeover Panel had stopped the clock on the bid timetable to allow more time for enquiries by the Office of Fair Trading, said the banker. The OFT had to decide whether to refer the takeover bid to the Mergers and Monopolies Commission but was not currently in a position to do so. It was good news, said Metcalf, because it gave Cook more time to work on his defence and a potential buyout. The sticking point for the OFT seemed to be the Lloyd Burton foundry, which William Cook had acquired from Triplex Lloyd in 1990. The prospect of it being paired with a rival operation at Triplex Lloyd had caused some concern among officials over the impact on consumers. Metcalf wished Cook a happy holiday and rang off. Cook joined the queue to board his flight when his phone rang again. It was the PR man Tony Carlisle.

"Andrew, there are more sleaze allegations. Journalists are digging around again. They have been told you have bought a Ferrari and a flat in the South of France with company money. No guesses who's been whispering into their ears."

"Tony, I can't talk. I am about to board a flight. Stonewall them for now and keep me posted," said Cook, weary from the whole battle. He had had enough of these bastards. He said goodbye to Carlisle and followed the other passengers across the apron to board the plane. It was starting to snow quite heavily. Blizzards were closing airports across the south of England. Feeling besieged, he just wanted to get up into the air and away from this damned country.

CHAPTER 26

A different sort of City

New Year's Day was spent skiing with the children at Portes du Soleil, a family skiing area spanning a galaxy of resorts between Mont Blanc in France and Lake Geneva in Switzerland. The sun was shining, the snow was perfect and Cook felt at ease in the mountainous surroundings, away from the twin pressures of business and Britain, yet he could not remain. Early the next day, a taxi took him to Geneva airport for the 7am Crossair flight to London City and a follow-up meeting at Electra Fleming. He read the morning's papers on the flight. Princess Diana was going to Angola as part of her campaign to ban the manufacture and sale of landmines. Tony Blair, the youthful leader of New Labour, was grinning about winning donations from a growing number of business leaders. The Bishop of Oxford was bashing the Tories for failing to put morality at the heart of government policy.

Margaret Young, who was still sniffling, and a junior colleague from NatWest Markets were awaiting Cook at Electra Fleming's reception in Kingsway. They had come along to help establish the ground rules for the management buyout discussions to proceed. There were some sensitivities around conflicts of interest, warned Young. In the meeting room, the host Tim Syder cheerfully welcomed his visitors, wished them a happy new year and offered tea and coffee. He had invited along BZW, the investment banking arm of Barclays which had arranged the loans for the aborted share buyback for William Cook. Its man turned to Cook, cleared his throat and cut straight to the point. "As chairman of the plc board, you have a duty to your shareholders to get the best possible price for William Cook and you are leading the orthodox defence on the argument that the Triplex Lloyd bid undervalues the company. You are also proposing to lead a management buyout of the company and presumably you will not wish to be paying over the odds. You have a problem here, don't you?"

Cook fixed him in the eye and replied he had no problem whatsoever. His job was to get the maximum value for shareholders and if a buyout was the best way to achieve that, he would be doing his job. The BZW man harrumphed. Both looked at Syder, who smiled and did not appear too bothered about any potential conflict and moved onto the next item on the agenda: pay and perks. This matter seemed to exercise Syder who told Cook he would need a letter of disclosure from him setting out exactly how much he got paid and who else was on the payroll, just so everything was out in the open. He added there would necessarily be some belt-tightening because Electra Fleming liked its portfolio companies to run a tight ship. Cook decided against arguing the point. He needed the backing. In any case, Syder seemed to have complete command of the situation and was combing through the details, grilling Cook on every aspect of his business. He seemed a master of the ritual and the craft.

Outside, the world continued turning and humankind's

battle over the control of scarce resources, the essence of economics, resumed after the festive pause. The stock market had closed on a record high at the end of 1996, but 1997 opened for business in tumultuous fashion with "bears on the rampage" and £7.5bn wiped from the value of shares in trading, according to the *Evening Standard*'s City Prices edition, which was lying on a table in reception. The Square Mile was becoming increasingly concerned about Britain's political situation, wrote Tom Winnifrith, author of the Market Report column. "Friday 13th could well be a grim day for the Tories as Parliament reopens with by-elections and further defections increasing the chances of John Major having to call an early election which he seems certain to lose," he wrote. Winnifrith added that Triplex Lloyd had extended its offer for William Cook until January 14. The predator claimed it had received acceptances on behalf of more than one million shares, equivalent to just under six per cent of the total. It was clear to anybody who was watching that Triplex Lloyd would have to increase its offer. It was just a question of when.

The meeting resumed the following morning, the number of people in the room steadily increasing with bankers of all shapes and sizes from Robert Fleming & Co, Bank of Scotland and Barclays jostling for space alongside teams from Electra Fleming and its law firm Ashurst Morris Crisp. Andrew Jackson, the co-founder of Intermediate Capital Group, arrived to offer the mezzanine debt, a type of high-risk finance used in management buyouts. Syder was conducting the group like an orchestra, clearly in his element. Cook was the centre of attention, momentum gathering around him. The room took on the appearance of a theatre when Cook pressed play on the corporate video, its voice-over introducing viewers to the steel casting – "versatile, tough, whether complex or simple, always practical" – and the largest producer in Europe with customers across five continents who depended on William Cook products, illustrated with a montage of moving images showing the defence, transport and mining industries in action.

After the corporate video, Cook showed the group an earlier film, dating back to 1986, to demonstrate the evolution of the company. Seeing his younger self on screen made Cook realise how much he had aged over the last decade, the result of the international travel, the long hours and the constant pressure of running a business with little margin for error. The combined effects had been compounded by the car crash. Still, he was in better shape than most businessmen at his age, who spent their lives sitting on trains, behind desks, at boardroom tables, in restaurants and at bars, thanks to his extreme fitness regime and abstemious lifestyle built up during the previous decade.

The questions kept coming from Syder and co, pressing for information about the defence business, relations with key customers like Vickers and the ultimate end user, the Ministry of Defence, and the impact of exchange rate movements on the company's finances. This was a very thorough going-over, the session continuing past 6pm, then 7pm and then 8pm, by which time Cook would have had to depart to catch the last plane to Geneva. He decided to keep quiet about his travel plans, in case it raised questions over his commitment, but someone else let slip that he was planning to go to Switzerland, a cause of some amusement to Syder, that the higher flyer was grounded for once.

It was gone 9pm when the meeting started to wind up.

Cook, who was no slouch himself, was impressed by the dedication of this lot, a different sort of City from the one he held in such contempt. At 10pm, Syder called it a night. The Bank of Scotland man, who had travelled down from Edinburgh for the meeting, hurried out to catch the last plane home, just making it, while Cook and Caldwell headed to the Waldorf Hotel in Aldwych and its well-stocked bar. Caldwell had one for the road, drank up quickly and dashed for the last train back to Sheffield but Cook stayed on, unable to relax and in the mood for more alcohol. He reached for the Nokia inside his coat pocket and scrolled through the contacts, looking for Emma Milligan's name.

CHAPTER 27

False mirror

In the parlance of estate agents, Dore Road was one of the most sought-after addresses in Sheffield with exceptional Victorian residences set in landscaped gardens along a tree-lined road, originally established by the Duke of Devonshire to connect the Derbyshire village of Dore to the station in the city centre. Behind the impressive façades and among the period features lived affluent families, some happy and others less so. The Salisburys were next-door neighbours but one from the Cooks and they had also grown rich from industry, but more recently. Bill Salisbury was a self-made man, a Rolls-Royce driving Labour supporter from Wales who had invented an ingenious method for repairing cracked castings. With his entrepreneurial zeal, he expanded into property development, enzyme manufacture and corrosion protection for naval vessels. He was the type of man that McTurk's generation disliked, representing new money and a threat to the established order, but Cook got on well with him, identifying another outsider. Later in life, Salisbury would say to the young industrialist: "When I heard you were sleeping in your office, I knew you would be successful."

Salisbury had two sons and a daughter. Emma remembered

playing in her garden as a young girl and losing her ball over the hedge in the garden which backed onto hers. It belonged to a tall, frightening man, "a monster" who treated his own young children, Andrew and Angela, like dogs. Later, she would hear people say that McTurk was grief stricken by the loss of his wife. But she thought he was a man who just wanted to die.

Emma recalled Cook as a strange schoolboy. Unlike his peers, he would dress in a gentleman's coat and carry an umbrella. McTurk had instructed his son to wear good suits and always trust in the Almighty Lord. Despite the unlikely beginnings, Cook and Emma started dating in the Seventies. They would go to the cinema together to see films or head off to Europe on skiing trips. They watched *Close Encounters of the Third Kind* together in Zermatt. Cook was a superb skier but as his involvement in the business grew he became prone to cancelling holidays at the last minute because of some crisis or other at the company. They never had a steady relationship because his commitment was to William Cook, to which he had devoted himself. In those years, Emma found him full of ideas for the future and possessed of an innocence not yet worn down by experience. He was finding his way in the world.

Cook also had an arrogance, which she believed was born out of the solitude his father subjected him to. He could look down his nose at people but he never did so with the men in his factories. He loved being with them, wearing his blue overalls and solving engineering problems, and never felt alone when he was on the shop floor. He knew them all by name and understood there would be no company without their sweat and toil. In contrast, he loathed the City and its grown-up public schoolboys with cut-glass accents from the Home Counties who reminded him of his traumatic childhood. Emma thought he had a chip on his shoulder about being a boy from Sheffield in a world ruled by men from the right backgrounds.

Undoubtedly he had been damaged by the loss of his mother, fate depriving him of the strongest bond a child can have. Emma believed that feeling of belonging would elude him for most of his life, even in his marriage with Alison, not least because of his commitment to the company and the extraordinary demands it placed on him and the anxieties it fuelled. On paper, he was a highly successful man: he was rich, resourceful, engaging and on occasions very entertaining but it was a false mirror. On reflection, she thought he might be on the autistic spectrum. He could only understand some interactions retrospectively. He had a profound sense of right and wrong. She also believed he had a good heart and he showed this by supporting her during some dark and difficult times in her own life for no reason other than pure, unerring loyalty. They both experienced unhappy marriages and would confide in each other, discussing each other's problems, usually on the phone given Cook's continuous and impulsive travel. In her eyes, he had an unusually high degree of intelligence and preternaturally sharp awareness and was a great force for good who was incapable of acting dishonestly. It was a powerful combination. If it had not been for the company and having to take up the mantle for his sister and then provide for his own children, whom he adored, who knows where his talents would have taken him? He might have had a stellar career in politics.

It was after 11pm when Emma arrived at Good Godfrey's bar at the Waldorf to meet her lifelong friend, who was sitting alone at a corner table with his back to the wall and a bottle of champagne and two glasses before him. She spotted him before he saw her. He looked tired but his eyes lit up when he saw her and his face cracked into that familiar smile. She had never seen him look so wrung out. He poured her a glass and unburdened himself while she listened. He told her all about the troubles that had befallen him since Triplex Lloyd launched its hostile takeover bid nearly two months ago and the exciting new opportunity he had to take the company private and end the association with the City that McTurk had commenced all those decades ago. He told her about all the mudslinging and the terrible, untrue things they were saying about him in the press, all this stuff about flats in the South of France, Ferraris and non-existent company helicopters. It was so outrageous that people could behave like that. Emma could see exactly how he had fallen foul of the institutions, with his outwardly arrogant manner and unwillingness to play the game by courting the kind of people he could not stand. When he needed their help, they weren't there. Unloved by institutions, his company was a sitting duck for a ruthless predator like Triplex Lloyd. Cook topped up their drinks and picked up a handful of nuts. The bar was getting noisy.

Emma said: "It sounds to me like you might have a mole in your camp, feeding information to the other side. In any event, you've got to get a move on Andrew. The clock is ticking and this opportunity won't last forever. What's to stop Triplex Lloyd coming back with a bigger offer and your shareholders, PDFM and the rest, taking the money? You look knackered. This is killing you. You've got to get the buyout done or you'll regret this for the rest of your life."

He knew she was right. At that moment, Cook's phone

rang above the din. It was Alison, calling from Switzerland. He looked at his watch. It was past 1am. Where had the time gone? He answered, cupping his hand over the receiver and promising his wife he would be on the first British Airways flight to Geneva the following morning. Yes, he was still out and was with Emma, who Alison knew as his childhood friend and would not suspect she was anything more.

That weekend, the Cooks played host to their friends, the industrialist Tony Langley and his wife Mandy at Champéry, and in the evening dined at Grand Paradis, a traditional Swiss chalet at the head of the valley and housing the village's best restaurant. The overwrought Cook relaxed in their company, having known the Langleys for many years. Langley had first got in touch to complain about the poor standard of British industry, one of Cook's companies receiving an order from one of his and performing badly. Cook suggested they meet in person to talk it over and Langley had accepted. In person, they soon recognised they shared similar outlooks on the world and stayed in touch. Langley would ask for advice on occasion and Cook, who was five years older and then the richer of the two, would give it freely. Cook considered the sports-loving Langley less driven than himself and a man who clearly enjoyed his recreations – he owned a yacht, a helicopter and a twin-engined jet. Langley had recruited and retained some very capable and trusted lieutenants, who afforded him the time to pursue his interests outside work. He also knew Langley was a very shrewd entrepreneur who made some excellent acquisitions, especially in Germany, which would later propel him to billionaire status. "You have to be careful not to become a professional sailor and amateur businessman," he once told *The Times*.

Over cheese fondue, the friends talked and drank Swiss Fendant white wine long into the evening. Langley asked Cook about his trouble in the City. The party quietened as Cook told them about the management buyout he was working on and his potential backers at Electra Fleming who seemed keen on providing the private equity funds to take the company private and appeared to be a different sort of proposition to the usual City sharks. Alison, Tony and Mandy listened intently. Cook said Electra Fleming's support would likely come with significant costs to him personally: he would have to accept a big pay cut, give up many of the perks he had become accustomed to and stand down as chairman of the company founded by his forefathers that he rescued from certain death. Without a moment's hesitation, his wife and his friends told him to go for it and take the terms on offer. What was there to lose? Even if he succeeded in seeing off Triplex Lloyd and William Cook remained an independent public company, he would have to give up most of his pay and perks and chairmanship anyway to satisfy his existing shareholders and would probably remain a slave to the institutions for the rest of his days. The decision seemed obvious to his wife and friends. Cook said: "You've been in a few tight spots yourself, Tony. You know what it's like looking into the abyss. It's a comfort to me to discuss this problem with someone who is on the same wavelength." Langley, smiled and raised his glass in toast. They clinked glasses.

The Langleys and Cooks spent the next day skiing. They did the spectacular Ripaille–Grand Paradis run, a 10km piste described by the local guides as starting with wide, groomed slopes and giving way to rolling bumps and "a thigh-burning schuss in the middle" before levelling out onto a wonderland path through silent, snow-covered forests. Cook noticed how skilful the young William was becoming at skiing. It wouldn't be long before he would be overtaking his father.

CHAPTER 28

Heaven forbid and perish the thought

In medieval London, Gutter Lane was home to a community of goldbeaters. In the 13th century, Gregory de Rokesley, the Warden of the Mint and one of the capital's richest goldsmiths, ordered England's new coinage to be of the fineness "commonly called silver of Guthuron's lane". Named after its one-time owner, the designation alluded to the Latin word for throat, clearing the way for the proverb "all goes down Gutter Lane". An apocryphal tale from more recent times tells of a major accountancy firm acquiring a site in the street off Cheapside and asking the City of London Corporation if it could change the name to something more fitting, presumably involving an acronym of its founding fathers. The corporation reputedly retorted: "We don't allow people to change historic street names. But feel free to change your company's name to Gutter plc."

Andrew Cook thought the address appropriate as he arrived for his 11am meeting at Schroders, the investment banking advisor to Triplex Lloyd, a big shareholder in William Cook plc through its fund management arm and a signed-up supporter of its hostile bid. It was another fabled City institution, being founded in 1818 by prototype merchant banker Johann

Heinrich Schröder, a member of a prominent Hanseatic family of Hamburg who settled in London and became expert at the financing and shipping of commodities. Like Robert Fleming & Co, Schroders made its fortune in railway finance, issuing bonds for overseas borrowers on the London market and raising funds for infrastructure development across the US, Europe and Asia. By the late 20th century, Schroders was the biggest independent institution of its kind in Britain, generating hundreds of millions of pounds in annual profits from investing in securities and advising on mergers and acquisitions.

Andy Brough was waiting for Cook in reception. A qualified chartered accountant by profession, he had joined Schroders in 1987 and was in charge of its UK smaller companies fund, giving him considerable influence over the fortunes of the listed businesses in which he managed stakes. Judging by his subsequent media coverage, Brough was not averse to engineering mergers and acquisitions activities, writing to boards in his portfolio encouraging them to launch bids for rivals. Cook knew of his reputation and did not know quite what to expect but in person Brough had an easy manner, his bookish spectacles and boyish features belying his commanding position. He was also a huge music fan and would later present his own *Jazz FM* radio show called Jazz in the City. Settling into conversation, Cook hit the notes with his value argument for William Cook, rehearsing his lines about the bid undervaluing his company and its future prospects. Brough nodded along, tapping his foot in time. Cook found it difficult to square the agreeable man before him with the stance of the institution behind him. Schroders the investment bank was acting for Triplex Lloyd and Schroders the fund manager had accepted its offer. Yet here was Brough making upbeat noises about the value argument in a seemingly straight-up way to Cook. Beware appearances, Cook said to himself as he left the building; the City is filled with illusions, its players profiting handsomely from perceptions, regardless of the reality. On the face of it, Schroders was clearly conflicted, having a financial interest in both parties but like its peers would insist the existence of Chinese walls prevented any unethical behaviour within its hallowed halls, heaven forbid and perish the thought. Like so many old-school City institutions, they were beyond reproach.

Across the Square Mile at Fleetbank House in Salisbury Square, civil servants at the Office of Fair Trading pondered the growing pile of paperwork relating to Triplex Lloyd's proposed takeover of William Cook. Would they refer the case to the Monopolies and Mergers Commission? An official leafed through a manilla foolscap file, considering its contents. One letter stood out – it was from Major General Alan Sharman, director general of the Defence Manufacturers Association and until June 1996 director general of land systems in the Ministry of Defence, responsible for the procurement of all army equipment including armoured fighting vehicles. In this capacity, he had got to know William Cook well as suppliers of track, turrets and other components. Sharman added he had also become aware of the personal part that chairman Andrew Cook had played in the success of the business. "This awareness culminated in the recommendation, sponsored by the then chief of defence procurement, for the award to Mr Cook of the CBE in recognition of his towering contribution to defence, exports and the foundry industry," he wrote. Cook was duly awarded the honour in the New Year Honours of

1996 for services to the steel castings industry. Sharman went on: "I am of course unqualified to comment upon the rights, wrongs, validity or viability of the Triplex Lloyd bid. I believe however that in considering the case you should be aware of the importance of the personal contribution made by Mr Cook to UK defence and the defence industry and the risks that could arise for the public interest were this contribution to be lost." The bundle contained a raft of letters from other industrial customers, pledging their support to William Cook.

Cook had tasked his team with getting as many customers as possible to write to the OFT about the public interest element of the bid, namely that a group representing nearly two thirds of the UK market for a basic building block of the engineering and capital goods sector should decline in the future due to poor management by Triplex Lloyd. William Cook was the sole or main steel casting supplier to blue-chip companies including Vickers, Caterpillar, General Electric and GKN, not to mention the MOD. They would inevitably have to look abroad for their castings, where quality was inferior. The UK defence industry could become reliant on a German manufacturer for its tank tracks. All of this could not be in the public interest, or so went the argument.

North of King's Cross, Cook was sitting in a first-class train carriage alongside the grey men in their grey suits and the occasional red tie, a sign of the changing times, and catching up with the media coverage of his *battle royale*. He saw the business sections had covered the latest press release prepared by his PR man Tony Carlisle and issued in response to Triplex Lloyd's announcement that it was extending its bid for further acceptances. William Cook's announcement had sought to counter the relentless barrage of criticism with an attack of its own, based on some research about the track records of the business-men leading the hostile bid. The chairman Colin Cooke had sat on the Triplex Lloyd board since 1988 and should accept responsibility for the series of losses, failed acquisitions and decline in sales that have occurred during his tenure, according to Cook without an 'e'. The CEO Graham Lockyer was singled out for the collapse in profits at his previous employer Dowty Aerospace when he was managing director in the early Nineties. "Given the lack of industrial logic behind Triplex Lloyd's bid and the poor record of its 'new management team', this bid is not in the interests of shareholders of either company," said the William Cook release, claiming the bidder had made losses in three of the last six years and its results had been flattered by property disposals and exceptional items. It was testy stuff, but would it have any impact on the institutions? Cook was doubtful. Triplex Lloyd hit back, saying "in stark contrast to Andrew Cook, Colin Cooke has succeeded in strengthening the board of the company" and the management team had increased profits and strengthened cash flow. It dismissed as nonsense the claim the companies were in completely different sectors and there would be no significant savings from merg-ing the two head offices. "If Andrew Cook cannot see where substantial head office savings might come from, he cannot be looking very far," said Triplex Lloyd. Cook felt his fists tighten and muttered a Germanic oath under his breath.

Elsewhere in the business pages, Cook read a speculative report in *The Star* that Sheffield Forgemasters could be launch-ing a reverse takeover of an unnamed publicly quoted UK engineering business to gain a stock market listing. It was a virtual replay of his pre-Christmas dinner party conversation with Sarah Grunewald, the corporate financier. The Sheffield business community thrived on such gossip and he was glad to be out of it.

The Independent's Jill Treanor informed her readers that City law firms had reaped rich rewards from last year's boom in takeover activity, scooping a record £500m in fees, a 50 per cent increase on 1995. "I would have expected partners to have had one of their best years for quite a number of years," said David Woolfson of legal expert Chambers. The *Acquisitions Monthly* magazine estimated that total fees paid out to investment bankers, lawyers, accountants and public relations advisors hit £1.1bn in 1996. The soaring stock market, low interest rates and expectation that a new Labour government would tighten tax and competition policy had created a boom in mergers and acquisitions and a bonanza in fees for the professionals. It would be left to chumps to pick up the bill.

A headline stood out in *The Times*, 'Protection for high-flyers is a policy that makes good sense', about the safety net offered to businesses by key-man insurance. "As he rose into the Morocco skies yesterday aboard the Virgin Global challenger balloon in his attempt to circumnavigate the world, Richard Branson left behind a £150,000 key-man insurance policy," wrote the journalist Gavin Lumsden. "If disaster does strike on the 18-day flight, Virgin will receive £30m to compensate for his loss and to fund the search for a replacement." Key-man insurance started in the United States but took off in the UK following the death of publishing tycoon Robert Maxwell. Barely three months ago, the multi-millionaire vice-chairman of Chelsea Football Club Matthew Harding had died in a helicopter accident on the way home from a game in Bolton. He was insured for £30m, reported *The Times*. Cook shifted uncomfortably in his seat, remembering that he held such a policy himself.

The next day, Cook had organised a private bus tour around William Cook plants for Tim Syder of Electra Fleming and bankers from Robert Fleming & Co, Barclays and Bank of Scotland. NatWest had tagged along to ensure adherence to the City's rules and regulations on takeovers by monitoring information presented to Electra Fleming. How the City loved its rituals. Syder had a heavy cold – it was catching – but was determined to get around the plants. One of his colleagues clearly didn't like being outside London: commenting loudly that north of Watford was bad enough, let alone the North East and South Yorkshire, which reeked of social and economic deprivation. It was a world away from the handsome Georgian townhouses and leafy garden squares of west London where City bankers lived in blissful ignorance of the vast swathes of England being left behind by the macro trends of globalisation and deindustrialisation. To them, they were mere numbers on a screen. Anyway, an election was around the corner and New Labour was promising to create regional development agencies to devolve decision-making powers to all corners of England and promote investment, stimulate employment and enhance the knowledge-based economy. "Apparently it is called the 'bottom-up' approach," said the banker in a bored voice as they drove past dilapidated housing, abandoned slag heaps and decrepit mills. To titters from the back of the bus, he added: "Why don't these people just get off their backsides instead?"

Syder sniffled away with his heavy cold but seemed to stay

focused on the plants and what Cook was telling him about their individual and combined performance. The tour took in the company's sites at Guisborough, Weardale, Leeds, Penistone and Sheffield. It was a long day with a lot of information and by late afternoon the party was looking bedraggled and ready for the train back to London. The bus was ready to depart from Parkway for the train station at Doncaster, but Syder told Cook he wanted to see more. They waved the others off and then headed to Holbrook for one final plant tour. Syder continued with his questions, listening intently to the answers above the noise of the operations. After all, he was proposing to put a lot of his employer's money at risk. Cook drove them over the Pennines to Manchester Airport with Syder using the Motorola car phone to buy himself a plane ticket to Heathrow with his gold card, arriving at the airport with 15 minutes to spare. Cook drove home to the Manor House, listening to a radio documentary about the growth of a new form of telecommunication, which allowed mobile phone users on the same network to send and receive text messages. He arrived in time to put the children to bed and then disappeared into his study.

William Cook's site managers, shop stewards and factory workers had been busy lobbying constituency MPs about the threat of the Triplex Lloyd takeover and the disastrous effect it would have on the company and the general engineering industry, urging them to press the Office of Fair Trading to refer the case to the Monopolies and Mergers Commission. In a memo to colleagues, one of the site managers, Greg McDonald of Lloyds Burton, wrote: "It is important to remember that it is an election year and all politicians, MPs and hopeful MPs are looking for opportunities to show their constituents how caring and attentive they can be."

Their efforts resulted in a meeting at the Houses of Parliament on Monday, January 13. Arriving at the venue, Cook instantly recognised the friendly face across the room. It was Richard Caborn, the member for Sheffield Central since 1983 and opposition spokesman on matters including trade, industry and regional affairs. Caborn was an energetic man with a straightforward manner and quick smile who could rub along with anyone. He had left school at 15 and served as an engineering apprentice before entering the trade union movement and becoming convenor of shop stewards at his employer Firth Brown. Cook had known Caborn for years and found it difficult to reconcile the one-time radical activist with the sharp-suited operator before him in Parliament who seemed certain to get a ministerial job if, as early polls were suggesting, New Labour won power. Caborn quickly agreed to put forward an Early Day Motion calling for the Monopolies and Mergers Commission to carry out a detailed evaluation of the bid and requesting that financial institutions properly evaluate the industrial strength of the steel castings sector and "base their decision on the long-term interest of the investor and the customer, not short-term gain".

Caborn was joined by several Labour colleagues including Harry Barnes, MP for North East Derbyshire, Kevin Barron, MP for Rother Valley, Clive Betts, MP for Sheffield South East, David Blunkett, MP for Sheffield Brightside, Michael Clapham, MP for Barnsley West and Penistone, Derek Fatchett, MP for Leeds Central, David Hinchliffe, MP for Wakefield, Helen Jackson, MP for Sheffield Hillsborough, Bill Michie, MP for Sheffield Heeley, Dennis MacShane, MP for Rotherham,

and Dennis Skinner, MP for Bolsover. As a gathering of prac-
tising and reformed socialists, it was hard to beat but at least
they showed up and seemed willing to help.

Cook left the Labour contingent to his site managers and
wandered over to the smaller group of Conservative MPs lurk-
ing in the corner of the room. His sister Angela Knight, the
Conservative MP for Erewash and a ranking member of the
Major government as Economic Secretary to the Treasury,
had gathered them together in an effort to help her brother
out. Compared to the confident and lively members of the
Opposition, they were a rather lacklustre bunch, perhaps sensing their time was up. Among them was Sir Irvine Patnick,
a Sheffield-born businessman who was notable for coining
the phrase "the socialist republic of South Yorkshire" and
his smearing of Liverpool football fans in the aftermath of
the Hillsborough stadium tragedy. He was sporting a deep
Mediterranean suntan and appeared even more laidback than
usual despite facing some stiff competition for the once safe
seat of Sheffield Hallam from the Liberal Democrat upstart
Richard Allan, a future lord and lobbyist for Facebook. Cook
was upfront with the Conservatives, explaining that he was
trying to put a management buyout together to save William
Cook from the clutches of Triplex Lloyd and just needed time
to get it away. He ran through the arguments for an inquiry by
the Monopolies and Mergers Commission. Their response was
positive but non-committal. The Tories would try but couldn't
promise anything. Cook left the meeting wondering whether
it had all been a waste of time and reminded himself never to
rely on politicians.

A couple of days later, Cook was heading to London by

train when his Nokia started chirping outside Hitchin in Hertfordshire. He recognised the number as Simon Metcalf's. An announcement from the Office of Fair Trading had just flashed up on Bloomberg terminals across the City.

"What does it say then, Simon?"

"No material threat to competition, I'm afraid. The clock is ticking again and I hate to say it but it looks like we might be running out of time."

CHAPTER 29

A world away from the dark satanic mills

I f hostile takeovers are a field day for City advisors, they are a bloodsport for financial journalists. "With so little action in the markets to amuse us at the moment, we have to give thanks to the executives at William Cook and Triplex Lloyd for providing such enormous entertainment in one of the most bitterly fought takeover battles for years," wrote City columnist Michael Shanahan in the *Evening Standard*, who gleefully told his readers "the two metal-bashers have been going at it hammer and tongs since mid-November".

Behind the humour, the writer was making a serious point: few people in the City followed William Cook and it was generally assumed the offer, representing a 30 per cent premium to the price of shares on the day, was reasonable as the target had "a fairly desultory track record" and CEO Graham Lockyer would have little trouble sewing the deal up. "How wrong could they be," observed Shanahan, a self-confessed lover of fine wine, food, slow horses and, it seemed, corporate dust-ups. Andrew Cook, he wrote, may be one of the most corporately incorrect company executives in the country – borrowing an earlier line from Christopher Fildes in *The Spectator* – but he had launched and carried through such a determined defence of the independence of his company that he had won the grudging admiration of even his most critical detractors. There was no doubt that Triplex Lloyd would have to put more money on the table if it was to win but there were doubts that Lockyer could afford to go for the knock-out blow, according to the commentator. Cook would do himself no harm if he addressed the thorny issue of corporate governance in his final defence document, which was due out in a few weeks' time. Appointing a top-flight chairman, a clear-out of the non-executive directors and a reduction in the length of his employment contract could just be enough to win the day, Shanahan predicted.

In the newspaper industry, the *Evening Standard* was an outlier. Nominally a 'local' paper for the capital, the title behaved like a national in thought and deed and with its multi-edition model was able to break and update important stories during the day, up until the West End Final edition. It also had a slightly different sensibility from its industry peers, being based in the more rarefied atmosphere of Kensington High Street as opposed to the earthier Wapping or blandly corporate Canary Wharf. Yes, it was conservative in its outlook, like powerful stablemates the *Daily Mail* and *The Mail on Sunday*, but it relished its editorial independence under editor Max Hastings, one of the big beasts of Fleet Street, a former editor-in-chief of *The Daily Telegraph* who had made his name as a fearless war correspondent with his despatches from the Falklands. The *Standard*'s City coverage was bang up-to-date and widely read by Square Mile commuters returning to the Home Counties at the end of every day.

Someone at NatWest Markets had presumably got some ideas from Michael Shanahan's column, which appeared under the headline 'How metal-basher Cook can forge a victory', and decided that Cook ought to renew his efforts to find a new chairman and put an end to the issue of corporate governance. The bank had lined up a firm of headhunters which specialised in recruiting non-executive directors and apparently could solve all of Cook's problems for a consideration of just £25,000 plus VAT. After much huffing and puffing, the recruitment consultant came up with just one name: David Hubbard, the former chairman of Powell Duffryn plc, a shipping services and energy group which could trace its origins back to the 19th century coalfields of South Wales. Under Hubbard, the group had won the bidding for the Tees and Hartlepool Port Authority, the first British trust port to be privatised, and would later become known as PD Ports. Cook, who always liked to pursue all possibilities, agreed to meet him the following day, January 16.

Cook spotted the man as soon as he stepped off the train onto the platform at Doncaster station. Dressed in a long camel overcoat and wearing the navy blue and red zig-zag tie of the Royal Artillery, Hubbard gave every impression of being a decent and dependable fellow. He certainly seemed to be well connected, being a Freeman of the City of London, a one-time industrial appointee of the Takeover Panel and a member of the Lucifer Golfing Society. Cook gave him a tour of the plants in Leeds and Sheffield and scrutinised Hubbard closely. Could he picture him gunning for William Cook in the City? As the cold day wore on, Cook thought he could. Hubbard had warmed up and was clearly impressed with the company's operations – "they're a world away from the dark satanic mills I was expecting" – and Cook as an individual. As he prepared to depart at Doncaster station, he looked Cook in the eye, shook his hand and told him he would be happy to serve as chairman and help him see off Triplex Lloyd and its outrageous bid. He was a damn sight better than Tonk Rogers of Newman Dougs, or whatever his name was, thought Cook as he drove home to the Manor House.

Cook was back in London the next day for a morning meeting with Simon Metcalf of NatWest Markets at 135 Bishopsgate, the giant City office block that Thatcher had hailed as "a monument to the virility and vitality of our times". Metcalf poured the coffee and asked how it went with Hubbard. Cook replied affirmatively, that Hubbard was a chairman straight out of central casting, seemed a safe pair of hands and what's more, had come to realise over the course of the day that in fact William Cook was a decent company and he was a decent man. Metcalf took a sip of coffee and placed the cup on the table and started to explain that since the headhunters had put Hubbard forward as a candidate some other information had come to light about Powell Duffryn's share price performance during his tenure and NatWest was hearing he was not every institution's cup of tea. "This is getting ludicrous," said Cook. "I can't go on wasting my time spending days trawling prospective chairmen around the company at your behest, only for NatWest to go cold on them afterwards because they aren't everybody's cup of tea. As lead defence advisor, you advised me to engage these recruitment consultants who have so far managed to put forward a grand total of one individual for a cost of £25,000 and then you tell me afterwards he is actually not quite right for the job. This classic defence we have been working on is getting us nowhere Simon. There is only one thing that is going to settle this and that's money. Money solves everything because it is at the root of most problems."

That afternoon, Cook returned to Kingsway for an appointment with Lawrence Banks, the deputy chairman of Robert Fleming & Co and Electra Fleming's nominee to be chairman of the buyout company. He was different from the regulation chairmen he had met to date. Banks was old school, hailing from one of England's landed families. His ancestor Sir Joseph Banks was a famous botanist who joined Captain James Cook's expedition to explore the uncharted lands of the South Pacific. The Banks had owned the 1,000-acre Hergest Croft estate at Rington in Herefordshire for more than two centuries and cultivated one of Britain's finest collections of trees and shrubs, notably Maples, Birches and Zelkovas. In person, Banks was a weathered man dressed in a well-made but crumpled suit who descended from a line of bankers and lawyers. Like his famous ancestor, he was a passionate gardener and served as treasurer of the Royal Horticultural Society during the Eighties, mixing blue blood with green fingers. His wife Elizabeth was an award-winning landscape gardener who would later become the first female president of the RHS. Banks had a worldly-wise air about him as he scrutinised Cook through wafts of heavy cigar smoke. He was joined by Fred Vinton, the chairman of Electra Fleming and a former high-flying investment banker at JP Morgan and NM Rothschild & Sons. Cook knew he was in the presence of City grandees and almost felt comfortable in their company. The feeling seemed mutual and the meeting was short and amicable.

Cook left Kodak House and hailed a Hackney cab for Victoria train station. He was catching a train to Gatwick

Airport and then a scheduled flight for a weekend in Guernsey with his family. How he missed the children. They missed their father, too, with him being absent for such long periods to fight this battle. The taxi driver switched off the roof light and asked Cook how his day was. In that private, contained space, Cook unburdened himself and shared his problems. The driver listened intently, occasionally looking back at the intense silver-haired man in the mirror as they weaved through the rush-hour traffic.

"If it all comes down to money, why don't you get the unions to put up some dosh? They're not short of cash, judging by the amount they pay their leaders," said the driver.

Cook thought it a long shot – when would a trade union ever back a management buyout? – but the driver was dead right about one thing: it would all come down to money. It always did. Arriving at Victoria, Cook took the driver's phone number and promised to let him know the outcome. He would keep his word.

Cook made it in time for the last flight of the day. As the plane taxied down the runway, he reflected on a rare piece of supportive media coverage. On the face of it, fund managers at Schroders had changed their mind about William Cook and withdrawn their acceptances of Triplex Lloyd's bid, taking £1m of shares out of the enemy's camp. The *volte-face* reduced total acceptances by 5.44 per cent to just 0.39 per cent. Cook knew the move was down to an administrative error within the City's biggest independent investment bank but it had handed him a propaganda win. He wondered whether it also represented a change in his fortunes. Writing in *The Independent*, Patrick Tooher said the episode was clearly a setback for Triplex Lloyd, which had made much of the high level of acceptances at the first closing date and would have to increase its offer to prevail before the final deadline of February 12. Cook checked himself; he would not tempt fate by contemplating victory. Graham Lockyer, CEO of Triplex Lloyd, said shareholders should not regard the withdrawal of this acceptance as any form of comment on the logic of his offer. Lockyer had been briefing the *Financial Times* that his company was trading strongly and winning new multi-million pound contracts with aerospace and automotive customers in the United States and Japan, largely the result of its development of new castings technologies. Triplex Lloyd was on the up and winning high-tech work under its dynamic new management team, or so the story went.

The jet soared into the sky and immediately flew into turbulence, the cabin juddering violently as it navigated chaotic currents. Something was clearly in the air. The stock markets had endured their biggest single-day fall in years after Alan Greenspan, chairman of the US Federal Reserve, had warned investors against what he was calling "irrational exuberance". William Cook's share price was unmoved.

CHAPTER 30

Fools' illusions everywhere

Graham William Stafford Lockyer had risen to the top largely without trace. With his neatly combed side-parted hair, square spectacles and finely striped suit, shirt and tie, he could have passed for any middle manager leading a blameless life in middle England. Born in 1947, the quietly ambitious engineering graduate started his career at the General Electric Company, the British industrial conglomerate and one of the country's biggest private sector employers with 250,000 staff. He trained with the turbine generation division, including a stint on the shopfloor of a foundry, and steadily worked his way up through the ranks. After 21 years with GEC, Lockyer spread his wings and left to become production director at Dowty Rotol, a Gloucestershire-based manufacturer of aircraft equipment. In 1991, he was appointed managing director of a new business unit called Dowty Aerospace just as the aviation industry dived into recession. Significant redundancies followed as healthy profits turned into substantial losses but Lockyer survived and in 1994 came to the attention of Colin Cooke who was in the midst of restructuring Triplex Lloyd. He promptly hired the 47-year-old as group operations director. Within months, Lockyer won promotion to the top job.

Explaining the rationale, Cooke told the *Financial Times*: "We need a strong operations guy – we're a very technical company."

In a double-headed profile, the *FT* said the two leading players in the bitter takeover struggle between William Cook and Triplex Lloyd seemed miscast. The domineering Cook had earned his reputation by staging a boardroom coup against his own father and then ruthlessly acquiring and rationalising much of the UK steel castings industry yet was on the back foot in having to defend his independence and promising to be more friendly to the City. By contrast, the pink 'un described Lockyer as a mild-mannered team player who seemed more at home building a kit car – one of his favourite pastimes – than waging war in the City. "Lockyer believes he can build a successful foundry group around his collegiate management style," wrote Midlands correspondent Richard Wolffe. "Prior to the bid he had already won analysts' support for his work at Triplex." According to the *Herald*, Lockyer was "canny and conservative" and his adversary "one of the most ebullient and individualistic of the engineers". This fight was finely balanced.

After landing a blow with Schroders' withdrawal of acceptances, PR man Tony Carlisle was advising Cook to maintain momentum and try to further undermine investor confidence in Triplex Lloyd. They should use Ford Motor Company's latest announcement of 1,300 job losses at its Halewood factory in Merseyside to their advantage. Ford was a customer of Triplex Lloyd's. In an opportunistic press release, William Cook challenged Triplex Lloyd to "come clean about its own prospects" and make a trading statement against a background of negative reports on the UK and European automotive components markets. The other side swung back immediately. In a curt response issued to *The Independent*, a Triplex Lloyd spokeswoman said: "Clearly William Cook does not understand Triplex Lloyd's business. Our automotive business is very much commercial vehicle related, with Perkins being the main customer. To talk about Ford is completely irrelevant." The company had no intention of making any trading statement, she added. Cook followed up the left-hand jab with a right-hand cross: William Cook was lifting its profit forecast for the year to more than £11m, a rise of 30 per cent on the previous year, due to strong trading and new orders for defence, mining and construction equipment and as a result would be increasing its final dividend for shareholders. Lockyer dismissed the update as "immaterial" and said it did nothing to address the sustainability of the next year's profits. As for the proposed dividend, Lockyer said the payout was lower than in 1991, the year that William Cook lost direction. And so it went on.

Back in London after a weekend's respite in Guernsey with his family, Cook returned to Electra Fleming's office at Kingsway where the bankers and associated professionals were busy arranging the finance for the management buyout. Behind all the drama, this would boil down to a simple financial transaction, an agreement between a buyer and a seller to exchange an asset – in this case the company bearing Cook's family name – in return for money. Barclays and the Bank of Scotland had to raise £45m between them, which was not proving too difficult given they had already agreed a similar sum in principle for the share buy-back scheme before Triplex Lloyd launched its hostile bid. Intermediate Capital Group had stumped up £15m in mezzanine debt. The remainder would be supplied by Electra Fleming and, it transpired, Andrew Cook who would have to roll over his shares in William Cook plc plus his pension fund into the new company, a total of some £3m. His sister Angela would cash out her shares, worth £2m.

Backed by the combined capital resources of Electra Investment Trust and Robert Fleming & Co, together worth an estimated £1.47bn, Electra Fleming was not short of money but in the new scheme of things, Cook would be. He had been a multi-millionaire on paper for the best part of a decade and would be sacrificing that status to protect his life's work. The reality set in as Cook scrutinised the draft legal documents, which valued William Cook at £90m, more than £30m in excess of Triplex Lloyd's offer. Tim Syder studied his expression as he did so.

"Not having any second thoughts, are we Andrew?"

"I don't think I have any choice, do I? Better this way than the other," replied Cook.

Syder wanted to speak with Cook's customers as part of his due diligence, the essential process of exercising care before any potential investment. He was not only risking Electra Fleming's money but also his own reputation in the City. Syder had instructed KPMG to help him with the task and its man had been touring the plants, interviewing staff and asking searching questions in an effort to uncover any hidden nasties that lay buried in the business. Cook enjoyed excellent relations with his customers and gave Syder a list of names and numbers of his key accounts. As he handed over the paper, he warned him not to mess them about by missing any appointments. Without those customers, the company would not exist.

Darkness had set in and the professionals were still hard at work, notching up the billable hours in service of their clients. By 8pm they had moved on to the Appold Street offices of Ashurst Morris Crisp, legal advisors to Electra Fleming. Founded in 1822, this was one of the UK's oldest law firms and had the unusual distinction of George Harrison writing a song about its wildly eccentric co-founder. "See the Lord and all the mouths he feeds," sang the ex-Beatle in his 'Ballad of Sir Frankie Crisp'. With the voluminous documents of indemnities, new contracts of employment and irrevocable undertakings being drafted and amended, the lawyers certainly wouldn't be going hungry. All of this legal work made Cook feel he wasn't entirely trusted. For a self-confessed autocrat, some of the proposed limitations on his power in the new company were simply out of the question but he resisted the urge to say as much and just let it roll in case he deterred his potential backers. Cook recalled his maxim: pay out the line and do not economise on the bait; you can always get tough once they are on the hook. On the law firm's part, a tall and attractive employment lawyer succeeded in obtaining his approvals, soothing Cook as he swallowed this bitter pill. "There, there," she might have said as the poison was taking hold. The room started to blur as the lawyers, bankers and investors passed their bundles of papers around, annotating this and that with increasing intensity, their chatter becoming a roar. The process was accelerating and taking on a life of its own, swirling around Cook, the power of capital now the dominant force. This was Electra Fleming's buyout, not his. He was just the instrument by which it was achieved. The ideal of independence was draining away. Cook had an unusually vivid dream during the night: the opening to a desert cave, a large boulder blocking his way, metal objects glinting in the light. "Fools illusions everywhere," went the George Harrison song. The sleeping pills weren't working very well.

The next day was Tuesday, January 21. The headlines concerned the wellbeing of Russian President Boris Yeltsin, who had not been seen since entering hospital earlier in the month. His American counterpart Bill Clinton was inaugurated for a second term, his approval rating higher than at any time since becoming the most powerful man on earth. Colonel Tom Parker, the man who discovered and managed Elvis Presley, had died in Las Vegas at the age of 87. In a speech to a business audience, the shadow chancellor Gordon Brown promised not to raise the top rate of tax in the life of the next parliament, wooing the City and wrong-footing the Conservatives. The tide appeared to be turning.

Cook was back at Electra Fleming's office by first light. Shortly after 7.30am, Syder walked into the room waving a piece of paper. Triplex Lloyd had made its move and was raising its offer for William Cook to £72.8m, up from £56m. It was offering 400p per share in cash and shares or 380p per share in cash only. CEO Graham Lockyer said William Cook shareholders had a clear choice between the certainty of the bid or to hope that its target's "newly discovered bright prospects" would survive after the offer had passed. Chairman Colin Cooke was on the media offensive, telling *The Yorkshire Post* his counterpart's contractual arrangements were "obscene" and lawyers were working on a legal challenge to minimise any payout to Cook on his departure. He told *The Independent*: "From buying in shares and saying there is no future for the garden, now we are seeing sunshine in the air and daffodils in the garden. It is time shareholders got some fair treatment from Mr Cook." To the *Daily Mail*, Cooke predicted he could make even more cost savings at William Cook's head office. "We don't need two cars and a helicopter," he sniped.

After absorbing the announcement, Cook called Tony Carlisle and the two of them hashed out a statement rejecting the offer to feed hungry hacks. Cook said: "Triplex Lloyd's new offer may no longer be ludicrously low but it remains manifestly low. The bid fails to take account of William Cook's substantially increased profits in the current year, the imminent completion of its modernisation programme and its excellent growth prospects. The suspicion continues to grow that Triplex Lloyd needs to buy our earnings on the cheap to make up for problems they face in their own business – not least the well-chronicled pressure on automotive castings, which is nearly half their sales." The statement added the company was making significant progress in finding new directors and could soon announce appointments. That should be enough to keep the press hounds at bay, Cook and Carlisle thought.

The *Birmingham Post* said most City analysts continued to believe that Triplex Lloyd would win the battle. One big shareholder in William Cook told the *FT*: "There is still a lot to play for, but this offer is probably enough. We were hoping someone else would come in with a bid but it now looks like this is not going to happen." John Sharp, analyst at stockbroker Albert E Sharp told the *Daily Mail*: "It is a generous offer. They should win, though it is hard to read the minds of institutions." William Cook shares rose 5p to 380p while Triplex Lloyd shares slipped by 11p to 192p, the biggest decline since it launched the hostile bid, its final offer being at the top end of analyst expectations. "There is time for a late recovery, but Triplex is in danger of being outmanoeuvred," wrote Kirstie Hamilton in *The Express*. In *The Times*, Carl Mortished commented that Triplex Lloyd had "brought out a hammer" after accepting that its fellow metal-basher had more life in it than the City expected but might "regret cracking this particular nut".

The meeting room at Electra Fleming was full again with fee-earning professionals. Syder, conductor of the orchestra, filled Cook's cup with coffee and offered him a KitKat. "You've got to decide now," he said. "It's us or them. What's it to be, Andrew?" Cook simply nodded his head, realising at last that his chances of staying independent had been zero from the very beginning. It was only ever going to come down to who was prepared to pay the most money to gain control of the company that he had saved from near-certain death. Syder patted him on the back and told him it was time to go and get some rest because they had some busy days coming up. As Cook walked out of the reception and into the freezing night air, his Nokia rang again for the umpteenth time that day. He answered it and heard a familiar female voice. It was Fiona Walsh, the seasoned City correspondent of the *Evening Standard*.

"Now then, Andrew. What's this I'm hearing about a buyout?"

CHAPTER 31

The ungodly hour

PDFM was having a nightmare. The fund manager had slipped from first to 15th place in industry league tables for new business won in 1996, losing its crown to scandal-hit rival Morgan Grenfell Asset Management whose star fund manager Peter Young had turned rogue trader accused of a £220m fraud and later appeared in court dressed as a woman. "The stresses and strains of working in the City are legendary. The relentless pressure to make money means traders burn out fast," observed *The Guardian*. Young suffered life-threatening injuries after attempting to castrate himself.

PDFM's own star manager, Tony 'Dr Doom' Dye, was convinced the stock markets in London and New York were about to come crashing down and had assembled positions in cash and bonds for when his prophecy would come to pass. The trouble was the markets kept rising and PDFM was being left behind, underperforming by six per cent according to City tables. Sheffield-born Dye, another product of High Storrs grammar school, was years ahead of his time and could only watch as Schroder Investment Management became the new king of the castle as Britain's biggest independent investment manager. PDFM was under pressure. Not only was it failing to win new business, it was bleeding clients as well.

Andrew Cook had a headache of his own. A pounding one, after a late dinner rounded off with port at the Waldorf Hotel the night before with finance director John Caldwell and Andrew Harrison, a young corporate lawyer from Cook's preferred local law firm Irwin Mitchell who had been helping with the paperwork. They hadn't been hitting the bottle too hard but by God, Cook's head was throbbing the morning after. He had taken the call from Fiona Walsh of the *Evening Standard* and declined to comment directly on any management buyout, though he had reiterated his position that he would not let the company go on the cheap and would do anything in his power to stop it being sold to Triplex Lloyd. The hotel's baroque dining room was deserted when they arrived at 11pm. The men went their separate ways at midnight. Cook needed to be alert the following morning but was struggling with a singular hangover. It was going to be a long day, he thought as he arrived at NatWest Markets for a meeting with banker Simon Metcalf and lawyer David Cheyne to resume work on the classic defence. As far as they were concerned, appointing a non-executive chairman could still repel Triplex Lloyd and convince erring shareholders to stick with Cook. Unlike Cook, they were sceptical about the buyout, giving it only a 50-50 chance of success. Chugging glass after glass of water, Cook found their focus on finding a chairman almost farcical at this stage of the game. Apparently, NatWest Markets had found a perfect candidate who was well respected in the City and also close to PDFM and would be visiting the office shortly for a meet and greet. Wearily, Cook went along with the charade and nodded his approval. Predictably, it was a waste of time, the man in question being wholly indistinct and more like a professor than a business leader. To Cook, who was unusually monosyllabic during the exchange, the issue was becoming academic anyway. Matters were coming to a head and he must decide whether to carry on with this classic defence, which appeared increasingly pointless, or do the management buyout.

A secretary entered the meeting room and announced that Mrs Alison Cook had arrived and was asking for her husband. Metcalf and Cheyne leapt up from their seats and intercepted Alison in the hallway before the pensive Cook could move.

"Alison, how are you? You are looking so well. And the children? Very good. Listen, Andrew is under frightful strain and seems virtually incapable of speaking, letting alone making a decision. You must help."

Cook regained his power and rushed into the corridor.

"Thank you, gentlemen. Alison, come with me." They walked around a corner to a quiet spot in the corridor. "Don't listen to them, I am absolutely fine, more or less. The time has come for me to decide what to do. I can persist with the classic defence, which would amount to appointing a professional chairman to deal with this corporate governance issue and hoping the shareholders stick with me, or I can go for the management buyout and be rid of the City. My defence team doesn't rate the chances of the buyout but they don't know Electra Fleming like I do. They are the proper City people and they have been combing through the company accounts to make sure the numbers stack up and they have been talking to our key customers. I think they are serious and they will go with me. Metcalf and Cheyne can say what they like but I don't rate the chances of the classic defence because it leaves me at the mercy of external shareholders and what they make of it."

Cook paused for breath. The act of explaining the situation to Alison had cleared his mind. He knew exactly what to do. She, a talented lawyer, understood the situation perfectly. It was obvious to both of them. He must call PDFM immediately and ask directly if he were to appoint a chairman and sort out the corporate governance at William Cook, would his biggest shareholder stay with him?

The question hung in the air as the high-powered investment bankers scrambled to find a phone with a working intercom for the all-important call. For all its astronomical fees, NatWest Markets was struggling to provide basic amenities for its clients. In a rather half-arsed way, the facilities manager attempted to explain they had none available at this time. Cook could feel his temper rising. Here he was in what felt like a life-or-death situation, fighting for his life's work, and his defence team was incapable of providing a squawk box. Eventually, the facilities manager returned to the meeting room with a dusty brown telephone, which he laboriously connected to a socket. Cook picked up the handset, dialled the number for PDFM's switchboard and asked to be put through to Hugh Sergeant. Metcalf and Margaret Young hovered behind Cook silently, barely breathing.

The receptionist at PDFM took Cook's name and connected him to the senior fund manager sitting upstairs. The statue of Mercury, standing on a globe on top of Triton Court, looking down on all in the City streets below.

Sergeant picked up the phone, his other hand subconsciously rising to cover his nose and mouth when he heard the familiar voice down the line.

"Hugh Sergeant here. How can I help, Andrew?"

Dispensing with the niceties, Cook put it to him straight: "Corporate governance plus acceptable chairman – do you stay with me?"

Sergeant replied: "We rather see corporate governance as an issue to be settled ex-bid."

Cook tried again: "But do you stay with me if I sort out corporate governance and appoint an acceptable chairman?"

Speaking through his hand, Sergeant said: "Andrew, we will make our decision when we have seen all the arguments, seen both parties and seen the price on the table. The issues of corporate governance and a chairman aren't particularly relevant to us at the moment."

Cook thanked him and hung up the handset. He looked at Metcalf and Young and repeated what Sergeant had told him. He suspected it all along but now it was clear as day: it was money on the table that was going to sort this out. The team at NatWest Markets had been trying in vain to counter Triplex Lloyd's cleverly assembled arguments, claims and allegations in the final defence document but words alone wouldn't change anyone's mind in this world. Cash is king.

There and then, Cook knew what to do. He told his advisors: "Abandon the classic defence, do the buyout."

With the momentous decision made, he exhaled and slumped back into the chair. He had had enough for the day and just wanted to get back to his children and away from all of these people. At that moment, the noises, the smells, the crowds, the demands, the threats and the darkness of the City repulsed him.

"The buyout can wait until tomorrow," he said. "I'm going home."

He rose and started gathering his paperwork when his Nokia rang. It was the PR man Tony Carlisle, smoking away at the other end. "Andrew, how are we? Brace yourself old boy, I've just heard the *Evening Standard* is going to break the story of your buyout plans in half an hour. I'm waiting for their City editor to call me back. I have some favours to call in and I'm going to try to buy us some time."

Cook relayed the message to the people in the room and watched as their faces sank into expressions of dismay. From the depths of exhaustion a moment earlier, Cook felt instantly energised, an adrenaline shot jolting him back into action. This disclosure would bring matters to a head. He called Tim Syder, told him the news and arranged to meet at Ashurst Morris Crisp, legal advisors to Electra Fleming. He turned to finance director John Caldwell and the young man from Irwin Mitchell: "No port tonight chaps. We're doing a management buyout."

At that moment, the prospective chairman walked back into the meeting room, the supposed perfect candidate lined up by NatWest Markets who was apparently close to PDFM. Metcalf took him to one side and quietly informed him that Cook and co were off to do a buyout and his services would not longer be required. His face reddening, the man cursed about time wasting and marched out in a huff.

Moments later, another man arrived, a noticeably lighter presence. It was Julian Briant of Robert Fleming & Co who had come to secure NatWest's agreement to a recommended offer. Briant was an urbane individual in his early forties and a seasoned dealmaker who had joined the bank in 1983 and worked his way up to director of corporate finance and, appropriately given his smooth-talking manner, senior relationship manager. This sort of activity was second nature to him and he soon started trying to talk a few pennies off the agreed price. Cook and Syder had agreed £4.25 per share but Briant was mooting a range of £4-£4.10.

"Hold on a minute here," said Cook loudly. "I can't possibly support a buyout unless there is sufficient daylight between our price and Triplex Lloyd's. It's £4.25 or nothing."

Briant agreed and so did NatWest Markets on the condition that a new committee be set up, independent of the board, to consider if the offer should be recommended to shareholders. It would be made up of the reliable old hands Porter, Pickford and Pratt and, on paper at least, should satisfy the Takeover Panel that codes of conduct were being observed.

Day turned into night and Cook walked the short distance to Ashursts at Broadwalk House, a prominent corner building designed by Skidmore, Owings & Merill as part of Broadgate, the Square Mile's largest office scheme. At least 15 professionals, including half a dozen lawyers, had congregated in one of the meeting rooms and all seemed to be speaking at once. On his arrival, they swarmed around Cook, jabbing multitudes of documents at him. To proceed, he must secure the resignations as company consultants of his father McTurk, his wife Alison and the long-serving Pratt. Cook reached Alison at the Manor House by phone and explained what was required. She quickly understood and, waiting for the faxed pages to arrive, telephoned her father-in-law, apologising for disturbing him so late at night but it was very important and concerned the future of the company. True to form, McTurk decided to make things difficult for his son. If it was so important why isn't the boy on the phone? Was he too important to speak to his own father? Furthermore, McTurk added, it was asking a lot to ring him up at night and ask him to sign away his consultancy with the company, just like that without any time for reflection. Actually, if she didn't mind, he would not be resigning that evening at all. He needed time to give it due consideration and perhaps speak to some of his friends in the City next week to get their opinions. They really understand these deals and have a lot more experience than Andrew who is out of his depth here. In any event, where was his payoff for all his efforts over the years? Cook was not privy to what Alison said to her father-in-law in response but evidently it worked and in half an hour's time, the signed document arrived by fax. Even at this crucial moment in Cook's life, the son felt his father's grudge. Ronald Pratt, who had joined William Cook in 1949 and become a director in 1953, signed his resignation by return, despite having no real nest egg.

Another problem reared its head, this time with the Inland Revenue and the prospect of Cook's shareholding becoming liable for taxation at 40 per cent, potentially landing him with a £1m tax bill. Cook was punch drunk by this point, his head spinning with numbers, but could not accept this blow without a fight and remembered an accountant friend, Steve Lindley, who was expert in these type of tax matters. Lindley, who had been raised from the land of nod in Huddersfield, explained sleepily how it could be done and learned counsel agreed, the scare passing.

Pizzas arrived, melted cheese still hot, boxes stained with

grease, followed soon after by bankers from the Bank of Scotland and Barclays and their lawyers. It was now 2am and yet the money men were well groomed, besuited and unruffled – no creased shirts or loosened ties here – despite the ungodly hour, this being precisely what they thrived on. Their fees would be eye-watering. Cook asked one if he had actually been to bed but didn't catch the answer. The money men got to work while a man from Robert Fleming & Co drafted a press release to announce the buyout offer. Still the documents flowed forth, the resignations, the warranties and now the indemnities: Cook would be on the hook for £400,000 if anything went wrong in the buyout process. He wasn't entirely happy about that, in fact the anxiety rose within him as his mind raced through anything that might crop up in the future and trigger the clause. He fixed on Unitcast, the one unmitigated disaster in his business career, the failed US acquisition that had flushed $12.6m in investors' money down the toilet. He visualised the two framed dollar bills above the toilet in his head office, all that remained from the ill-fated venture. Cook raised it quietly with the lead lawyer from Ashursts, an easy-going man called Charlie Geffen, who assured him it was nothing to worry about.

The lawyers continued with their lawyering, producing the bank documentation for Cook's signature, some 24 separate documents in total agreeing the £80m funds raised by Barclays, Bank of Scotland, Intermediate Capital Finance, Electra Fleming and Cook himself. Cook casually wrote out a cheque and handed it to Syder who read the sum and laughed, asking Cook how much his house in Guernsey was worth. "Mind your own business," said Cook, mindful they would be asking for further guarantees if he wasn't careful. The buyout sum covered, the legal discussions turned to the topic of fees. This was the payday for the advisors. NatWest Markets was in line for £1.2m as the lead defence advisor followed by UBS with £750,000, despite it doing virtually nothing in Cook's eyes, having failed to identify the attitudes and intentions of the large shareholders and being unable to offer any meaningful guidance, advice or information on share dealings. And yet here it was, second in line for fees, come what may. Word reached Cook that one of its senior officers, an individual who had sight of both the investment banking and PDFM operations, had remarked that William Cook plc was "going to go anyway and it was only a matter of price". After NatWest Markets and UBS, Cook had to pay £500,000 in arrangement fees to the banks, then the legal fees for Linklaters and Ashursts and lest we forget the PR man Tony Carlisle, who had indicated a fee of £275,000 for Dewe Rogerson's services. Cook quietly recalled Carlisle's words to him at the beginning of this sorry saga: "Don't expect any change out of £80,000." William Cook had certainly been in the headlines, but most of them entirely unwelcome. It would take many man-hours of work on the shop floors of the seven sites to clear these fees, thought Cook as he signed them away. Harrison, the lawyer from Irwin Mitchell who was brought in to safeguard Cook's interests in the minutiae of the documentation, started laughing wildly at some obscure point in one of the agreements. The small crowd paused, unsure of the joke. It was pushing 6am and they had been at it for the best part of 24 hours. The pressure of working through the night on a multi-million pound life-changing deal was having some curious effects. Still, there were no attempted castrations.

The paperwork largely complete, the principals left Ashursts and headed off in their various directions, Cook to his flat in Maida Vale, situated in a leafy avenue of large terraced housing subdivided into roomy apartments. The sun was coming up and exhausted or not, he could not rest as he had more business to attend to, the board meeting of independent directors scheduled for first thing that morning. After a quick bath and change of clothing, Cook hailed a taxi and headed back to NatWest Markets in the City, collecting Caldwell and Harrison from their hotel along the way. Martin, Cook's loyal driver, had collected Pickford and Porter in the middle of the night and driven them to the Lansdowne Club in Berkeley Square in preparation for the meeting, at which they would receive and consider the offer from the newly formed bid company. The team assembled at Broadgate for the 8am start time but Margaret Young was running late, stuck in traffic. It was approaching 9am, though time itself was losing its meaning with the cumulative effects of stress and sleep deprivation. Cook felt a sharp pain in his hip, a reminder of the old injury. He paced around the meeting room in an attempt to walk it off as David Cheyne, the Linklaters lawyer, looked out of the window at the skyline of the Square Mile, clouds emerging from behind the steel, glass and stone structures, filled with hundreds of thousands of human souls devoted to the pursuit of money. Shortly afterwards, Young arrived and the meeting could formally begin. Pickford and Porter both looked up at Cook, the silver-haired son of the widower, acknowledged receipt of his offer, read out the terms on the table and said they would be delighted to recommend it to shareholders for their acceptance.

CHAPTER 32

I suppose he thinks he's saved it

A ndrew Cook left the City for King's Cross and his train
home, falling asleep soon after he flopped down in his seat.
It was January 23 and the press release announcing the management buyout bid was finally approved by NatWest Markets.
Under the storied name of Robert Fleming & Co, it read: "Steel
Castings Investments Plc and William Cook Plc announce that
they have agreed terms for a recommended cash offer for the
ordinary share capital of William Cook, other than the ordinary
shares beneficially held by Andrew Cook, to be made by Robert
Fleming & Co Limited on behalf of Steel Castings Investments.
Steel Castings Investments is a company recently formed for
the purpose of making the Offer with financing arranged by
Electra Fleming. Electra Fleming has reached agreements for
Andrew Cook, who has been William Cook's chairman and
chief executive for 14 years and has built the company into
the market leader in the UK steel castings market, to be Steel
Castings Investments' chief executive and for John Caldwell,
currently William Cook's group financial controller, to be
finance director. It is intended that William Cook's existing
management team, including Roy Henson, will continue to
run the business following the successful completion of the

offer. A total of 21 managers will be offered the opportunity to invest in the equity of Steel Castings Investments."

The offer, recommended by the independent directors of William Cook, Robert Pickford, Ian Porter and Ronald Pratt, valued each William Cook share at 425p in cash, valuing the company at approximately £80m, representing a premium of 76 per cent over the price on November 14, the day before Triplex Lloyd announced its hostile bid, and a premium of 10 per cent over the increased offer made on January 21, which valued the company at approximately £72.4m. Lawrence Banks, the chairman of Steel Castings Investments and green-fingered, blue-blooded deputy chairman of Robert Fleming & Co, said: "This cash offer of 425p per share offers good value to shareholders and is in the best interests of the company, its customers and employees. Electra Fleming looks forward to working closely with the management team who successfully built William Cook into the UK market leader in steel castings." John Sunnucks of City spinners Brunswick, the PR agent for Flemings, distributed the release far and wide as Cook slept dreamlessly in the first-class carriage hurtling north to his homeland.

As the train pulled into Doncaster station, John Caldwell nudged Cook's arm three times to awaken him. Martin the loyal driver was waiting for them in the car park and drove the weary pair back to William Cook's head office in Sheffield, where Cook briefed his senior executives as well as he could before going back to the Manor House, where his wife and family awaited him. "Even if you lose," said Alison, her husband slowly walking down the hall, "you will have done everything you can." Cook had the best night's sleep since the whole waking nightmare started some 10 weeks earlier.

The press lapped up the news, the hungry hounds feasting on this surprising turn of events in what had already been a classic of the genre. The *Evening Standard* scooped its rivals, apparently based on a leak, telling readers that "battling" Andrew Cook had put together a bid to thwart Triplex Lloyd but under terms of the Takeover Code, the predator was now free to increase its own offer. In *The Express*, City columnist Kirstie Hamilton said that while engineering was rarely her favourite subject, the battle was proving fine entertainment. "In the saga so far, Andrew Cook has turned out to be surprisingly adept at defending his company from the clutches of Triplex," she wrote. "No one in the City was too keen on the man initially, mostly because Cook refused to play the game the way investors like it played. He avoided talking to investors unless absolutely necessary and insisted on keeping an iron grip on the firm by remaining chairman and chief executive. Terry Smith, our columnist, was one of the few voices to speak out on William Cook's behalf." Hamilton, a future City editor of *The Sunday Times*, noted that Triplex Lloyd had time to consider whether to raise its bid and although the market was convinced none of its options looked good – shares had fallen on news of the management buyout offer – the best bet for the company might be to press on. If Triplex backs off, the mud slung by William Cook and its advisors will inevitably stick and Triplex will end up looking like a loser, she said. In a world where perception is everything, nobody could afford that tag. "Either way," wrote Hamilton, "Andrew Cook is not a man I'd like to play cards with."

Nobody saw this coming, the Albert E Sharp analyst John

Dean told *The Independent*. "It is a very unusual form of 'white knight'," he said, using the term applied to the saviour of a company subject to a hostile takeover bid and taken from the game of chess. What was the Square Mile if not a board for battle formation?

Eric Barkas, City Editor of *The Yorkshire Post*, described Cook's move as audacious and if successful would rank as one of the great Houdini acts in recent City history, noting the last time such a defence was mounted was in 1985. This was when entrepreneur Philip Ling led a management buyout at listed engineering group Haden MacLellan in the face of a hostile bid from conglomerate Trafalgar House. Ling was a pioneer, becoming the first manager to take a British public company private in such a way. His backers included Electra. Cook's exit from the listed company scene would not be unwelcome, an unnamed analyst told *The Yorkshire Post*, although the author added there was no doubting his passion for the family business and his fierce determination to prevent it falling into the hands of Triplex Lloyd.

The Scotsman speculated that chairman Colin Cooke and chief executive Graham Lockyer would almost certainly decide to call it a day but would not wish to be seen acting too quickly. Reading this, Cook had to stop himself getting carried away with thoughts of victory. There might be more twists in the tale to come. Lockyer was telling journalists the buyout bid was not a surprise: "It is the logical conclusion of Andrew Cook's strategy of retreat."

In an interview with the *Financial Times*, Lockyer said Triplex Lloyd would wait to consult with its advisors, Schroders, before making a decision on the next move. He added: "This chap has run this business like a private company with very little regard for the codes that we all try to work to. I do not think it is much of a jump from that to a management buyout. The offer is obviously a higher price than ours but it cannot get away from the fact that only a combination of the two groups can bring the synergies we have outlined in the longer term." Speaking to Fraser Nelson at *The Times*, Lockyer said: "If the company's not in Triplex Lloyd's hands, I suppose he thinks he's saved it."

The Guardian poured scorn on both sides, describing the entire battle as a poor advert for British business. Although Cook may now keep his job, the newspaper said he had conceded plenty of the arguments along the way, notably his lavish contractual arrangements; at the same time, Triplex had been punished for failing to talk about the benefits of the deal for its stakeholders, instead taking the easy but ill-advised option of attacking Cook. Investors had accordingly voted with their feet, driving down the value of Triplex's cash and paper offer, preventing it from winning control of a company that richly deserved to be taken over, concluded *The Guardian*. The newspaper also laid down a marker, noting Cook was the brother of Treasury minister Angela Knight.

In its Comment column, *The Independent* said Cook always did run his company like a private fiefdom and now it was actually going to become one; the buyout bid meant the Cadbury and Greenbury codes on corporate governance and pay, which never seemed to mean a great deal to him, could be safely buried altogether. "Now up pop some venture capitalists who not only believe his valuation arguments but don't appear to give a fig about all those corporate governance concerns either," the newspaper added.

The Times lived up to its reputation as the paper of record, outside of Yorkshire at least, with an extended comment piece under the legend 'William Cook – The Movie'. (Netflix commissioners take note.) "There is a strong whiff of 1980s Wall Street – the market and the movie – in the attempt by William Cook to evade seemingly inevitable takeover by Triplex Lloyd. Consider this plot. Small family firm is about to be swallowed by ruthless asset-stripping conglomerate more concerned about profit than the future of the employees. Energetic, photogenic chairman, in last-minute dash around the moneymen, scrapes together enough cash and goodwill to fight back. Tearful appeal to shareholders – some things are worth more than money. Family honour restored. Cut from shot of angry asset-strippers. Pull back from face of old retainer, tears of joy running down his cheeks, to take in smiling workforce around him. Fade."

Except, said *The Times*, there are a few scenes in this script that did not fit into this picture. Namely, this had been a badly behaved takeover bid from the start. The company had been run in a way that contravened every code of corporate governance, a policy which undermined the share price and encouraged institutions to approach Triplex Lloyd to bid. The terms of the buyout had been available on the streets of the capital mid-morning, prompting questions about the source of the leak to the *Evening Standard* newspaper and if anyone had dealt shares before the official announcement. Triplex Lloyd had the option of making a higher offer, but the board would be cautious because its shares had been falling on concerns it was bidding too high already. After detailing its charge sheet, *The Times* concluded: "William Cook has been dragged, kicking and screaming, into the latter half of the 20th century by a hostile takeover bid, which is one justification for the existence of such a process. Triplex arrived because the company was undervalued, as it was not seen as run for the benefit of shareholders. Just one message for Mr Cook, who was known to chafe at the normal constraints of corporate governance. Just see how you enjoy being run by a clutch of hard-headed venture capitalists."

Not to be outdone by its old rival, *The Daily Telegraph* also devoted its City Comment to the story, pointing out there were very few moments when a company's board could launch a bid for the enterprise they were paid to manage, the conflict between their duties as directors and what constituted an attractive price was near absolute, which was why such proposals were once-in-a-decade affairs. It said: "The buyout bid prices the company for sale and if Triplex can offer a penny more, then it would win the day." Chairman Colin Cooke coolly told the newspaper: "Electra have done their due diligence. They may know more than we know. If they do, it would justify us coming back."

The story even made the *Daily Mirror*, under the punchy editorship of Piers Morgan, which painted Cook as a winner whichever way the takeover tussle went. If Triplex Lloyd won, he would pocket a £1.7m payoff – five times his £350,000 salary – plus £3.5m for his shares. But if Cook's bid succeeded, the new owners would buy his stake for £4.6m and he would stay in charge. The Labour-supporting paper of the workers squeezed in mentions to his wife's employment as a £35,000-a-year advisor and his father's £15,000-a-year retainer. The politics of envy was alive and well.

Lex, the flagship *FT* column aimed squarely at the owners of the means of production, told readers "barbarians are at the foundry gate" with the buyout bid carrying echoes of the 1989 battle over US food giant RJR Nabisco, the "grandaddy of all takeovers" in the words of *The New York Times* and the subject of a best-selling business book by Bryan Burrough and John Helyar. The cover of *Barbarians at the Gate* featured a besuited devil in silhouette against a red background, lighting a cigar with a burning wad of dollar bills.

Lex said the leveraged buyout looked a clever response, as taking on a large amount of debt would generate a substantial tax shield for profits and high borrowings and along with generous share options would motivate management to perform, but it also raised tricky issues. Lex urged shareholders to consider that only last October the company issued a downbeat trading statement and bought back 5.5 per cent of shares at 248p while Cook bought shares for his pension fund at 239p and the company took powers to buy in a further 10 per cent of stock to put into a long-term incentive scheme for directors. Just three months later, management was bidding 425p a share. "Since the bid is in cash, shareholders may not care, but it does leave a bad taste," the column summed up.

Cook finished leafing through the faxed cuttings in his office and looked out of the window across the blackened factory roofs to the Sheffield skyline beyond. Jane, his secretary, knocked and walked into the room, carrying a tray with a steaming pot of coffee, a KitKat and the latest correspondence, including a message to call his father McTurk, who was unhappy with the media coverage, especially that damned article in the *Mirror* and he wanted Andrew to do something about it. Cook groaned inwardly. It would have to wait as he had a busy day ahead. Lawrence Banks, the chairman of the buyout company and in theory Cook's new boss, was due to visit for a full tour of the plants. Cook was more concerned about Triplex Lloyd's next move. Under the rules of the Takeover Code, NatWest Markets had to disclose all the financial information that William Cook had shared with Electra Fleming. The projections were much more upbeat and long term than anything in the public domain. The new information could easily justify an increased offer from Triplex Lloyd. And the onslaught would begin again.

CHAPTER 33

They are going to fight to the death

In Andrew Cook's eyes, business is war. Throughout his life, he was always fighting against one form of adversity or another, whether it was competitors bent on his company's destruction, customers determined not to pay the price that his goods warranted, workforces demanding remuneration beyond his capacity to pay or governments imposing ill-considered and costly regulations. In Cook's book, all is fair in love and war. Withholding wages from men about to go on strike to make it more difficult for them to achieve their objectives was perfectly legitimate, even if such ruthless tactics shocked his management team on occasion. But once he had secured victory, he would make concessions out of principle to let the other side save face and maintain some morale, seeing it as ultimately being in the best interests of his customer and workforce relations not to have a totally defeated opponent, one more likely to be harbouring feelings of malice, retribution and revenge.

"Magnanimity in victory is not just a rule of mine, it is in my nature," he explained. "But firstly, victory there must be." Always the outcast, Cook considered his philosophy to be completely at odds with the Establishment, defined as the dominant power structure in social and economic life, and its adherence to the prevailing trends of the day, the focus on corporate governance being a good example. He saw members of the Establishment as corporatists by nature, seeking safety in numbers with their fondness for committees, boards, associations and clubs. The inner circle of this group tended to look after its own, providing new jobs for such useless members who lost their old ones, explaining the peculiarly British phenomenon of failing upwards. At least they had the redeeming feature of loyalty to their own, Cook believed. The same could not be said of members of the outer circle, who followed one rule only: look after number one and watch your back. Slavish conformance to currently fashionable thinking was one way this rule could be maintained. "The loners, like me, who seek to fear nor favour anyone and follow the principle of doing the right thing as laid down by one's conscience have no place in either circles," he would later write.

Cook had another reasonably good night's sleep and awoke on the Saturday morning feeling refreshed, rather than hunted, and was enjoying the company of his children when the phone rang. Alison answered and called through for her husband. It was Robert Pickford, the independent director and Sheffield solicitor, with news for Cook. Actually, it would be more accurately described as hearsay, one of the most frequently disputed forms of evidence in a court of law but, like eavesdropping, a useful device for driving plot development in drama. In hushed tones, Pickford relayed the story of how his wife had overheard a conversation in a private setting which seemed to point to a former company lieutenant as the mole in the camp. Cook felt sickened at the prospect, any sense of relief he had enjoyed over the last couple of days evaporating and being replaced by a feeling of foreboding, fear and anxiety. Cook thanked Pickford and hung up the phone and looked at Alison, his face ashen. "These people aren't going to just roll over and surrender," he told her. "They are going to fight to the death. I know it. There's worse still to come."

The weekend newspapers signalled he might be right. The *Financial Times* said William Cook's forecast of a 30 per cent rise in pre-tax profits this year was likely to be cancelled out by £2.5m in defence costs incurred fighting the hostile bid. It was a reminder of who the real winners were in these takeover battles – the City advisors, most of whom got paid regardless of the outcome. The *Mail on Sunday* joined the fray the following day, informing the Middle England readers of its Markets column that Schroders was evaluating the new information released by William Cook under Takeover Panel rules and "hopes to have new terms to put to Triplex's institutional shareholders in days". Reading the report and running through the argument as rationally as he could, Cook could see that Triplex Lloyd would have problems returning with a higher offer. Even Paul 'Compo' Compton, the engineering analyst who had been agitating for change, seemed to think the game might be up, telling the *FT* the previous day that "Triplex's share price was looking ropey enough as it was before the buyout was announced. I am not sure they have the firepower to come back". The mud that Cook and co had flung back was surely starting to stick, investors raising questions over the underlying strength of Triplex Lloyd's business. Ominously, *The Daily Telegraph* reported that fund manager Mercury Asset Management had cut its holding in Triplex Lloyd by more than a half. Company advisors told the newspaper the move was not a vote of no confidence but probably reflected a move at Mercury to reduce its holding in small engineering stocks.

Back in London the next morning, January 27, Cook went to Robert Fleming & Co at 25 Copthall Avenue to meet with PR advisors Brunswick and help drum up some positive media coverage for the management buyout by getting employees and customers to speak directly to the press. Founded by Alan Parker in 1987, the company was supposed to be one of the City's best connected PR advisors and represented up to a third of the FTSE 100. On the day, Cook found the firm a bit wanting and while a PR flunkey fussed over a press release, he hit the phones and managed to track down Alan Potts, a long-standing customer and industry ally, who was waiting for a flight at Cape Town airport and in fine spirits after a good lunch and a successful trip selling mining machinery in South Africa. Potts agreed to be quoted in the release, as did Roy Henson, William Cook's barrel-chested production stalwart, who said that if Cook went, so would he, or words to that effect. They also added the best bits from the Defence Manufacturers' Association letter to the Monopolies' Commission, which stated Cook's value to the UK defence industry. Big guns assembled, Brunswick pressed fire on the release.

The buyout team turned to the topic of what to do about PDFM, the biggest shareholder in William Cook. Should they, or should they not, attempt to buy out its shares before being assured of victory? It was a risk and could leave Electra Fleming with a minority stake in a listed company if the buyout failed, which would be fairly disastrous for Tim Syder's career as a big bucks venture capitalist. Cook was for it, believing that his backers should call up PDFM there and then and offer to take

227

the stake, sensing the fund manager was a willing seller. The fund manager had been performing poorly and would welcome the chance to cash in on one of its few successes. Syder was reluctant, understandably given the dire consequences for him if it backfired, and raised questions about the technicalities of the offer and how it would be paid for, given the banking arrangements agreed with the lawyers would not come into effect until the offer went unconditional. Christopher Kirkness, director of asset management at Robert Fleming & Co, and his colleague Julian Briant, director of corporate finance, signalled their support for the move and made the call to the chairman of Electra Fleming, Michael Stoddart, who was on a shooting trip in Dumfriesshire, to approve the £20m required for the offer. Stoddart, a Marlborough-educated City grandee who founded Electra Investment Trust in 1974, gave the go-ahead and Kirkness nodded to share salesman Ed Burke to phone Hugh Sergeant at PDFM and put it to him. The room went quiet as Burke walked out to make the call. Would this be it, thought Cook, the defining moment of the whole affair? Three minutes later, Burke returned to the room and told the waiting group that Sergeant had gone home for the day. Cook uttered an oath, frustrated at the delay which he blamed on Syder's unwillingness to take risks.

"January 27," Cook said loudly to the room. "The day the bid was lost."

"You shut up," shot back Syder. "You're beginning to piss me off."

The others froze, all heads turning from Syder to Cook for his response to this outburst. He paused to compute the situation with his analytical mind; Syder's volley was needlessly impolite but Cook decided to make allowances as the man was clearly under pressure and unable to see things as clearly as he could. Defusing a potentially explosive situation, he calmly announced to the room they should all pack up and go home for the night and get some rest.

Cook hit the bottle hard on the train home with finance director John Caldwell, the pair necking back a bottle of wine each by the time the express pulled into Doncaster, deadening the feelings of dismay at the day's events and, back in bed at the Manor House, lowering him into a dehydrated and restless slumber, punctuated by moments of wakefulness in the small, dark hours of the morning.

The next day, Cook got on with business as best he could. The to-do list had turned into a mountain of tasks. If this saga had cost millions of pounds in fees, Lord knows how much it had cost in missed business opportunities. London's financial and professional services industry would prosper regardless of the outcome for what remained of the rump of British manufacturing. Any thoughts about what might lay ahead were disturbed by the cheeping of his Nokia. It was John Sunnocks of Brunswick, PR agent to Electra Fleming and a former Life Guard. The cavalry has arrived, but for what?

"Bad news, Andrew. An anonymous letter has been faxed to the newspapers and institutional shareholders. It contains some pretty inflammatory stuff."

CHAPTER 34

A personal fiefdom

At first glance, the typed correspondence purporting to be from the girlfriend of one of the directors closest to Andrew Cook would represent a red-letter day for a libel lawyer, given its litany of allegations made against the chairman of William Cook plc and his use of company money. "I have a lot of inside info which you may be able to use," the author announced in her, or his, opening gambit, describing Cook as a "bully who uses people to get what he wants" and was detested by all.

The letter claimed his sister Angela Knight, the Conservative MP of Erewash and the Economic Secretary to the Treasury, had a pension, car and private medical insurance all paid for by the company and was until recently paid as a consultant, all of which might have been undeclared to the taxman. It added Emma Milligan, Cook's lifelong friend and confidant, was in fact his mistress and had enjoyed the use of a car, fax machine and accommodation at the expense of the company, an arrangement dressed up as her being a supplier of potted plants to William Cook's offices. The anonymous correspondent claimed the company paid for an all-expenses, champagne-fuelled sailing holiday in the Caribbean for Cook and his cronies, their wives and girlfriends and a trip to Venice on board the Orient Express. It also claimed the company paid for the family's nanny, her accommodation and car; the largesse even stretched to Cook's cleaner who also enjoyed the use of a company car.

The letter alleged that Cook was in trouble with the taxman over his family's frequent trips to a home in Guernsey with all travel costs paid for by the company. It claimed the company also paid for a luxury boat he kept on the island for entertaining clients and Cook was in the process of buying a company aircraft in the United States and had already booked a hangar at Sheffield airport in preparation. The letter alleged the company had paid for a large extension at the Manor House and met most of the bills associated with running the home. Further, it claimed the company paid for most of Alison Cook's 40th birthday celebrations with the costs hidden in invoices for work carried out at its foundries. His wife spent freely on the company credit card, it alleged. The letter also claimed the company paid for Cook and friends like the Lartundos to regularly stay at Cliveden, the five-star country house hotel in Berkshire made famous by the Profumo affair which scandalised British politics in the 1960s.

The correspondent turned to the subject of Cook's pension arrangements, claiming he had extracted a huge lump sum from the company scheme to fund his own private pension and "everybody thinks there is a Maxwell fiddle going on", in a reference to the disgraced publishing tycoon who raided his employees' retirement savings to keep his empire from collapsing. It also claimed the company paid Cook an above-market rate for a flat he owned in the South of France. Finally, the letter said Cook's father was subsidised by the company and spent most afternoons getting drunk at his club in Sheffield and then making a nuisance of himself at the Parkway plant or running up a small fortune on private medical treatment. The letter had all the ingredients of a juicy scandal: a fat cat row engulfing a Treasury minister in a Conservative government rocked by a series of sleaze allegations.

Cook called his PR man Tony Carlisle, who answered on the first ring. Lighting a cigarette, Carlisle explained that he had picked up on this poison pen letter which had been circulating news desks and the main shareholders and was clearly an attempt to destabilise Cook's relationship with Electra Fleming by implying he had his hand in the company till and had run the business in a manner designed solely to benefit himself. The trouble was a lot of the contents were gross distortions intended to create false impressions rather than outright lies, said Cook, adding that his sense of foreboding at the weekend had been proved right.

"*The Guardian* has the story and is planning to publish. I can only hold them off for so long," warned Carlisle. "I suggest you contact Syder and square it off with him and then get down to London."

Cook rang off and called Tim Syder at Electra Fleming to deal with it head on. "No doubt you'll be suing over this," said the venture capitalist. Cook sensed the comment was partly tongue in cheek and suspected Syder believed some of the claims to have the ring of truth about them. Cook led Syder through each one, explaining the *actualité*, believing it was better to be upfront than be caught later on because, sooner or later, the truth will out and carry the day. Syder appeared reassured, thanked him for his frankness and they would speak again soon after Cook had taken legal advice.

That advice came the next morning in the palatial London offices of PR firm Dewe Rogerson. Tony Carlisle was playing host as Cook and Linklaters' defamation partner John Holden went through the contents of the letter in minute detail, the subject clarifying matters of fact as he saw them under the sceptical cross-examination of the hard-bitten lawyer and the quiet scrutiny of Carlisle. Alison had come along to show support. Eventually, they were done and the Linklaters man delivered his verdict: "Unless all the allegations are completely false, without a shred of truth or even a semblance of a basis of truth, a defamation case will not succeed and neither will an injunction. My advice is do not proceed with legal action. Jurors do not like rich men." Cook looked at Alison and then back to the lawyer and PR man and nodded his agreement, acceding to the professional's judgment and years of experience in advising clients at the sharp end, but he had to do something: the truth would always come out, but how long could he afford to wait?

Not long, it turned out. At 5pm, Carlisle phoned Cook who was back in Sheffield to say *The Guardian* was to publish its story in its next edition and there was nothing he could do to stop it. Cook thanked him and hung up. What to do? He would do what he had always done. He took a deep breath, picked up his Nokia and dialled the number for *The Guardian* journalist, a respected story-getter named Paul Murphy. Murphy was steeped in the City, a graduate of the London School of Economics who started his reporting career at *The Banker*, a trade paper, on Black Monday in 1987, the day of a sudden, severe crash in the global stock markets. Someone, somewhere had passed him the poison pen letter and he was preparing to file his story when his phone rang and was slightly surprised to hear the subject on the other end of the line. Cook introduced himself and invited Murphy to take him through the allegations one by one, which he did, and Cook responded to each with his own account of the truth. After 10 minutes, the journalist had exhausted his line of questioning. "That seems to be about it," said Murphy. Cook said goodbye and quickly pressed the red button on his Nokia to terminate the call. He had done his best and would have to wait for the outcome. He called Carlisle to let him know he had spoken with the journalist and gave instructions to fax him a copy of the story when the first edition hit the streets.

Cook joined Alison later that evening at the Peacock, a stone-built manor house hotel in the Peak District village of Rowsley, where she was hosting a dinner for the health authority she chaired. The other board members, a mixture of time-served NHS managers and retired professionals, smiled greetings at her husband when he arrived midway through the main course. He had been in the press more or less non-stop since November and must have been under frightful strain. He looked drawn but managed a smile and a humorous remark as he took a seat next to his wife at the oak table in the long dining room and tucked into his dinner.

At 6am, Cook walked down to reception and asked for any correspondence in his name. The receptionist handed him a fax with a cover note from Dewe Rogerson. It was *The Guardian* article with the headline 'DTI urged to investigate Wm Cook share dealings' emblazoned across the front page of its finance section with a large photograph of Cook grimacing at the camera and a picture of his minister sister inset. The author Paul Murphy told readers the Department for Trade and Industry was being asked to open an insider dealing inquiry into the company "at the centre of one of the most acrimonious takeover battles of recent times" over its decision to buy back 5.5 per cent of its own shares at the end of October, just three days after a downbeat interim trading statement. Six weeks later, having come under attack from Triplex Lloyd, William Cook issued a much more upbeat trading statement and had since tabled plans for a management buyout, the correspondent added. *The Guardian* reported there was a widespread belief in the City that the complaint to the DTI had come from one of Triplex Lloyd's City supporters. The newspaper included a barrister-style rebuttal from Cook high up in the copy, claiming there was no basis for the DTI to be interested in the activity as the share repurchase was "perfectly legitimate" and no-one had tried to suggest the statement on October 25 was incorrect. Murphy wrote the matter put further pressure on Cook who was fighting claims he ran the business as a "personal fiefdom" and drew an over-generous salary and enjoyed a string of other benefits. *The Guardian* pointed towards the anonymous letter sent to a number of City institutions which made allegations about his stewardship of the company. It included his rebuttal of the contents as "a mixture of lies and distortions of the truth", which he blamed on unnamed former employees. "I do happen to be one of the largest shareholders," Cook was quoted as saying. "I am running the show. Some of these people cannot abide by the fact that I have succeeded. I run William Cook as an autocrat, certainly, but I do not run it as my own private company."

The Guardian stated the anonymous letter included details

of emoluments said to have been enjoyed by Cook's sister while she acted as a consultant to William Cook. It reported that Angela Knight, a chemist and metallurgist by training, had resigned her consultancy post upon joining the government in the summer of 1995. Her spokeswoman told the newspaper that all her pay and benefits for work carried out was in line with her expertise and had been correctly declared. Still, a national newspaper headline calling for an official probe into potential insider dealing at a publicly quoted company closely linked to a Treasury minister will have made uncomfortable reading in government circles. Murphy and his newsroom colleagues had done their job, closing with a proviso there was no evidence the anonymous letter emanated from Triplex Lloyd or any of its advisors. A spokeswoman for the company told the newspaper: "Triplex has made some criticisms of Andrew Cook's corporate practices. But they have no knowledge of this letter."

Cook finished reading and exhaled in relief. That could have been a lot worse, especially had he not picked up the phone and spoken to the journalist about the letter, the sick feeling in the pit of his stomach dissipating somewhat. He wandered through to the lounge, picked up the *Financial Times* and a coffee along the way and opened the pink paper. William Lewis, an ambitious young reporter at the *FT*, had joined the fray, sharing a byline with Richard Wolffe, on the story headlined 'DTI asked to quiz William Cook on trading forecasts'. Echoing *The Guardian*, the article informed readers the Department for Trade and Industry had been asked to investigate "apparent discrepancies" between a downbeat trading statement from William Cook and financial information the company gave to its bankers a month earlier. The *FT* said the memo in question was prepared by the company in September to help secure a credit facility and appeared to show increases in turnover and profit to March 1997. A letter seen by the newspaper – and disclosed by unknown parties – called for a DTI probe under the Companies Act 1985.

It was big news in the City. Graham Lockyer, chief executive of Triplex Lloyd, told the *Daily Mail* that "throughout the bid we have made many comments about corporate governance at William Cook and the sudden change in its trading fortunes. This could be quite a serious matter". The *Birmingham Post* would later quote a source close to the Triplex Lloyd camp admitting the company had asked the DTI to investigate allegations of irregular share dealings.

To Cook, the implication he had manipulated the share price by giving false or misleading information was an outrageous tactic but one which would still have to be countered. Unlike many in the City, he knew how business orders could ebb and flow and one month's optimistic situation could change very quickly the next. Still, there was a lot of money at stake in the bid battle including huge fees for Triplex Lloyd's army of advisors and Cook believed they would stop at nothing to secure their objective.

The *Evening Standard* also picked up on the call for the DTI inquiry and the anonymous letter with its lurid allegations. Cook had wearily told the journalist Fiona Walsh that "malicious allegations or actions must always raise the question of motivation. It cannot be right for alleged anonymous or inspired statements to gain either credence or effect. I see no possible justification for statements of this kind to be retailed.

If this type of innuendo is raised, by whatever source, I begin to despair of natural justice". Unfortunately, the interests of natural justice and the profit-seeking motives of capitalism were not always aligned. City analysts told the *Investors Chronicle* that Triplex Lloyd could afford to match Cook's buyout offer. "Triplex aren't out of this by any means," said Sandy Morris of ABN AMRO Hoare Lovett. "They could offer more and still enhance earnings." The influential weekly, part of the *FT* stable, concluded that although a victory for Andrew Cook remained the most likely outcome, Cook shareholders would be wise to hold onto their shares for now.

CHAPTER 35

Whence had they derived their power?

"The suspense is killing me," said Andrew Cook, standing in a toilet cubicle between the first and second-class carriages in a Midland Main Line train rattling towards London. He had managed to get hold of Mark Powers, who was Hugh Sergeant's boss at PDFM, William Cook's biggest shareholder. Cook believed his side had missed an opportunity in failing to persuade the fund manager to sell its stake in the company and he was having another go. It was approaching midday on Friday January 31 and the first-class carriage was packed with civil servants, prompting Cook to seek a quiet place to take the call without distraction. "Look, can't you just accept this offer? My wife is taking it very hard," said Cook, not altogether truthfully because Alison was a strong woman but he judged it was reasonable to suggest that anybody's health would be suffering in this set of circumstances. A powerful smell of perfumed detergent filled his nostrils as he waited for Powers to reply. The response was as expected: PDFM was well-disposed towards his offer but until it was clear that a better one would not be forthcoming, they would have to sit tight and wait. "I'm sure you will understand Andrew," said Powers. "Yes, I do," replied Cook, thanking Powers and terminating the call. He understood only too well: this whole thing was about money and if lives were broken in the process, then so be it. The biggest amount would win the day, whatever the costs and consequences. So much for corporate governance and social responsibility, he thought to himself as he unlocked the cubicle and walked back to his seat.

In the City, the men from Triplex Lloyd and their advisors were engaged in a series of meetings with William Cook's shareholders, making the case for their cash and shares offer. The clock was ticking and tens of millions of pounds were at stake. In Whitehall, grey-suited officials at the Department for Trade and Industry were raising their eyebrows at representations about William Cook's share-dealing activities in light of the Companies Act. Cook arrived at Electra Fleming's office by early afternoon, the now familiar Art Deco block in Kingsway, that broad stretch of road between High Holborn and Aldwych, the broadest in London, for a meeting to take stock with his buyout team. The teas and coffees had just been poured when a Nokia ring tone filled the room. Half-a-dozen heads reflexively looked towards their devices. It was Cook's and it was Tony Carlisle, the PR man. He thumbed the button to accept the call.

"More trouble, Andrew, I'm afraid," said Carlisle. "The *Mail on Sunday* has got hold of some speech you made to the Institute of British Foundrymen in which you are said to have made racist remarks and were drunk and slurring your words."

"This had to be some kind of joke," said Cook. He cast his mind back to the address he made at the business luncheon the previous summer, in which he had shared what he and the audience thought were humorous stories about his experiences of international foundries to illustrate the challenges and opportunities facing British industry. As for being drunk, it was before lunch and the only liquid that passed his lips was water. Cook, who had left the room to take the call, said as much to Carlisle. "Surely they can't be serious, Tony?"

"I'm afraid so, Andrew. This is *The Mail on Sunday*. They don't mess around."

Cook returned to the room and saw that John Sunnucks, Electra Fleming's PR man, had joined the meeting and was whispering something to Tim Syder, who was staring at Cook.

"It's not this speech, is it?" asked Cook.

"Yes," said Syder. "*The Mail on Sunday* has been in touch and wants to speak to me about your supposed racist remarks and drunkenness at an industry lunch. This could be serious, Andrew."

The three of them decamped to another meeting room and Sunnucks dialled the number for Northcliffe House, the Kensington High Street home of *The Mail on Sunday*. The *MoS* was one of the most influential newspapers in the land and also one of the most aggressive in the pursuit of its prey, usually the rich and the powerful. It was led by the charismatic and slightly eccentric editor Jonathan Holborow (who reputedly carried a white handkerchief named 'Oswald Nosely'), a product of Charterhouse School and career rival of Paul Dacre, editor of the *Daily Mail*. The Associated Newspapers approach was famously deadly: the *MoS* would chuck in the hand grenades at the weekend and the sister paper's shocktroopers would storm in afterwards. It was a formidable operation.

Sunnucks spoke to the journalist Allan Piper, editor of the Financial Mail section, and handed the phone to Syder, whispering the words: "He is an absolute shit."

Cook and Sunnucks listened as Syder batted away the questions, the journalist pushing him again and again about the contents of the speech and the allegations contained in the anonymous letter. Cook paced up and down, listening with growing outrage at this latest apparent attempt to drive a wedge between him and his would-be backers. As firmly as he could, Syder told Piper: "It is certainly not going to affect how we see Andrew Cook. There have been far more serious allegations that we have checked as part of our due diligence, and we are 100 per cent supportive of him." Syder finished the call and Cook thanked him for giving it his best shot, but he was not convinced they had got the message across and decided to confront the matter head on by calling the journalist himself.

Syder and Sunnucks listened in silence as Cook gave his account of his comments to the Institute of British Foundrymen at the Castcon 1996 industry event.

The plastic VHS cassette provided plenty of ammunition for Piper as Cook, wearing a signature double-breasted suit and gesticulating flamboyantly, spoke for an hour on the future of the UK foundry industry, including a lengthy section on his experience of overseas foundries, much to the amusement of the audience assembled in Bolton, Lancashire. It was played for laughs but included a serious underlying message about costs and competitors, namely that Britain's foundries could still rule the world.

Cook said the whole German industry, foundry or otherwise, shut down on Friday afternoon and was on the way out. "All they can do is play football and they can't do that very well," he said, in one of many throwaway lines. In Portugal, where he had been looking at a potential acquisition, he said it was not uncommon practice for a £100 wage to be drawn on Friday and spent entirely on drink over the weekend. The almighty hangover that followed was good reason for calling in sick on Monday, Tuesday and Wednesday and then workers would creak in on Thursday in order to draw a wage packet again on Friday. In India, he described a visit to the foundry which employed a form of corporal punishment to maintain order and told the audience how the management came across four sleeping workers during their tour of the site. The slowest one to recover received a cuff around the head. "I said that's a jolly good idea," Cook said. "Unfortunately, this behaviour is rather frowned upon in the UK." He described farcical scenes observing locals trying to use outdated telephones as "like watching Mr Pastry or the Marx brothers". In China, Cook recalled interactions with a train passenger who "looked like a Triad" and a quality controller who resembled the character Plug from the Beano comic. "The Chinese are very, very short on software – I mean this sort of software," he said, tapping his head, in reference to the nation's perceived weaknesses.

It was hardly Bernard Manning in the racist comedy club stakes but taken out of context it could be enough to raise question marks. Cook was adamant, telling Piper his speech was "a lighthearted review of my travels through several countries" and his remarks were all true and they were not influenced by drink. "I often wave my arms about and sway when I'm talking. If there is a slur in my speech on the video it must have been a fault on the recording," said Cook. "I am not a racist and I am not a drunk."

Piper made non-committal grunts on the other end of the

line as Cook explained himself. Sunnucks was sitting opposite, nodding his approval while Syder stood and stared out of the window, bolt upright. After 20 minutes, Cook finished the call and exhaled loudly. Sunnucks patted him on the back and told him he had probably done enough to defuse it but Cook was not so sure. An hour or so later, Cook again found himself balancing in the vestibule between two train carriages, clasping his Nokia to his ear and straining to hear the chairman of the Institute of British Foundrymen above the noise of the diesel locomotive. The voice was faint at the other end but Cook heard the words he wanted to hear: the IBF chairman and his secretary would contact *The Mail on Sunday* and tell Piper the allegations were total rot. Cook thanked the man and next phoned the defamation partner at law firm Linklaters, who was at a dinner party with friends. He knew the in-house lawyer at the *MoS* and would contact him immediately with the threat of a writ if they called Cook a racist and a drunk. Calls finished, Cook walked back to his seat, feeling weary. The phone was nearly out of battery. It hadn't been charged for a week.

On Saturday morning, the Manor House was filled with the sounds of young children playing and laughing. Their father was home and despite the contents of the morning's papers, which had thudded onto the mat at dawn, he was relaxed and playful. The *Financial Times*, *Daily Mail*, *Guardian* and *The Yorkshire Post* all carried big follow-up stories about the Department for Trade and Industry probe into the discrepancy between William Cook's downbeat trading statement in October and upbeat financial information given to the company's bankers in a memo a month earlier. The *FT* led the pack with confirmation that Triplex Lloyd was behind the request for the investigation. Schroders, investment banking advisor to the company, told the *FT*: "We confirm that Triplex has sent a letter to the DTI." The newspaper added that Schroders was disassociating itself from other correspondence circulating the City containing allegations about William Cook and its chairman. Cook smiled to himself when he read that his advisors had lodged a formal complaint with the Takeover Panel about the use of the memo in the complaint to the DTI. Lawyers for Cook argued on technical grounds that a confidentiality agreement between William Cook and Triplex Lloyd had been breached. Cook gave a cursory glance to the other headlines of the day: Oasis star Noel Gallagher claimed that taking drugs was no different from having a cup of tea, Britain's arms industry had captured a quarter of the world's defence market with record sales in 1996 and double-barrelled socialite Tara Palmer-Tomkinson had been named best dressed woman of the year. Cook was relatively sanguine about the DTI investigation, knowing he could demonstrate the ebb and flow of business orders, less so about *The Mail on Sunday*.

Alison knocked on the door of Cook's study and suggested they get away for the weekend. It felt like they were under siege from this relentless press attention and it would do all of them the world of good to break free. Cook recalled the Siege of Malta, one of his favourite boyhood books, and his own assailants at Triplex Lloyd and their pin-striped hordes in the City of London. He agreed readily and they packed a couple of bags for a night at the Chester Grosvenor hotel and a family trip the following day to Chester Zoo. The family piled into Alison's Range Rover and sped away from the Manor House with Cook at the wheel, checking his rear-view mirror for anything out of the ordinary, any feelings of calm giving way to anxiety tinged with paranoia: these people and their agents would stop at nothing to catch their quarry. Had that black Ford Mondeo been following him? He tightened his grip on the steering wheel and glanced at his children in the backseat. His mind went back to his car crash of 1990, his chauffeur-driven car veering out of control on the M1 near Lutterworth, cannoning into the central reservation, jumping over the barrier and propelling Cook feet-first out of the passenger door, leaving him in a crumpled heap on the embankment with a shattered pelvis. The car was a total write-off, but Cook's driver was unscathed. An ambulance rushed him to the Hospital of St Cross in Rugby and its accident and emergency unit, where doctors transferred him to intensive care, concerned about his life. But Cook came round. He stopped daydreaming and saw the junction for Chester.

The Tudor-revival Grosvenor was as comfortable as you would expect for a five-star hotel and in the morning the family had a fine breakfast beneath the hand-painted glass skylight in the brasserie, their father pointedly ignoring the Sunday newspapers placed around the dining room entrance for guests, resisting the temptation to see what *The Mail on Sunday*, Britain's biggest-selling middle market newspaper, had written about him. He knew it would ruin the rest of his day and could tip his fragile mood into a state of despair. Cook led his family outside for some fresh air and walked out of the hotel and into the cobbled streets of Chester, grey skies and light drizzle creating a hazy, ethereal atmosphere. Any contemplation was lost with the sound of ringing bells. It was coming from the cathedral and its free-standing bell tower. Cook answered the call and turned to the direction of the chimes. He entered the precinct and walked into the red sandstone and battlemented building, planned in cruciform after the Christian cross. He found a stall near the rear of the gathered congregation and quietly sat, gazing at the interior of the building, the creation of countless master craftsmen over multiple decades. Masters of their craft, each and every one of them. Whence had they derived their power? There was something about the sanctuary of the setting that moved Cook and, for the third time since the launch of the infernal bid, he wept. Heads turned among the worshippers, eyes alighting on the bereft silver-haired man in scarf and overcoat, weeping to himself, and wondering to themselves if he had suffered some terrible bereavement. They turned back to the clergy, Sunday service floating over the tide of human affairs. Cook lingered at the end and slowly followed the small flock out of the cathedral.

A clergyman, probably the provost, caught his eye.

"Now my friend," said the robed man. "Can we offer you some coffee?"

"Thank you but no," replied Cook. "I feel much better now. I'm on my way to rejoin my wife and children."

They were waiting outside, where William was thinking things must be really bad if his father was praying to God.

CHAPTER 36

The eleventh commandment

On his post-surgery ward rounds, the consultant ortho-paedic and trauma surgeon stopped at Andrew Cook's bed in the private wing at the Hospital of St Cross and told its occupant in a matter of fact way that he had been a very lucky man. The car crash had fractured his pelvis in four places and ruptured his urethra. They had patched things up as best they could and bed rest was the order of the day – 12 weeks of it. That's unthinkable, thought Cook; he couldn't be doing with that. First, he would have to run his business from his hospital bed and second, he would have to get himself up and about as soon as possible. The company couldn't wait and his customers certainly wouldn't. As the soporific effect of the anaesthetic wore off, Cook spent increasing amounts of time on the phone, switching between the handset next to his bed and his brick-like Nokia Cityman mobile phone, arranging meet-ings, dictating letters, chasing up his managers and gobbling down opiate-based painkillers. The effect of this bed-bound activity was two-fold: it satisfied his sense of determination and will but dismayed his wife who saw her husband doubling down on work instead of resting and recuperating as the good doctor had ordered. Within three weeks, Cook was hobbling around on crutches. Never mind that his upper half felt disconnected from his lower half, he battled on, discharged himself from hospital and moved back home, equipping the bedroom and dining room with telephones, fax machines and coffee makers to assist him with running the company. It was WFH, 1990-style. In the days after the accident, Cook had not felt particularly alarmed about his precarious position, but even so, he knew he had had a narrow escape, a brush with death. Being tossed out of a speeding car on a motorway could not kill him, but losing his life's work surely would.

During the course of his life, Cook had developed a number of maxims, some based on his own experience in business and others inspired by his readings of great historical figures. On the question of when to act, he believed that one could always find a reason for not doing something and if in doubt, do nowt. Cook also believed, like Henry Kissinger, that whatever must be done ultimately, should be done immediately.

With this in mind, and with his life's work at stake, he picked up the phone and called the Department for Trade and Industry and asked for the officer handling the William Cook case and within minutes was put through to a young civil servant with a polite voice. Cook introduced himself and said he intended to write a letter setting out exactly what happened and when, so as to fully satisfy any concerns he had not acted entirely within the law when he had been preparing his statements to investors in the City of London. The civil servant listened to Cook and said he would look forward to receiving his correspondence in due course and it was nice to hear from him. Cook thanked him for his time and ended the call, looking over to Margaret Young who had turned quite pale during the course of the conversation. She had advised Cook against contacting the DTI, considering it too risky and best left to the lawyers. Cook knew Margaret's higher-ups had been implicated in the Blue Arrow fraud affair that had scandalised her employer County NatWest in the late Eighties and understood why she was jumpy, but he pressed ahead anyway, confident in his position.

Young called for more coffee to be sent to their meeting room at NatWest Markets and the pair set about drafting a letter to the DTI, pointing out the figures contained in the memo to Barclays had been prepared some seven months ahead of the company's interim statement to the City in October, during which time profits and orders had fallen considerably before strengthening in November and December, allowing the company to make a more upbeat forecast as part of its bid defence. In longhand, Cook wrote "the reference to yourselves by Triplex Lloyd and the corresponding leak to the press is a gross misuse of confidential information, was motivated by malice and designed solely to cause disruption to the Electra-backed counter bid". Draft complete, Cook faxed the letter to lawyer David Cheyne at Linklaters and his accountants at KPMG, drained the rest of his coffee and snapped off a finger of KitKat as he picked up the latest pile of press cuttings.

The Mail on Sunday story had been and gone. Headlined "Cook 'joke' speech triggers a race row", the article by Allan Piper and Henrietta Lake claimed that "a speech full of abusive and racist remarks" by the chairman of William Cook, the brother of Treasury minister Angela Knight, had sparked new controversy over the acrimonious takeover bid. They added that many of the company's overseas clients were now seeking a copy of the videotape, the implication being the "blunt remarks" could jeopardise export sales. It was as rotten as Cook had expected, but he felt less concerned: in fact, he had a sense that everything was going to be alright in the end. (He still took the time to send a copy of the videotape to libel specialist Peter Carter-Ruck and Partners to seek opinion on whether to take proceedings against the newspaper. In the event, they advised him against any action.)

The Sunday Telegraph told readers the bid had "degenerated into one of the most vicious smear campaigns the City has seen" and included a categorical denial from Bob Mitchell, finance director at Triplex Lloyd, that his company had been in any way involved. He said: "This so-called smear campaign is unhelpful to us because we'd prefer people to concentrate on the more substantive issues that we have asked the DTI to look at."

The Sunday Times had the last word: "Ignore the scuttlebutt about the Department for Trade and Industry inquiry at the engineering group. The bottom line is that the management buyout led by Andrew Cook and backed by Electra has put 425p on the table, and that looks much better than Triplex is able to offer."

In the *Evening Standard*, City Editor Anthony Hilton wrote there was something "deeply distasteful about the increasingly personal attacks" on Cook. The commentator, a 30-year veteran of financial reporting, added: "In previous bid battles where the dispute has become personal it has been possible to trace the rumours to the other side. There is, let me stress, no evidence of that in this case, though if anything that makes the tales more unpleasant. These rumours are utterly irrelevant. The bid is now about money on the table, and here Andrew Cook has a clear advantage." *The Scotsman* said Electra Fleming was standing by its man and the threat of the DTI enquiry made the venture capitalist even more determined to win. Tim Syder told the newspaper all the allegations made were "a distortion of the truth at best – others are just totally fake". Eric Barkas, City Editor of *The Yorkshire Post*, observed that Cook's manner had made him enemies. "When the Triplex bid was launched, advisors told him to curb his habit of opening his mouth and putting his foot in it," wrote Barkas.

Cook finished his KitKat, screwed the silver foil and red wrapper into a small ball and tossed it into a bin. Young returned to the meeting room, smiling and holding a piece of paper from the fax machine. She handed it to him. Still warm, it was a statement from the Takeover Panel, which had just been released to the news wires. In matter of fact terms, the statement announced: "On January 21 Triplex Lloyd posted its increased offer for William Cook. On January 23 Steel Castings announced a higher and recommended offer for William Cook. On January 24, as required by Rule 20.2 of the Code, William Cook passed certain information, which had already been passed to Steel Castings, in confidence to Triplex Lloyd. On January 30 Triplex Lloyd's solicitors wrote a letter to the Department of Trade and Industry (the DTI) which made reference to some of the information passed to Triplex Lloyd by William Cook. On January 30 Citigate, the public relations advisors to Triplex Lloyd, spoke to journalists at the *Financial Times* and *The Guardian* on the instructions of Triplex Lloyd, and showed a draft of the letter to the DTI to the *Financial Times*. Both papers carried articles on the subject the following day. As explained in earlier Panel Statements on such issues, all parties to an offer (whether directors and officials of companies or their representatives and their advisors) must take extreme care in discussions with journalists. It is reprehensible, as in this case, intentionally to leak to the press during an offer a letter which contained references to a piece of confidential information supplied under Rule 20.2. Accordingly, both Triplex Lloyd and Citigate are criticised."

Cook finished reading the fax. The word "reprehensible" struck home – he remembered using it on the phone against Colin Cooke when his adversary called him at home to announce the forthcoming bid. Turning to Young, he said "criticise" didn't seem as strong a word as "censure" but the beaming banker paid no mind to the difference, the Panel had delivered its verdict and it was utterly damning as far as she was concerned. The damage had been done and the black mark could make it much harder for Triplex Lloyd if it tried to go back to its shareholders to raise the funds necessary to increase its offer for William Cook. Young had not looked so happy since the whole affair had started. Cook was more circumspect, seeing his foe as a wounded animal and dangerous as such. If Triplex Lloyd didn't pull off this deal, careers would be ruined. He knew Schroders would be on a mega-bucks success fee and believed the advisors would do everything in their power to win.

Another fax arrived. It was a press cutting from the West End Final edition of the *Evening Standard*, reporting the board of Triplex Lloyd was understood to be keen to come back with a fresh offer for William Cook and could be considering a bid worth about £85m or 450p a share. The article added that Electra Fleming would increase its offer if a higher bid emerged.

Citing a source close to the William Cook camp, the newspaper reported: "Cook will go to any legal means to prevent his company being sold to Triplex Lloyd. He will fight to the end. Also, Electra is perfectly capable of making a revised offer. Plans are in place for them to be able to do so." The picture of Cook's smiling face appeared alongside the article.

The following day was Wednesday, February 5 and Cook was back in Sheffield, walking the factory floor at Parkway, dressed in blue overalls bearing the company logo and catching up with his employees, the familiar odours of the casting process filling his nostrils again, a smell he had known virtually his entire life. Cook had been consumed by an inner feeling of calm since Sunday, the gnawing feeling of anxiety in his stomach was in full retreat. The press coverage of Triplex Lloyd's rebuke was damning and widespread, stretching from Fleet Street to Auld Reekie; Cook's delighted advisors had devoured it all. John Gapper of the *Financial Times* noted that Schroders was absent from the Takeover Panel's ruling, adding drily that "merchant banks usually take the role of managing the actions of public relations advisors on behalf of corporate clients". Patrick Tooher of *The Independent* reported the Takeover Panel had exonerated Schroders: it was understood – journalistic shorthand for being told something off the record – the investment bank only discovered that Triplex Lloyd and Citigate had agreed to leak the letter after it had already been shown to the press. The guilty parties coughed up. A spokeswoman for Citigate said: "We always work as hard as we can on our clients' behalf and always seek to operate within the Takeover Code. We have successfully advised on over 40 takeovers and in this instance we have acknowledged the Takeover Panel's criticism." Some observers might have questioned whether that was an apology or a sales pitch. In an article headlined 'The eleventh commandment', *The Times* said the City authorities, including the august Takeover Panel, had been looking for a scapegoat in the public relations industry, which many in the Square Mile believed was getting above itself. Sardonically, the paper of record said: "Julian Redbrace, the account holder, is to be publicly thrashed; Caroline Alice-Band, who pours the drinks so delightfully at City lunches, must henceforth hide her charms under the thickest sackcloth and ashes." Taking a more serious tone, the article claimed the Panel knew perfectly well what firms like Citigate were up to and was merely concerned to keep an eye on the most outrageous examples – those where practitioners get caught. It added: "The bars of the City will still be packed on Thursday evenings with public relations advisors and Sunday paper journalists plying their respective trades. No-one gets hurt. But if you want a villain, go to Triplex itself, whose instructions Citigate was carrying out, on pain of their client finding another willing firm to do the job." That was, and is, the way of this world.

Cook finished his tour and returned to his office, saying a cheery hello to secretary Jane as he walked past the framed century-old certificate of his family company's incorporation hanging on the wall and settled down to a plate of sandwiches brought in by his driver Martin. On his desk was the latest edition of *Punch*. Cook turned to the Insider Dealing column penned by his old friend, ally and fellow grammar schoolboy Terry Smith at the back of the magazine and scanned the copy through to the footnote at the end.

Smith wrote: "Some of you may recall my article about

Andrew Cook, chairman of William Cook, who was on the receiving end of a hostile takeover bid and was short of friends in the City because of his outspoken, accurate criticism of the Cadbury and Greenbury codes. Events have taken an unusual turn in this bid battle. Andrew Cook has decided to rescue himself. He appeared to me to be winning the war of words with the bidder, Triplex Lloyd, but all of these fine arguments looked as though they were for nought when Triplex raised its price. Andrew Cook had been arguing his company was worth more than Triplex was bidding. Now he has put his money where his mouth is and has raised the money to launch his own higher bid. By most reckoning, this type of defence against a takeover has not been seen in the City for at least a decade. For his action, Andrew Cook becomes the first winner of the Punch 'City Testosterone' Award for putting up instead of shutting up."

Cook finished the article and made a note to call Terry when he had a moment. His Nokia rang – he looked at the black digits against the grey screen and recognised the caller as Margaret Young. He glanced at the Swiss Railways Clock on the wall of his office. It was 5pm.

"Andrew," she said, voice filled with glee. "Triplex has withdrawn!"

"You mean, they have dropped their bid and accepted defeat?"

"Yes! You've done it!"

House rule number one

It was 6am and the sun had already been up an hour when the sleek white yacht motored gently out of Lulworth Cove where it had anchored overnight. Powered by a quiet and smooth engine, the 47ft Wellworthy left the still blue waters of the secluded pocket of the Jurassic Coast and steered out towards the horizon. At the helm was Paul Compton, the 42-year-old City of London engineering analyst, and his 33-year-old girl-friend Hannah Gutteridge, a press officer for the Italian sauce maker Saclà. Captain Compo was showing his young charge the ropes aboard his brand-new £250,000 pride and joy and it was all very exciting with things going swimmingly – until the weather started to turn.

Over to Miss Gutteridge and the *Daily Mail* for what happened next. She said: "I'm not massively experienced. Paul was teaching me to sail. I'd never sailed such a big boat before. I was steering at the time. Paul had gone down below to check the satellite navigation system and I was at the wheel. All of a sudden I just heard a loud crunching noise and realised we'd hit something. It was very, very scary. The boat just filled up with water and I honestly thought I was going to die. We found a rock and jumped on it. We just watched the boat sinking under the waves and prayed someone would come."

After calling mayday, a lifeboat and coastguard helicopter staged a dramatic rescue from Anvil Point. Compton managed to leap aboard the lifeboat but Miss Gutteridge had to be winched off the rocks. She was left badly shaken by the ordeal, telling *The Daily Telegraph*: "I haven't slept. I've been reliving the experience over and over again. We both lost everything, including passport and clothes. I don't know if I'll ever sail again." There was more bad news to come. A City associate of Compton's told the *Daily Mail*: "Poor old Paul. The insurance company said he failed in his duty of care by leaving his inexperienced girlfriend at the helm. But he earns a lot so nobody's feeling too sorry for him." Compton bought himself a near identical boat a few weeks later. Easy come, easy go.

Compton's yacht was not the only vessel that ended up on the rocks. Triplex Lloyd's hostile bid to buy William Cook, an enterprise egged on by analysts like Compton agitating for change at the listed company, was also holed below the waterline. A day after the humiliating reprimand from the Takeover Panel, the company announced it was letting its offer lapse. In a statement to the City, chairman Colin Cooke said: "We correctly identified that William Cook was an undervalued company and would like to have acquired it at a price we could have justified to our shareholders. In the event, this was not possible. I am confident that Triplex Lloyd has the management team and the vision to develop its existing businesses for the continuing benefit of its shareholders." Chief executive Graham Lockyer added: "We could have put together two companies and furnished shareholders a more valuable organisation… We could not afford to keep going back with a higher offer – if we were going to make a bid it would have to have been a decisive one. In the end, we decided we could not put something together with sufficient security." All it had to show for its efforts was a £2.1m bill and a boatload of negative headlines.

For Cook, a man who was never entirely satisfied, the victory had a pyrrhic feeling. As the Sheffield management team popped champagne bottles bought from the Makro cash-and-carry next door and toasted the decision to withdraw, Cook was withdrawn. He remembered the Duke of Wellington's famous lines that it had been "the nearest-run thing" and "nothing except a battle lost can be half so melancholy as a battle won". Cook rued his loss of cash and freedom, swapping the pay and perks of a public company chairman for a big pile of debt and ruthless new owners determined to make their money back.

In Fleet Street's eyes, Cook had gone from zero to hero and his Nokia rang incessantly with journalists calling for comment. He told them: "No-one said we would win but we have. I have said all along that persistence and determination alone are omnipotent. I thought Triplex Lloyd's tactics throughout were frankly reprehensible. But as far as bitterness is concerned, we've got a business to run." And shareholders to win over, he might have added as Cook and Electra Fleming still needed to secure acceptances from the outstanding institutions. But it was just a matter of time as one by one, they fell into line and the offer turned unconditional with William Cook delisting its shares from the London Stock Exchange and becoming a private company for the first time in more than four decades. It was a new beginning for the company with a new board of directors for Cook to answer to including the green-fingered banker Laurence Banks as chairman and Tim Syder as non-executive director. It was a new beginning for Britain too as New Labour swept to power with a new set of apparently progressive policies, not least a light-touch approach to regulation of the City of London, which coupled with a strong pound heralded a new era for the financial services industry, increasingly the overlord of the British economy. What could possibly go wrong?

In *The Sunday Telegraph*, financial journalist Judi Bevan penned a victor's profile of Cook, observing that he would do well in Grand Opera: "He has the right kind of looks – plumed white hair swept back from a sharp-featured face with strangely-piercing eyes; and he has the temperament – high on passion and given to mercurial swings of emotion complete with temper tantrums." In the absence of Don Carlos or Figaro, she said the hostile bid provided an admirable vehicle for his talents from which he had emerged as the conquering hero in spite of being cast as the villain of the piece at the start of the story. Beneath his robust manner, Bevan opined that Cook had a tender skin and was wounded by the vilification that came with the bid. Probing deeper into the makings of his unusual character, she wrote: "The absence of a mother and a distant relationship with a broken-hearted father may well account for his childlike intensity and the passion he has for the company. It is as though he has transferred the love he should have had for his parents to the business."

Local newspaper *The Star* sought out another personal angle – an interview with Cook's wife Alison. She told the paper: "Perhaps my most poignant memory was Andrew in a cowboy fancy dress outfit playing at being Wyatt Earp just two days after hearing of the hostile bid because it was our son William's eighth birthday party. Andrew had so many things on his mind, he was facing a real battle, but there he was on a foggy field playing at cowboys with a group of young children because he would not let business worries spoil his son's birthday."

Much of the coverage passed Cook by, his mind preoccupied by other things, such as his relationship with his new investors. At a celebratory dinner at Claridge's hotel in London to mark the successful buyout, he gave a speech in which he joked that Captain Cook had commanded the expedition to the new world but Joseph Banks, the botanist ancestor of chairman Laurence Banks, had paid for it. The gag was greeted with a smattering of derisory applause and plenty of stony faces among the assembled money men and their paid advisers. Relations would sour further still. Cook was not a man who liked to answer to anybody, beyond his customers and his family.

One particular tale did catch his eye, however. It came from the left-field of Fleet Street – from the backstreets of Soho to be precise. The satirical magazine *Private Eye* prided itself on being a scourge of the establishment and the cosy club of old public schoolboys running Britain's institutions and the fast-and-loose chancers on the make. Perhaps it identified another outsider in Cook. The Eye noted the torrent of bad publicity he had endured – the coverage of his "drunken, racist" speech to the Institute of British Foundrymen, the potted plants provided by his lady-friend Emma Milligan and the non-existent company helicopter – and pointed out that "not one scrap of balancing criticism of the business methods of his rivals at Triplex Lloyd has appeared in any Fleet Street organ". This, said the magazine, was despite most news desks being aware of a document sent to Greater Manchester Police which claimed that Triplex

Lloyd had once engaged a Manchester model agency boss who was subsequently convicted of serious sexual offences. The Eye reported that Peter Martin, a former policeman and an associate of the controversial Blackpool FC tycoon and Labour Party donor Owen Oyston, had worked for Triplex Lloyd on a consultancy basis in 1993 in relation to a piece of litigation against the company and had received a fee of £110,000. The magazine added the company directors were "absolutely shocked" when they learned of his crimes.

If that seedy story wasn't enough, the Eye told readers about Triplex Lloyd's stewardship of its foundries and a court case involving a subsidiary in Sheffield which had, in the words of a judge, "closed its eyes to the risks to its employees" by leaving a defective guard on a casting machine after repeated accidents. Two tonnes of molten metal had burst through a gap in a mould spinning at 245mph and hit three workers, one of whom suffered 40 per cent burns and spent 12 weeks in hospital. Prosecutors told the court the 1995 accident happened because of "complacency and corporate inaction". Two years earlier, a worker had needed skin grafts after an accident on the same machine. It seems William Cook's workers had a lucky escape.

In summer 1997, Triplex Lloyd announced the exit of £252,000-a-year chief executive Graham Lockyer by mutual consent and with immediate effect. Chairman Colin Cooke said his CEO had contributed significantly to the performance of the group over the past three years but added, with a sting, that "differences of opinion about strategic direction have become evident recently and, as a result, Graham and ourselves have mutually decided to pursue separate paths." City analysts speculated Lockyer was paying the price for failing to ensnare William Cook, which would have increased earnings by 30 per cent. One told *The Independent*: "Colin has a bit of a reputation as a hatchet man. Graham was a lovely person and well liked, but he wasn't the ideal one to lead on these decisions. It's probably a fair decision to let him go." Cooke denied the departure had anything to do with the bid and said his company continued to look for acquisitions. In reflective mood, he told *The Independent*: "I do regret this bid. The cost was heavy. It was going to give us substantial synergies and it was a very undervalued company. But if I could go back I would not do it again."

In January 1998, Triplex Lloyd agreed to be acquired by Doncasters Group, an international aerospace manufacturing group, in a deal worth nearly £200m. Later that year, Dewe Rogerson, the PR agency advising Cook, merged with Citigate, the PR agency advising Triplex Lloyd (and publicly reprimanded for its efforts), with Tony Carlisle, the victorious advisor, crowned executive chairman of the enlarged firm.

Cook struggled with not being the master of his own house and was left with the sense that he had swapped one kind of hostile shareholder for another. His new masters certainly did not take kindly to him firing off a letter to UBS complaining about its astronomical fees – £750,000 for its services during the bid defence – and accusing it of complicity with its fund management arm PDFM in encouraging the Triplex Lloyd takeover. The letter prompted a blazing boardroom row between Cook and his new chairman Laurence Banks. Cook had to seek a humiliating accommodation with Malcolm Le May, the red braces-wearing head of European investment banking at UBS, who addressed him as a public school prefect might do a recalcitrant fifth former and agreed to chip off £50,000 from the bill. Cook had forgotten house rule number one: the bank always wins.

Angela Knight, Cook's sister, lost her parliamentary seat to one of Blair's Babes, Liz Blackman, in Labour's landslide 1997 election victory but as a former Treasury minister she soon found lucrative work in the financial services industry. Knight first served as chief executive of the Association of Private Client Investment Managers and Stockbrokers and then CEO of the British Bankers' Association, becoming one of the City's most prominent spokespeople.

Terry Smith, one of Cook's few allies during the hostile bid, left the City in 2017 for the sunnier climes of Mauritius in the Indian Ocean where he runs Fundsmith, which manages funds worth £43bn "away from the noise of London", he told the *FT*.

Andrew McTurk Cook passed away in 2007. His son sent him a letter of forgiveness before he died, written with the intention that he could die in peace. The act had no such effect on Cook, who was left with feelings of outrage, puzzlement, horror and loathing about his father, the motherless child inside deprived of love, affection and understanding.

After several unhappy years as a wage slave, Andrew Cook succeeded in persuading Electra Fleming to sell him its stake in 2004 – for a reported loss of £10m – restoring William Cook to full family ownership and control for the first time since 1956 when McTurk had floated the company on the London Stock Exchange. At the time of writing, the company is in strong financial health with son William as a director. As for Cook himself, he resides in Switzerland and is married for the third time. He remains chairman of William Cook Holdings and retains an active involvement in the company he rescued from near death in 1982 and hostile takeover in 1997. Cook travels frequently, the sense of being safe in transit applying some balm to his troubled soul.

THE END

A note from the author:

This book is based on diaries, interviews, press cuttings and corporate archives. Some scenes have been dramatised but overall the story is a depiction of events as experienced by the protagonist and is the authorised account. After all, history is written by the victors.

Chapter 30 includes lyrics from *Ballad of Sir Frankie Crisp* (Let It Roll) by George Harrison.

If you enjoyed reading *Outcast*, please do leave a positive review at Amazon.co.uk.

About the author:

Bernard Ginns is a former newspaper journalist who served as business editor of *The Yorkshire Post* from 2008 to 2016 and was previously editor of an award-winning media start-up and a staff reporter at *The Mail on Sunday*. He lives in West Yorkshire and runs the specialist communications consultancy Branksome Partners.

Printed in Great Britain
by Amazon

his feet and mirrored the stance of the bull-like man on the stage. A kerfuffle ensued as Briggs Senior charged forwards and Andrew jumped up to support Joe, forgetting the personal implications for his small family if the development were not to go ahead. The crowd jeered and hollered, and Daisy felt like she might faint as Rob's strong arms came around her to protect her from his father's wrath. Bunch appeared up front, grabbed the bouquet from earlier, and slammed it down on the older Briggs' head. To what avail, Daisy had no idea, since it barely stopped the man in his tracks. It simply added to the farcical nature of the whole scene.

Probably a few minutes too late, Cluero appeared from the back of the hall with several uniformed officers in tow. He had watched and heard everything from the small balcony above and was quick to have his colleagues restrain Robert Briggs.

"It's not slander if it's true," Daisy said, as she watched the large man being handcuffed whilst he shouted threats and protestations of innocence.

That he had committed murder in the case of at least two of the three recent deaths, Daisy was sure, but what she really wanted to know was whether the landowner could've killed her grandmother all those years ago after her refusal to sell the flower shop to him.

Daisy had come so far, she couldn't stop now without knowing the truth.

21. THE EVIDENCE WILL SPEAK FOR ITSELF

Of course, Daisy was also asked to accompany the police down to the station to provide proof to back up her accusation, much to Joe's horror. There would be no allowances made this time, she knew.

"I'll follow on the bike, lass," he whispered, but Daisy simply shook her head as she followed Cluero out. She had known this would need to be done, that it would be the first – of many, no doubt – prices to be paid for accusing the wealthiest landowner in the town of such a heinous crime. And not only the one, either, but of three murders to be exact. Daisy knew she would have the wrath of those who considered themselves the 'top set' of Lillymouth society hailing down on her for the foreseeable future.

"It's her you should be locking up," Violet Glendinning's shrill voice pierced the excited chatter that continued all around, as Daisy felt a tug on her elbow, "The mad bat obviously returned with her own agenda!"

"Dee-Dee, that's my dad that you just accused," Rob said, holding her gently to the spot, his eyes pained though his voice was not harsh, "I hope for all our sakes you're right, otherwise there'll be hell to pay. You know how he holds a grudge. Believe me, you don't want him as your enemy."

"The evidence will speak for itself," Daisy said, with more confidence than she actually felt, pulling her arm back and leaving the man standing at the doors.

It was late that night when Daisy was dropped back to the vicarage in a squad car. She felt she had been washed up, wrung out, and hung to dry under the barrage of questions which had seemed as though they would never end. Before they could interrogate Robert Briggs, it seemed that the two detectives were determined to look at Daisy's evidence from every angle, to dissect her accusations, and even to turn them back on herself.

"Aye you sure you don't have anything to atone for, Vicar? Coming back to this town after fifteen years and immediately hunting down a supposed killer? Are you perhaps not compensating for the fact that you should've been put behind bars all those years ago?" Detective Michelle Matlock had been unrelenting, her disbelief plain to hear.

Daisy had held her nerve and had spoken her truth, however, sticking to the facts of the current crimes and refusing to be led into an emotional exploration of her past. To the point that even the tenacious detective had to finally admit it was time to move onto the real suspect, with one last dig at the woman in front of her, "You couldn't just leave it to the professionals could you? Had to have your spot in the limelight."

"After the police's abject failure to find my grandmother's killer? It's hardly surprising I refuse to put my faith in the 'professionals.' And while we're speaking so bluntly, I certainly don't have as much to atone for as you, Michelle," Daisy rallied as she knew her interrogation in this room filled with ghastly memories was coming to an end, "you caught me off guard when I first arrived, what with there being a dead body beside my new church. But hear me now, I don't like bullies, and you have clearly never repented that title."

"What? Are you going to send the wrath of God down on me?" The detective mocked.

Daisy had simply flashed a cold smile and decided it would be best to bide her time, instead she turned her attention to Detective Cluero as he walked her out of the station, the man having been cowed by his colleague's animosity towards Daisy for the last few hours, "You must promise me you will ask Briggs about my grandmother. He can't be innocent, not if he's capable of murder now, then he must've been capable of it back then. Please, detective." She could hear the desperation in her own voice and Daisy forced herself to stop before her pleading became embarrassing.

"Reverend Bloom, it's a fifteen year old cold case, I doubt I'll even persuade our boss to reopen it," the man sighed heavily and shook his head sadly.

"But you will try, especially if new evidence comes to light whilst you're questioning the man back there," Daisy had pushed.

"I will try," Cluero had conceded, and Daisy knew that was as much as she'd get for now.

Any hope of slipping quietly into bed had disappeared when Daisy saw the light still on in the kitchen. Feeling bad that Sylvia had sat up waiting for her, Daisy limped her way into that room, in desperate need of some painkillers and rest. Sitting on the small, wooden chair in the interrogation room had done little for her physical wellbeing, leaving her body almost as battered as her mind.

"Daisy lass," it was Joe who stood first as Daisy entered the room, "I came down but they wouldn't let me in to see you."

"It's okay, it was something I had to do alone," Daisy whispered, looking round and seeing two other sets of eyes also watching her sympathetically.

"Are you okay?" Rob asked softly.

"Shouldn't you be more concerned for your dad?" Daisy asked, regretting it immediately when she saw the flash of hurt wash across the man's features, "Sorry, I'm tired, thank you for waiting."

"It's okay, I'll be off now. Do you, ah, do you think they'll charge him?"

"Honestly, I don't know," Daisy said, accepting the

man's kiss to her forehead, despite it making her tense up uncomfortably.

"I'll get you a cup of chamomile tea," Sylvia broke the tension, "I'm sure Bea would've come round too, but she has the baby an all…"

"I think I may have a few bridges to repair there," Daisy admitted morosely, and Joe too kissed her goodbye.

"That Bunch bloke, the creepy one, wanted to stay too, but we sent him on his way," he said.

Daisy was grateful and sank down onto a chair as Sylvia showed the two men out.

"Maybe we should get some more locks for the door. Dead bolts, perhaps," she said as she returned to the kitchen and filled the teapot.

Daisy nodded, feeling sick to her stomach. The righteous path was not an easy one to walk, she knew, but today had been the hardest for a very long while.

22. EMOTIONAL BAGGAGE

The next few days passed in a blur. Violet Glendinning, it seemed, had taken it upon herself to do her civic duty and to report the unacceptable actions of the new parish incumbent to the Bishop, who not so subtly suggested Daisy take a step back from normal services for the next few weeks and ask a few of the lay readers to fill in for her.

"But I've just arrived," Daisy had retorted.

"Yes, and already you have caused such a commotion that I've been told half the town is pitted against the other," the man had brooked no argument, "despite the fact I sent you there to do the very opposite and to promote community cohesion. Certain town leaders are livid, and we can't ignore the very generous donations they regularly make to church funds…"

"I see," Daisy had replied, seeing, as always, that it all came down to politics and money. She had ended the call quickly, promising to remain in the background for the rest of the month.

This, at least, gave the vicar the chance to do some personal reflection and soul searching of her own. She eschewed the offers of meals and company from those who she could consider her allies, though not surprisingly no such kindness came from her best friend, Bea. The silence from that quarter was very loud indeed.

Even Joe, who suggested film nights and even boat trips, had been turned down gently in favour of time spent alone, as Daisy passed her days walking the coastline and beaches, sometimes even heading onto the moors in search of a peace that she couldn't seem to find. She tired her body to the point of painful exhaustion, but couldn't seem to quieten her mind.

The police had been back to the vicarage several times, both to take more of Arthur's belongings for evidence – which they should have done in the first place, Daisy thought – and to question the vicar more.

On the basis of the statement the officers had taken from staff at the ecological society, who confirmed that they had spoken to Robert Briggs the day before Arthur's death, Cluero had told her they had been able to hold the man longer, hoping all the while for a confession that never came. The motive was clear, the means too, but the last piece of the puzzle – the definitive bit of evidence that would see the case watertight – eluded them.

Despite their vigorous efforts, interviewing Rob Briggs Junior and others who worked at the farm, as well as members of the planning department and council, the police came up with nothing that would stick. That was, until finally a young intern, who had initially been paid for his silence, could harbour the guilt no longer. Worrying for his own future, he confessed how the head of the planning department had taken money from Robert Briggs Senior in return for a guarantee that planning permission would go ahead without a hitch. Whilst this wasn't confirmation of Briggs guilt with regard to the murders, the fact that he had been unscrupulous enough to bribe officials, and to push his plans through at any cost, meant the detectives finally had enough to arrest the man.

Daisy felt a weight had been lifted from her shoulders. Not least because her actions were now seen by many – though not all – as having been justified. A killer had been caught, and the souls of Arthur and Nora could finally be laid to rest.

The funerals were a small affair, though serene and respectful, as Nora would have wished. Even singing the words of 'Amazing Grace' to the tune of 'All things Bright and Beautiful' didn't detract from the formality and peace of the occasion. It was the perfect service to mark her return to her chosen vocation, though Daisy had been on the sidelines for less than two weeks. She decided it was what she had needed to come to terms with her return to Lillymouth and all the emotional baggage she had brought back with her.

It was therefore a vicar light in mood and spirit who decided to make one final tribute to the three residents of the town who had perished at the hands of a despicable and greedy man. Determined to see the view that Arthur and Lizzie had died trying to protect, Daisy made her way slowly and, at times, painfully up the narrow, circular staircase in the church tower. She paused in the belfry and admired the church bells, catching her breath and taking a large sip from her water bottle, before ascending an even narrower set of stairs up to what was known as the lantern. This small room, below the spire, was framed on all sides by open, glassless windows, rectangular in shape and slightly arched at the top.

Bracing herself against the cold, stone wall, Daisy caught her first sight of the view, the beauty of the landscape caught in the last golden rays of the sun. She walked slowly around the full circle, seeing all three hundred and sixty degrees of the view – the town and surrounding countryside from all angles – and understood immediately what had made Arthur, and then Lizzie Briggs too, come up here so often. It was indeed a view to fight for.

"Admiring the view, Vicar?" The voice was familiar, but the harsh tone not so, "I'm surprised you could get yourself up here, it took you an absolute age. I'm sure even old Arthur would've beaten you to the top."

Daisy spun around, using her cane as a pivot, to face the man who had clearly followed her up here. Despite the fact he stood in shadows, the sight of his much-changed visage caused Daisy to gasp aloud. Gone was the warmth in his eyes, gone every softness that had previously graced his features, to be replaced by a scorn that etched the hard planes of his face in harsh lines and deep shadows.

For the first time since returning to the town, Daisy felt

real fear. It ran through her limbs like liquid ice and she had to force her legs to remain upright and her face to stay impassive.

23. INTO THE LIGHT

"Rob, it's beautiful up here, isn't it?" Daisy could tell immediately that the man had not come to discuss the merits of the local landscape, but she was equally aware that she needed time to think up a plan. Since he blocked the only exit to the first set of stairs she would need to get down, Daisy decided communication might be the key to buying herself some time, "The last rays of the sun over the fields, why don't you come into the light and admire it?"

"I prefer to remain in the dark," Rob replied, his ominous implication not lost on the vicar.

"Is that so?" Daisy left the question hanging.

"You broke my heart when you left Daisy," his voice, full of anger, filled the small chamber, "though I guess I should be grateful, since you did teach me an important lesson." He stalked to the side, like a caged animal who had spotted its prey.

"And what was that?" Daisy whispered.

 "That I should take what I want before it slips through my fingers, and everyone else be damned. No one can be trusted, not even those you're closest to – all will turn on you in the end."

"Robbie, you know that's not how it was, I had to go, I…" She hoped familiarity might play to the man's fonder memories of her.

"Please, don't with the stupid nicknames. I mean, Dee-Dee? Made me sick to even say it!" He scoffed at himself as well as her, but the knowledge that he had been fooling her these past weeks was not lost on Daisy. If she hadn't caught on to that already, then his next words certainly spelt it out, "And have you looked in the mirror recently? The thought that I could still be attracted to… that," he used the pause to rake his piercing glare over her body, leaving Daisy feeling even more vulnerable and exposed, if that were possible.

"I haven't sought your affections since my return," Daisy said, "quite the opposite." *No,* she thought, *I have simply been another pawn in your game.*

"Aye, and having to pretend I still had feelings was bad enough…" he stopped short, as if realising he was veering off track, "anyway, I suppose I should thank you."

"Thank me?" Daisy moved to the side as he came closer, aware that the sun had now almost completely set and they would very soon be standing in darkness. Stupidly, she had no phone, no torch. Daisy shivered, a tremor that ran the length of her body, and not from the sudden chill in the room.

"Why yes, Reverend Daisy Bloom, you and your do-gooder, amateur sleuthing saved me from having to do off with my father. I mean, you know you got the wrong killer by now, right?"

"It has dawned on me, yes," Daisy edged slightly more to the side, away from him and closer to the exit. Not that she had a hope of beating him in a race based on speed alone. "I'm guessing it was you, the Robert Briggs that the bat society spoke to and not your father, wasn't it?"

"That's the girl, finally catching on. I mean, you were

totally blinkered, weren't you? Completely determined it was him, I didn't even have to give you many hints in that direction."

How stupid I have been, Daisy thought, *just because his father was one of those I considered a suspect in my grandmother's case...*

"I ah," Daisy couldn't even force the words out that would prolong their conversation.

"But, you did me a favour, getting the old man out of the way so now the place is mine to do what I want with. Shame all those old buildings the bats love so much are going to burn to the ground. Won't be needing a survey then, will they? I mean, there is just the one loose end you've left me with..." He eyed her with a wicked smile, "And I'm going to enjoy this..."

"Tell me!" Daisy quickly shouted, as she bolstered her courage and felt the adrenaline coursing through her body, "Tell me one last thing, then, did you kill my grandmother too?"

That caused him to stop his creeping approach, long enough to answer, "Of course not, though it did teach me a thing or two about how to get away with murder. Let me demonstrate..."

Rob rushed forwards, his intention clear – to push Daisy through the open window space behind her, making it look like either a tragic accident or a deliberate suicide.

Daisy had her own intentions, though, and dying like this was not one of them. Lifting her walking stick and praying she remembered some of the self-defence moves she had been taught, she used the cane as a weapon, thrusting it swiftly into Rob's crotch and causing him to double over at the unexpected assault. Grabbing her chance, Daisy then used the same tool to apply swift pressure behind the man's knees and thus to whip her assailant's legs out from under him, causing him to land heavily on the stone floor. She had one chance she knew, and only a slim one at that. Having watched too many films noirs and Agatha Christie's books brought to the big screen with her grandmother as a girl, Daisy knew the chances of the victim escaping the faster, stronger murderer were not good odds. Add into that her own disability, the dark and the staircases and well…

Daisy brought the stick down heavily on Rob's temple for good measure as he made a thankfully futile attempt to grab the weapon from her. With an agility and pace that could only have come from Above she threw herself towards the small opening in the wall and down the stairs.

All too soon, though, Daisy heard the faint, clattering steps above that signalled she was indeed being chased.

24. DO NOTHING, DAISY

Daisy made it down the first staircase, across the flat landing that formed the belfry and onto the second with only her own ragged breathing for company. The steps behind her became louder, however, as she neared the ground and Daisy realised belatedly that it would've been a sensible idea to shout for help as she made her descent. Not that she had much breath to spare, however…

Tap, tap, tap beat her cane on the stone stairs, "You won't escape me Daisy!" shouted the man from just behind her now, and Daisy pushed through the pain and light-headedness to scream into the darkness.

"Help me! Someone! Help!" Daisy stumbled through

the small hallway at the foot of the stairs and out of the door, which Rob had thankfully not had the foresight to lock behind him. Into the shadow of the church building, the graveyard next to it shrouded in darkness now, she gasped for fresh air.

Knowing she would not make it to the vicarage before Rob caught up with her, and that her legs would not hold her up for much longer in fact, Daisy slowed and turned, ready to make her last stand, her stick gripped tightly and held ready.

What happened next was all so sudden, so shocking, that for a while after regaining consciousness later that evening, Daisy was sure she must've imagined it. For out of the shadows came another figure, dressed all in black, and carrying a small shovel which immediately made sharp contact with Rob's head. Her pursuer crumpled to the ground, whilst the man who had saved her life came rushing to Daisy's side.

"Are you okay?" Like earlier, the voice was familiar, but the tone and volume completely different. Daisy's brain was clearly lacking in oxygen as a result of her forced exertions, and she couldn't seem to place her rescuer, who was too familiar to be a stranger. Had she been thinking more clearly, Daisy might also have considered whether she should trust someone in a graveyard at night in possession of a shovel, but instead she clung to the man's arm as if to her only lifeline as her knees buckled beneath her.

"Vicar, are you hurt?"

"He, ah, is he..?"

"Dead? No, I hit him sufficiently hard enough to knock him out but not to kill him. He will have a concussion that is all. You should call 999, Vicar," so softly spoken, the words held none of the brash buffoonery of his usual demeanour, yet it was him, Daisy was sure of it.

"Gerald?"

"Shh, let's get you to the vicarage and then you call the police. I'll tie him up in case he wakes."

"But, but, you've saved my life," Daisy's brain was struggling to compute. Short sentences were all she could manage.

"Anyone would have done the same," without his lewd outbursts and exaggerated mannerisms he was a completely different man.

"I don't want to owe you, to be in debt…" Daisy said the words without thinking, but he seemed to understand that she meant no offense by them.

"Well then, I'll tell you what you can do to return the favour."

"O-kay."

"Do nothing, Daisy. Tell no one I was here. Allow me to continue my charade in public, please."

"Oh! Right, but what about the shovel? How should I say I got it?"

"Left over from the burials of course," he spoke as he lifted the vicar into his arms, despite her protests about her size, and carried her to the door of the vicarage, "look after yourself, Vicar, this town has many secrets that it doesn't want unearthed."

Three heavy knocks on the door as he settled Daisy back onto her feet and with that Gerald Bunch – if that even was his real name – was gone, into the night as silently as he had appeared.

"Call the police," Daisy blurted out to a shocked Sylvia the moment the woman answered the door, before staggering inside and promptly passing out in the hallway.

25. AN AMATEUR ANGLICAN

It was lunchtime the next day before Daisy awoke in her own bed to a cup of hot, sweet tea brought to her by Sylvia. A heavy weight on her legs, that in her nightmares had been a large stone attached to her ankles, dragging her down to the murky depths of the ocean, turned out to be Jacob, who refused to budge even when Daisy tried to tip the cat off her body from under the blankets.

"Isn't he a good lad, keeping you company all night," Sylvia fussed with Daisy's pillow, helping her sit up straight before handing her the hot mug.

"Hmph, is that a helicopter outside? It's not the police helicopter is it?" Daisy forced the words through her parched mouth, her head throbbing – her whole body throbbing in pain in fact – from the exertions of the previous evening. The police hadn't left till gone midnight, and Daisy had had hell's own job persuading her house guest and then Joe to refrain from calling the local doctor out. She had wanted nothing more than her bed, but the questions seemed never-ending and of course, Daisy had to be light with the truth about the blow which had felled her attacker.

"No lass, it's just Archie. He's picked up some new sounds from my police shows," she at least had the grace to look a bit sheepish.

"You didn't need to call Joe last night," Daisy said, knowing she sounded a bit like a petulant teenager.

"He would've had my hide if I hadn't, petal. Besides, you gave me an awful fright, you know."

"I know, Sylvia, I'm sorry. Argh, how have I made so many mistakes in such a short time since coming back? I'm meant to be saving souls not catching killers. Am I just an amateur Anglican, far too focused on my own agenda?"

"Well, as far as I see it, you didn't have much choice in the matter lass. Two of the deaths happened right here, so you could hardly ignore them. How could we sleep at night with a murderer targeting the vicarage? Besides, I think you may have been a bit…" she paused, obviously unsure whether to continue, but Daisy urged her to speak her mind.

"No, go on, really."

"Well, a bit manipulated petal. That Rob Briggs is a piece of work, and he played on your past relationship to make sure your suspicions were directed elsewhere."

"Was I just his puppet, then Sylvia?" Daisy felt the emotion swell in her chest and tears fill her eyes.

"I wouldn't say that, you've always had your own mind Daisy, and you certainly weren't swayed by his charm offensive but… well, he's a wily one that's for sure. Don't feel guilty, it's hardly like his father is an angel."

"But I do! I've made an even bigger enemy of Briggs Senior, who now he's free again will simply push through with his plans."

"There's still the bats though."

"I know, I know, but will that be enough? Was any of it worth losing my best friend over?"

"Only time will tell about the project, but as for Bea, she'll come round, just give her time."

"I hope so, Sylvia, I really do hope so."

26. OUT WITH THE OLD

Daisy stood at the pulpit the following Sunday as they sang the bright and beautiful final hymn of the service and said a silent prayer of thanks that she was here to see this day and to lead this congregation. She had spent many hours in personal contemplation and had managed to partly make her peace with recent events. For sure, she had faced peril in her new parish. She had had a mostly innocent man put behind bars – albeit temporarily – and had inadvertently caught a real murderer, with more than a little help from an unexpected quarter. She had inherited a whole menagerie of animals, not least a cat who considered himself the perfect plus-sized pet, had renewed some old friendships and damaged others.

Searching the audience for one man in particular, Daisy caught the eye of the town florist and gave an almost imperceptible nod. It was the first time she had seen Gerald Bunch since discovering he was not at all as he seemed, and Daisy was as yet unsure as to whether this knowledge would prove blessing or burden. Certainly, the man must have an important reason for his grating public persona, and one that he wished to keep secret from his neighbours. Not for the first time that week, Daisy wondered what had kept him in the town, and in his apparent disguise for the past fifteen years.

Winking overtly, Bunch stood as the song ended, making a show of walking up the middle aisle of the church to stand in front of Daisy, casting a few looks from side to side to make sure all eyes were on him as he did so.

"Daisy Bloom!" He boomed, loud enough for the whole town to hear, let alone the congregation, Daisy thought, "Daisy Bloom, I think it is public knowledge that I would like to make a bunch of blooms with you."

"Eugh," Bea's mum Morag, who was like a second mother to Daisy when she was growing up, made the sound of disgust from where she cradled her baby granddaughter, Daisy's namesake, on the second row.

Bea and Andrew themselves were noticeably absent.

Not put off in the slightest, Bunch proceeded to get down on one knee. Giving a smaller wink this time, one which only he and Daisy shared and which communicated between them the fact that this was merely an act, he went on to loudly and in no uncertain terms declare his undying love for the vicar.

Red faced and sweating, Daisy could do nothing but nod and smile before turning the man down in the same unequivocal fashion, loudly and for all their neighbours to hear.

"Even he could do a lot better," the salty remark came from the very front pew, where Violet Glendinning sat with her much put upon husband, Percy, and a rather handsome stranger. The younger man with his long hair and tie-dye t-shirt caught Daisy's eye briefly before commenting, "Do be quiet, mother," and earning himself a harsh glare from Violet.

Finally, someone who stands up to the bitter old crow, Daisy thought to herself, as Bunch made a show of looking dejected and heartbroken, announcing that he would try again next month in the hope the vicar would have changed her mind by then, as he strode off to the side door.

Daisy made a mental note to find out more about the Glendinnings' son, so different it seemed from both of his parents, as she accepted Sylvia's help to remove her robes in the vestry and looked forward to the Sunday roast they had prepared together earlier that morning.

One thing was for sure, everything was not rosy in the picturesque seaside town of Daisy's birth, but she was back now and there was still a murderer to be caught, one who had been resting on their laurels for far too long now.

Was Daisy the woman to do it? With God's help, maybe…

Will Daisy uncover her Gran's killer or will she unearth more dark secrets which the town would rather keep hidden?

Find out in "No Shrinking Violet" Lillymouth Mysteries Book 2

No Shrinking Violet

The Lillymouth Mysteries Book Two

Coming June 20th 2023

With two new, unexpected allies, a housekeeper who enjoys amateur sleuthing and the unwanted affections of an otherwise aloof vicarage cat, Reverend Daisy Bloom is back in this second book of the popular Lillymouth Mysteries series.

Tensions are high in Lillymouth as some of the locals attempt to move a group of environmental activists who have settled in the disused train station just outside of town. Leading the way is Violet Glendinning, wife of the local bank manager, head of the parish council, and self-appointed protector of 'the way things used to be.'

Daisy is reluctantly given the role of keeper of the peace, though she would much rather be focusing on her own personal conflicts.

When one of the newcomers is found dead shortly after an altercation with Violet, it is not long before she finds herself faced with uncomfortable enquiries.

Will Violet swallow her pride and ask Reverend Daisy for help, or will it prove too bitter a pill to swallow?

Available for pre-order now!

ABOUT THE AUTHOR

Rachel Hutchins lives in northeast England with her husband, three children and their dog Boudicca. She loves writing both mysteries and romances, and enjoys reading these genres too. Her favourite place is walking along the local coastline, with a coffee and some cake!

You can connect with Rachel and sign up to her monthly **newsletter** via her website at: www.authorrachelhutchins.com

Alternatively, she has social media pages on:

Facebook: www.facebook.com/rahutchinsauthor

Instagram: www.instagram.com/ra_hutchins_author

R. A. Hutchins

OTHER MYSTERY BOOKS BY R. A. HUTCHINS

Here Today, Scone Tomorrow

Baker's Rise Mysteries Book One

When the self-titled Lord of the Manor, Harold Baker, meets an untimely end, the residents of Baker's Rise believe that he has simply died from choking. It is fair to say that they are certainly not sad to see him go!

Former city dweller Flora Miller, new to the quaint English village and in charge of the recently restored Tearoom on the Rise, is the unlucky recipient of the late man's parrot. Her new feathered companion has no filter and a vibrant personality that cannot be ignored! Witness to Harold's murder, the bird won't let the matter lie, and it's not long before Flora becomes suspicious.

A quest to bake the perfect scone is put on hold whilst Flora helps the charming Detective Bramble to investigate Harold's death. She has set her hopes on writing the next bestseller, not on becoming an amateur sleuth, but life sometimes has surprises in store!

Will they find the killer before they strike again, and can Flora find the acceptance and friendship she seeks amongst her new neighbours?

Packed with twists and turns, colourful characters and a sprinkle of romance, this is the first book in the series of Baker's Rise Mysteries. It will certainly leave you hungry for more!

(Includes a traditional scone recipe!)

There are currently nine books available in this series.

ROMANCES BY THIS AUTHOR

The Angel and the Wolf

What do a beautiful recluse, a well-trained husky, and a middle-aged biker have in common?
Find out in this poignant story of love and hope!

When Isaac meets the Angel and her Wolf, he's unsure whether he's in Hell or Heaven.
Worse still, he can't remember taking that final step.
They say that calm follows the storm, but will that be the case for Isaac?

Fate has led him to her door,
Will she have the courage to let him in?

To Catch A Feather
Found in Fife Book One

When tragedy strikes an already vulnerable Kate Winters, she retreats into herself, broken and beaten. Existing rather than living, she makes a journey North to try to find herself, or maybe just looking for some sort of closure.

Cameron McAllister has known his own share of grief and love lost. His son, Josh, is now his only priority. In

his forties and running a small coffee shop in a tiny
Scottish fishing village, Cal knows he is unlikely to
find love again.

When the two meet and sparks fly, can they overcome
their past losses and move on towards a shared future,
or are the memories which haunt them still too real?

*These books, as well as others by Rachel, can be found on
Amazon worldwide in e-book and paperback formats, as well
as free to read on Kindle Unlimited.*

Printed in Great Britain
by Amazon